The Negro in American Culture

Margaret Just Butcher

Based on materials left by Alain Locke

REVISED AND UPDATED

A MENTOR BOOK from
NEW AMERICAN LIBRARY
TIMES MIRROR

To the Memory of
Mary Hawkins Locke
and
Ernest Everett Just

© MARGARET JUST BUTCHER, 1956

Copyright 1956 by Margaret Just Butcher. All rights reserved. No part of this book may be reproduced in any form without permission in writing from the publisher, except by a reviewer who may quote brief passages in a review to be printed in a magazine or newspaper.

Lines from "No Name No. 3" by Nikki Giovanni are reprinted by permission of Broadside Press from *Black Judgment*. Copyright © 1968 by Nikki Giovanni.

Preface and Postscript
Copyright © 1971 by Margaret Just Butcher

Grateful acknowledgment is made to Harper & Brothers for permission to quote a part of "Men of Careful Turns" from *Annie Allen*, by Gwendolyn Brooks, Copyright, 1945, by Gwendolyn Brooks Blakely, and for a part of "Heritage" from *Color,* by Countee Cullen, Copyright 1925, by Harper & Brothers, Copyright, 1953, by Ida M. Cullen.

Published by arrangement with Alfred A. Knopf, Inc.

 MENTOR TRADEMARK REG. U.S. PAT. OFF. AND FOREIGN COUNTRIES
REGISTERED TRADEMARK—MARCA REGISTRADA
HECHO EN CHICAGO, U.S.A.

SIGNET, SIGNET CLASSICS, MENTOR, PLUME AND MERIDIAN BOOKS
are published by The New American Library, Inc.,
1301 Avenue of the Americas, New York, New York 10019

FIRST PRINTING, OCTOBER, 1957

3 4 5 6 7 8 9 10 11

PRINTED IN THE UNITED STATES OF AMERICA

34963

CONTENTS

CHAPTER		PAGE
	INTRODUCTION	iv
	PREFACE *1971*	viii
I	THE NEGRO'S ROLE IN AMERICAN SOCIETY	11
II	THE NEGRO IN AMERICAN CULTURE	23
III	THE EARLY FOLK GIFTS: MUSIC, DANCE, FOLKLORE	38
IV	NEGRO MUSIC AND DANCE: FORMAL RECOGNITION AND RECONSTRUCTION	51
V	NEGRO FOLK POETRY AND FOLK THOUGHT	82
VI	FORMAL NEGRO POETRY	96
VII	THE FICTION AND POLEMICS OF THE ANTI-SLAVERY PERIOD	115
VIII	THE NEGRO IN MODERN AMERICAN FICTION	132
IX	THE NEGRO IN AMERICAN DRAMA	149
X	THE NEGRO AS ARTIST AND IN AMERICAN ART	164
XI	REGIONAL NATIONALISM IN AMERICAN CULTURE	189
XII	SOME PROSPECTS OF AMERICAN CULTURE	220
	POSTSCRIPT *1971*	229
	INDEX	243

INTRODUCTION

I first saw Alain Locke in December 1919. I was a girl of six; he and my father, the late Ernest Just, were standing at the door of the auditorium of the old Miner Normal School, where I was a first-grade pupil in the "practice school." I remember looking expectantly at each: I had just recited "The Night before Christmas," and was ready to be complimented. My father said dryly: "You forgot a line." Alain Locke said kindly, after glaring at my father: "You did very well." I last saw Alain in May 1954. He was at Mt. Sinai Hospital, New York, desperately ill, yet still able to be his old kind self. This time he was concerned that for the second time I had come to New York from Washington to see him in spite of the fact that I was on crutches as the result of an injury. He was unusually susceptible to sentiment that day, and smiled when I told him I had to come because it was Mother's Day and I was standing *in loco parentis*.

Through the years Alain Locke and I were warm and devoted friends. Oddly enough, in spite of his reputation for frequently being sharp and sharply critical, and mine for being almost equally so, we got along very well. In later years he regarded my husband, daughter, and me as his family. Living very near us in Washington, he often dined with us, and during one terrible illness of his in 1952, we prepared and took his evening meal to him daily for nearly three months. He always insisted that my cooking (which he likened favorably to that of the French) "saved his life"!

It was also during 1952 that Alain admitted that because of his poor health he could not get ahead with his book, *The Negro in American Culture,* for which he had signed a contract with Alfred A. Knopf in 1951. This book was to have been his *magnum opus.* For years he had written articles, collaborated with other authors, and delivered lectures at leading universities both here and abroad. Yet he had never written a comprehensive book summing up his broad interest in Negro art and culture as related to and intertwined with American culture as a whole. His famous Bronze Booklets, now out of print, included his studies of Negro music and art. His prefaces to his own *The Negro in Art,* as well as, for example, his introduction to *When Peoples Meet,* set forth some of his basic concepts concerning respectively art and art criticism, and the role of minorities in a democratic

Introduction

society. He had always wanted to bring all these smaller works into a broad whole. This ambition prompted him to plan for free time to prepare a book and to ask assistance from the Rockefeller Foundation. In January 1951, Dr. Locke submitted a request to the Foundation for a grant. This request was promptly honored; in February 1951, Dr. Mordecai Johnson, President of Howard University, accepted a substantial grant and agreed to Dr. Locke's request for leave beginning on March 31, 1951. Dr. Charles Thompson, Dean of the Howard Graduate School, was administrator for the grant, and Dr. Locke was committed to finish the book by April 1952. But by the spring of 1952 he had been critically ill. He was to face an even more serious relapse in June of that year, a relapse that culminated in his going to Valley Forge Hospital for the first of several periods of treatment.

My husband and I were deeply involved in this first trip. I had offered to help Alain with the book, and now, because Alain felt that he would not live through the summer, he insisted that I take all the manuscript, all the notes, books—that is, those on which we were basing the well as some basic references—from his apartment. And because he was alone and extremely weak, that my husband go with him to Valley Forge. M tells a story about their trip which reveals two t rather touching—sides to Locke. He loved to eat. train got to Baltimore Alain was ready to go to the car, even though, once there, he was barely able to touch the food he so carefully ordered. He loved to be recognized. Only when the waiter asked him (with obvious deference and admiration): "Aren't you Dr. Locke? *The* Dr. Locke?" did he, as my husband recalls, "perk up" enough to *try* to eat.

Throughout the summer of 1952 I struggled with the Locke material. There were boxes and boxes of notes, clippings; long, typewritten excerpts from all sorts of books, pictures, programs, lectures, magazines (some marked, some not marked); letters, at least four different outlines, a list of proposed titles, a copy of my doctoral dissertation, a bundle of his philosophy notes—and one chapter for *The Negro in American Culture*. I read all I could and did what I could, and fortunately by early fall Alain was well enough to return to Washington. So the boxes went back to his apartment.

During 1952-53, Alain was able to resume teaching. During that year I was committed to write the chapters on fiction, poetry, the drama, "and any others I could tackle." Locke had managed earlier, with my help, to get a chapter together for *New World Writing*. We fought over it, but it had appeared in the first issue of *New World Writing,* in the spring of 1952. Alain's affectionate inscription in our copy was: "To Margaret and Jimmy, with grateful remembrance of the help that made it possible."

By June 1953, Alain had decided definitely that he would retire from Howard, move permanently to his New York apartment, and finish the now long-overdue book for which several time extensions had been made by both the Rockefeller Foundation and the publishers. In November 1953, I visited Alain in New York. He was settled, but terribly discouraged about the book. The routine of caring for himself —he refused a housekeeper—which included a day-long routine of medicine-taking, so exhausted him, he said, that by the time he was free to write, he slept. But we had a cheerful dinner in Greenwich Village and later went to see the memorable film, *Martin Luther.*

When next I saw Alain he was dying, and he urged that if anything happened to him I would try to "do the book."

After Alain's death in June 1954 I conferred with Herbert Weinstock of Alfred A. Knopf and Victor Weybright of The New American Library. Mr. Weybright, Alain's longtime friend and loyal admirer, had negotiated a subsidiary contract for the book to be published in paperback form. Both men were interested in the fact that I had been working with Dr. Locke. Each agreed that I was the logical person to complete the work. Mr. Weinstock took the responsibility of negotiating with Arthur Fauset, Alain's friend and business partner of years' standing, who was one of the executors of the estate, to see whether or not the estate was agreeable to my finishing the book, and whether I could take the now famous boxes of material to Washington. That same summer we received Mr. Fauset's agreement to my doing the book; by late July I was able to bring to Washington all the familiar materials—about seventy-five pounds of it. But it was not until May 1955 that the final legal details were settled and I was free to sign a contract with Alfred A. Knopf. Although I had given the material some attention when I had time, I had had to give prior consideration to my heavy commitments as Special Educational Consultant for the National Association for the Advancement of Colored People and to my continuing responsibilities as a member of the District of Columbia Board of Education. Between May and November 1955, therefore, the heaviest work was done. There was more personal reading to be done, there were more trips to the Congressional Library, and more attempts to use the materials Alain had left. The biggest job was to edit and bring up to date the work he had completed—his booklets on music and art, for example. As for actual manuscript, Alain had left less than two complete chapters. I had helped on one of these, and I made certain changes in both.

The purpose of the book, as Alain conceived it, as he and I discussed it, and as I have tried to develop it, is this: to trace in historical sequence—but topical fashion—both the folk and the formal contributions of the American Negro to American culture. It aims, further, to trace and interpret the considerable influence of the Negro on American culture at large. Its main thesis is that by setting up an inveterate tradition of racial differences in the absence of any fixed or basic differences of culture and tradition on the Negro's part, American slavery introduced into the very heart of American society a crucial dilemma whose resultant problems, with their progressive resolution, account for many fateful events in American history and for some of the most characteristic qualities of American culture. On all levels, political, social and cultural, this dilemma has become the focal point, disruptive as well as constructive, of major issues in American history. In the pre-Civil War period, the issue was slavery versus anti-slavery; in the Reconstruction era it was discrimination and bi-racialism versus equalitarian nationalism. In the contemporary era, it is segregation and cultural separatism versus integration and cultural democracy. The Supreme Court Decision of May 17, 1954, it must be remembered, did not solve our dilemma; it merely gave legal sanction to people working for an integrated society and a true cultural democracy. Instead of a historical discussion of these issues, however, this book includes an analysis of them as they are reflected in the changing moral and ideological contexts of American literature and art. Here, it must be added, there has been no attempt to be all-inclusive in terms of individual artists and authors. Comprehensive trends and exemplary types, rather than minutely detailed categories, have been stressed.

It has taken effort and sacrifice on my part to complete Dr. Locke's work. My doing it has exacted a great deal of patience from Herbert Weinstock and Victor Weybright, for I have been slow. Now that it is done, I am happy to have done it—because I was devoted to Alain Locke, because I am proud of what the American Negro has accomplished, and because, as an American who is a Negro, I am proud of the fact that our American Democracy is truly "coming of age."

Howard University —MARGARET JUST BUTCHER

PREFACE
1971

Since 1956, when *The Negro in American Culture* was first published, both the American Negro and America herself have witnessed and undergone many and significant changes. School desegregation, for example, a social phenomenon fifteen years ago, is now accepted with equanimity in virtually every community where the Supreme Court Decision of 1954 was applicable. American Negroes have become increasingly vocal and increasingly active physically in the continuing drive for a real and, truly demonstrable role in this society. New leaders, both black and white, have emerged. Some have been lost either by natural causes or tragic circumstances. The deaths of Medgar Evers, Martin Luther King, President Kennedy, that of his brother Robert, and, most recently, that of Whitney M. Young, have left disastrous gaps in America's social and political leadership. There have been, in addition to the well known figures, countless "little people"—the unnumbered band who have all too often borne the brunt of implementing the processes of democratic action that big decisions and strong leaders set into action. Many years ago, when I served as an Educational Consultant for Thurgood Marshall, when he was Chief Counsel for the Legal and Defense Fund of the National Association for the Advancement of Colored People, I had occasion to see the hard, dedicated work of Southern preachers and pastors as they fought—often at the risk of severe sanctions against them by hostile whites—to initiate social changes in their given parishes.

Today we are still at war; we are still, in some parts of our country, battling poverty, illiteracy, and social deprivation; we are still frequently misinterpreted and misunderstood by both our friends and critics at home and abroad. Yet, on the positive side, Americans have made some dramatic advances, particularly in science: our moon landing represents the most spectacular one. Although we have yet to develop cures for modern man's most serious physical scourges (cancer, for example), notable efforts have been and are being made.

In reviewing the cultural history of the Negro in the context of the myriad changes that have defined America these past years, one is reminded of William Faulkner's character Dilsey, who observed, "I have endured." We American Negroes have endured, have remained loyal to the country that brought us here "by special invitation" (as my friend Jo Saunders Redding so aptly phrases it), and have maintained a steadfast faith in the intrinsic premises of democracy. We have consistently made significant physical and cultural con-

Preface 1971

tributions to America. One need only look, for example, to the magnificent wrought iron work that characterizes much of Southern, particularly Louisianan, architecture to be reminded of the skill of black artisans. The construction of railroads, bridges, wharves, and ditches necessitated hard, often brutal labor which Negroes performed, invariably. In the Old South, it was the Negro who maintained the cotton economy. He planted cotton, picked it, and, as we are so poignantly reminded in the American classic, "Old Man River," bailed it for shipment.

Yet the American Negro's cultural contributions to the land he was forced to adopt, although notable, are all too frequently either ignored or grossly minimized. That the Negro "is musical" and "given to rhythm" is taken for granted by many naive white Americans as well as by many Europeans. That Negroes have been active in all areas of American life—including the abolition movement as well as the long fight for school desegregation (which, of course, set the pattern for desegregation in other areas of American life)—is less well known.

In this book, I have essayed to trace in historical sequence —but topical fashion—both the folk and the formal contributions of the American Negro to American culture as a whole. Its main thesis is that by setting up an inveterate tradition of racial differences in the absence of any fixed or basic differences of culture and tradition on the Negro's part, slavery introduced into the very heart of American society a crucial dilemma whose resultant problems, with their progressive resolutions, account for many fateful events in American history and for some of the most characteristic qualities of American culture. On political, social, and cultural levels, this dilemma has become the focal point, disruptive as well as constructive, of major issues in American history. In the pre-Civil War period, the issue was slavery versus anti-slavery; in the Reconstruction era it was discrimination and bi-racialism versus equalitarian nationalism. In the contemporary era it is segregation and cultural separatism versus integration and cultural democracy. It must be remembered that the Supreme Court Decision of May 17, 1954 did not solve the American dilemma; it merely gave legal sanction to people working for an integrated society and a true cultural democracy. Instead of an historical discussion of these issues, however, this book includes an analysis of them as they are reflected in the changing moral and ideological contexts of American literature and art. Here, it must be added, there has been no attempt to be all-inclusive in terms of individual artists and authors. Comprehensive trends and exemplary types, rather than minutely detailed categories, have been stressed.

As an American Negro, I am proud of what the American Negro has accomplished. I am equally proud that within my own lifetime I have witnessed the fact that almost daily our American Democracy is "coming of age."

MARGARET JUST BUTCHER

Washington, D. C.
May 26, 1971

CHAPTER ONE

The Negro's Role in American Society

THE RIGHT and most effective way to look at the Negro's relationship to American culture is to consider it not as an isolated race matter and minority group concern, but rather in the context of the whole of American culture. Thereupon one inevitably—and rightly—becomes involved with the history and fortunes of both the majority and the minority groups. These fortunes are not separate; nor can they be separately evaluated or understood. They overlap and interlock as, through successive generations, the lives of the Negroes and whites are intermingled. Together, and only together, they have interwoven the vital, sturdy patterns of American society. Together they have been responsible for both the basic characteristic structure of American society and the dynamic social changes that distinguish a democratic society from others. In short, to understand either the Caucasian majority or the Negro minority in America we must trace and follow the history, be it social or cultural, of each. To undertake, as we do here, a cultural history of the American Negro, it is as necessary to describe the impact of the Negro on America as it is to consider the impact of America on the Negro.

Whether the social or the artistic aspect of the culture be our focus of immediate interest, we shall discover on closer scrutiny that the two will be found vitally interrelated. To cope with a subject matter as involved in historical happenings and sociological complications as that which relates to the American Negro, one must constantly keep in mind American institutional life as it conditions artistic and intellectual activity. It would profit the historian and the sociologist to take this linkage into account more frequently; certainly in the study of the Negro it is a significant, though frequently neglected factor. For the culture historian consideration of the correlation is imperative. The literature of slavery, for example, throws much additional light on the nature of slavery. Yet there is an almost completely neglected body of fugitive-slave narratives. Consideration of the slave narratives, as well as of other available reflections of the slave mind and imagination, would supply a great lack in our history—a sufficient and adequate account of the Negro's own reaction to slavery. Again, the traditional stereotypes of the Negro, though in many instances contrary to fact, nevertheless reveal, more subtly than statutes and historical incidents, the inner complexes of the white mind in its attitudes and policies toward the Negro. A stubborn stereotype may block understanding and adjustment for decades because the way two groups of people think and feel about each other is often more influential and determinative than what the two groups actually are. Finally, changes of social attitude are at least as important as changes of social condition, and such changes, reflected in literature and art, are often the best barometers at hand to signal shifts in the character and quality of race relations.

The main approach in this book is from the side of ideological and artistic culture, but as frequently as possible an attempt has been made to correlate the parallel lines of social and artistic development. Indeed, though one of the main intentions is to document the considerable, but little known, contributions of the Negro to American arts and letters, we must include consideration of the Negro in his more fundamental connections with our social culture, and we must consider too his important impact upon the artistic culture of the nation. Although generally unrecognized, the Negro minority's counterinfluence upon the life and culture of the dominant white majority has been considerable in both degree and extent. Indeed, at several points in the national history the Negro's influence has exerted decisive effect upon the artistic and social culture of the nation as a whole.

Few would care to deny or even to minimize the momentous effects of slavery on our institutional culture. This assumption is valid, I think, whether one looks upon slavery as the moral, the humane, or the economic issue of the Civil War. Slavery challenged "head-on" two of the most basic of our national traditions: political freedom and free labor. In his study *The American Philosophy of Equality*, T. V. Smith, a keen analyst, concurs: "Slavery proved to be the first great institutional test of the equality doctrine." Many would also understand, if they reflected deeply enough, the way in which the slow, consistently steady rise of the Negro's status since emancipation in 1863 has served as a base-level fulcrum for new freedom and wider foundations for American democracy. The Negro's progression from chattel to freedman, to legal citizenship, to increasing equality of rights and opportunities, to accepted neighbor and compatriot represents a dramatic testament to democracy's positive and dynamic character.

The Supreme Court Decision of May 17, 1954, is not to be interpreted as an isolated social, moral, or humanitarian phenomenon. It was a completely logical and foreseeable climax to the Negro's long struggle for equality of opportunity and for decisive recognition of the fact that color per se is not the measure of human worth or dignity. But here again the Decision was by no means a "Negro victory" in the literal sense. Those who recognize the insidious effects of segregation recognize them in reciprocal terms. Thus, the Education Decision of May 17 has significant and meaningful implications for the white majority. The progress of the Negro since his emancipation has in large measure involved, as the May 17 Decision exemplifies, revision or radically changed interpretation of the organic law of the land. Willis J. King sums up this point succinctly: "One of the significant contributions made by the Negro to American life has been the way in which his presence has helped in the development and extension of the American idea of Democracy." Stated differently, the test of a democracy's meaningfulness is to be found in the impact of its intrinsic philosophy upon minority groups. The shift in philosophy and intent of the Supreme Court, manifest in what Commager has described as "The New Jurisprudence," has paved the way for the formidable succession of affirmative civil-rights decrees in recent years. Finally, with reference to the Negro's influence upon America's culture, not many realize, but all should know how much evidence there is of the transforming effects of Negro folk idioms in such major areas of the American arts as music, dance, and folklore. These influences have been for the most part dominant, fundamental, and enduring, rather than merely superficial or transitory.

It may be safely concluded then, if these claims be successfully justified, that the Negro, in spite of his deprivations and handicaps—indeed in some respects because of them—has played two constructive roles in the course of his more than three hundred years in America. He has acted as what might be termed a potent artistic leaven in American arts and letters; he is serving, in the apt phrase of J. Saunders Redding, as a powerful "catalyst of American democracy." Recalling the extent of the Negro's physical and intellectual participation in the struggle for his own freedom as slave fugitive, slave insurrectionist, anti-slavery writer and orator, Union soldier in the Civil War, and civil-rights contestant thereafter, we might well add that the Negro is best identified as a proud collaborator in the advance of American democracy. Putting aside for the moment the matter of the Negro's artistic role and influence, let us turn to the even more important effect of the Negro in America on the social and institutional culture of the nation.

Really, it should be taken for granted that any minority as large and long-established as the American Negro would exert considerable influence on the national life. The Negro is America's largest and oldest minority group: for the past hundred years he has steadily averaged a fraction under or over one tenth of the population. In colonial times this percentage was higher; at the time of the first census (1790) Negroes comprised a full fifth of the population. In thinking of the situation realistically, we must add the factor of the Negro's heavy concentration in the southern states, in some of which ratios approximating half of the population have been and still are prevalent, and where in certain localities the Negro, on a strictly numerical basis, becomes an actual (though, of course, in matters of material power, an impotent) majority. Judging by relative rates of population growth, this racial ratio promises to remain nearly constant indefinitely, so that it has been reasonably suggested that to visualize the situation we think of the Negro as "America's tenth man." At the census figure for 1950, this was an impressive sum total of nearly fifteen million persons.

But the cultural and institutional importance of the Negro is not solely or even principally a matter of statistical ratios. His importance stems from his unusual historical experience as a group and from his peculiar position in American society. Both have paradoxically caused the Negro to exert an influence disproportionate to his numbers and his social status. To the extent to which the Negro was oppressed and segregated, his folk life became more distinct and its reactions more distinctive; the more slavery spread and deepened, the more the Negro became the concern and obsession of his enslavers. The more he was made an exception to the general condition, the stronger a moral contradiction he became in both the conscience and the institutional life of the country. As Gunnar Myrdal so penetratingly put it, the plight and predicament of the black minority became in time the "great American dilemma," a dramatic clash between incompatible ideologies and traditions: slavery and freedom, caste and consistent democracy.

Indeed, when the American colonists, in their hard task of conquering the new continent, reached out desperate hands to the African slave trade for conscripted labor, they took hold of one of the most fateful strands in American history. Simultaneously with the founding of a society destined to become a great political democracy, these men imported democracy's greatest antithesis—slavery and hereditary bondage. They could never have anticipated that the introduction of slave labor would in time produce civil war, precipitate American society's foremost social problem, and in recurring crises threaten American democracy's vitality and influence.

It was only by historical accident that a white indentured servant class did not bear the brunt of the labor load of the European settlement of this continent. In fact, the earliest Negro importees shared substantially the status and rights of the indentured English bondsmen and convict debtors, with the privilege of reselling their labor by contract and purchasing their freedom by individual enterprise. Hundreds of Negroes rose thereby to become free men and, sad to relate, in a few instances themselves became slaveowners. These facts show how basic the principle of economic caste was in the historical inception of American slavery and explain why, for both the Negro and the country at large, free labor was at stake with political freedom and citizenship in the issues that this antidemocratic tradition projected into the heart of American society. Only as it came into the American scheme, and again as it passed out in a life-and-death struggle over common human liberties, was slavery to be seen in its truest light, with the human issues dominant and the racial factor almost irrelevant. Indeed, the die of slavery was cast not primarily by difference of race, but by undemocratic ideas and class practices in the early scheme of American society. In two hundred and fifty years, however, slavery as the particular plight of the black man could mask its institutional inconsistencies behind the black exception thus protecting the expression of fundamental democratic principles which had been contradicted for many generations. Thomas Jefferson, clear-sighted democrat that he was, had the right emphasis when he said that when he considered slavery he "trembled for his country." The presence of the Negro, with outright purchase and an indelible color difference to confirm it, allowed this negation of democracy to develop into a deeper and more tragic scheme than that of mere class exploitation. The Negro took the brunt of transplanted feudalism, enabling it to be diverted from the backs of the poorer white settlers.

Too often, the American mind, lacking knowledge of these facts, and so without proper historical perspective on American slavery, follows the great cover-up tradition that makes the Negro bear the blame as well as the brunt of the situation; often it is assumed that his very presence in the body politic has constituted the race problem. J. Saunders Redding's shrewd pleasantry that Negroes were the only element of the American population which came by special invitation, passage paid, has scarcely sufficed to drive home the sober realization that the Negro was desperately needed and humbly but importantly effective in the settlement of the New World. His warrant for being here is beyond question, doubly so because his mass service of basic labor in the wide zone of the slave system was unrewarded for seven or eight generations. It is estimated that before 1800 the number of Negroes brought to America in the slave trade was more than twenty times that of all European immigrants combined. The terrific toll of lives taken may be realized from the fact that by the first census of 1790 the black population in the United States was only one fifth of the total. "The wealth of the New World," says Edwin Embree, "came largely by the sweat of this new race." In his *Gift of Black Folk*, W. E. B. DuBois rightly rates the Negro's labor as his first substantial contribution. No matter how the benefits be reckoned, it remains a fact that the Negro's begrudged share in American civilization was dearly bought and paid for in advance of delivery.

Slavery, moreover, planted the Negro deep in the subsoil of American life and made him culturally a basic American. The domestic and rural form that slavery took necessitated particularly intimate group contacts and both forced and made possible the rapid assimilation of the white man's civilization, language, religion, and folkways. This cultural transfusion was considerably reinforced by wide interbreeding and admixture of blood: according to the rough evidence of the census count of mulattoes, about twenty per cent of the Negro population is of obviously mixed descent. In scientific investigation of sample Negro groups today, Melville J. Herskovits discovers an even higher percentage of mixture and estimates scarcely a one-third remnant of pure-blood Negroes in the total of fifteen million. On both physical and the cultural bases, American slavery is revealed as the institution directly responsible for undermining its own chief contentions about color and cultural difference. Originally there were wide physical and cultural differences between the two races. Now there is mainly a contrary-to-fact tradition of difference. Until quite recently this tradition was embraced by those who stubbornly tried to deny the trends and consequences of slavery's own handiwork.

While breaking down these natural barriers, slavery and its supporting code of prejudice erected artificial and tyrannical substitutes. Doctrines of race difference and inferiority and a rigid etiquette of color caste were formulated. The sense of difference operated most forcefully in situations where actual difference was least in evidence; the white majority became fanatical wherever the Negro claimed the rewards of conformity or the privileges of assimilation. Out of these peculiar paradoxes the characteristic American variety of race prejudice was born or, rather, manufactured. In the official apologia for slaveholding, a doctrine was needed to offset every real and potential claim for the Negro's rights as a human being and citizen: it was necessary to devise counterclaims that nullified any expression of humanitarian or civil concern for the slave.

Against the country's debt to the Negro for service and labor was set the Negro's presumably incalculable indebtedness for the benefits of the white man's civilization. Christianity represents a strong case in point. It was indeed a spirit-saving solace, but emphasis on its moral benefactions was used both to inculcate submissiveness and to rationalize slavery as a social practice. Eventually, in the "Bible argument for slavery," Christianity was demeaned into justifying the very institution itself. Furthermore, to discount the Negro's really remarkable assimilation of the rudiments of American civilization, the legend of his "nonassimilability" was popularized. This legend wrote off the Negro's accomplishments as mere "imitativeness" and thwarted further effort on the score of "inherent mental inferiority." The doctrine attributing to inherent inferiority the Negro's imposed handicaps and disabilities has developed so strong a hold upon the American public mind that only in the last decade or so have scientific study and objective comparisons made any headway in correcting it. There persists also the fallacious doctrine of the Negro's childlike dependence upon a guiding paternalism. Rarely is there a frank recognition of the fact that the feudal system of slavery and its semi-feudal aftermath depended in large measure upon the perpetuation of paternalistic bonds. Fortunately, the Negro has resisted this old dependence with increasing vigor, and his present-day attitude renders the "doctrine" completely specious.

The worst paradox and perhaps the saddest irony of all, in the pattern of masking the facts of racial admixture and insulating its social consequences, was the promulgating of the doctrine of white ethnic integrity. The promulgation and arbitrary maintenance of this unscientific concept negated the normal claims of the mixed-blood group—claims that generally have been recognized in every other culture where considerable miscegenation has taken place. This last policy needs close analysis. It has been crucial in determining the patterns of the social and intellectual culture of the United States. It is the historical reason for the absence of a buffer mulatto group in the North American racial situation, and so constitutes the great cultural divide between the Anglo-Saxon and the Latin cultures in the matter of race relations. However, it is a difference we should approach objectively, for it has both good points and bad. Among the former, one may mention that because in the United States any traceable degree of Negro blood has classified a person as "sociologically" a Negro, a most unusual—an almost solid—psychological solidarity of the whole Negro minority has been produced.

These rationalizing dogmas of "race integrity" and "pure" Anglo-Saxon culture have had wide, deep consequences that must for a moment give us pause. In the first place, they have concealed the actual facts of the historical development of a mixed race and a composite culture. By becoming traditional in American ways of thinking, these dogmas have been the taproot of our most characteristic variety of chauvinism, the stock notion of American culture as exclusively Anglo-Saxon. This bias has affected a much wider area of group relations than those between white and Negro, and has indeed until quite recently disparaged many other non-Anglo-Saxon strains and traditions in the national culture. Further, the same attitudes have unquestionably fed and intensified the mind-sets of race prejudice and have extended themselves into a more generalized color complex. This complex has adversely dominated our external cultural relations, particularly those with the entire non-white world.

There are other more immediate reasons for keeping in mind the sharp difference between the Latin and the Anglo-Saxon racial attitudes and codes in America. First of all, it explains why emancipation by no means eradicated race prejudice. Under different circumstances it might have been wiped out in a generation or so; instead, in some instances emancipation actually intensified race prejudice. Racial dogmas became chronic; they could not die a natural death with the death of the system that had produced them. This psychological aftermath of slavery, persisting as the philosophy of the color line, has had the most serious consequences in the period from emancipation to the present. It still offers more resistance to the Negro's progress than all the practical difficulties of social advance combined, and it still obstructs many normal realignments of social, political, and economic adjustment. "Keeping the Negro in his place," or its compromise form of compartmentalized "segregation," amounts to prolonging in clandestine form the regime of slavery and leads to the same negative results for the Negro and for American society at large. Dual standards and biracial partitioning add up to the denial of democracy in actual practice and have led inevitably to an undemocratic and self-frustrating policy of keeping one tenth of the population in a condition of artificially arrested development.

These generalizations, basically true, must not give the misleading impression that there was no counterpoint of dissent and protest on the matter of slavery among the Anglo-Saxons of American society. From early colonial days, there were anti-slavery thought and anti-slavery action. The earliest of these came from Quaker sources: John Woolman, Anthony Benezet, and others urged the Friends to have no part in slaveholding. They were followed by a small dissenter minority, north and south, expressing the awakening conscience of the more radically evangelical Christian churches. Notable were Bishop Asbury and the proselyting Wesleyans. Here were the beginnings of what in several generations would culminate formidably as the organized protest of the abolitionists.

Significantly, too, in 1789, the very year of the nation's founding, Negro protest began with the anonymous publication of an anti-slavery pamphlet, *On Slavery*. The author was a Negro freeman who discreetly hid his identity under the pen name "Othello." Researchers surmise that he may have been the phenomenal Benjamin Banneker, who, in 1791, addressed a long letter in similar vein to Thomas Jefferson. The little-known but significant exchange of correspondence (for Jefferson replied civilly and sympathetically, stating that he had sent a copy to M. de Condorcet, Secretary of the Academy of Sciences at Paris and a member of "The Philanthropic Society," "because I consider it a document to which your whole colour had a right for their justification against the doubts which have been entertained of them") may have had much to do with Jefferson's doubts and fears about the rectitude and wisdom of slavery. Negro protest continued bravely but sporadically until it climaxed a generation later in the noteworthy collaboration of men like Samuel Ringold Ward, Charles Lenox Remond, Henry Highland Garnet, and Frederick Douglass. But all this was at best representative of only a small segment of the population, the majority of which in the North tacitly acquiesced in slavery. The South, despite a brave but minute quota of Southern abolitionists, was, of course, overwhelmingly committed to "the peculiar institution."

There is not only the interesting divergence between the Anglo-Saxon and Latin attitudes toward differences of race; there are also important divergences in their typical social and cultural consequences. The Latin tradition is happily free from a priori prejudice: there is more likelihood of individuals being judged on their merits rather than in terms of categories. The triple inheritance of the French Revolution, Catholic universalism, and Latin social tolerance doubtless is responsible for this democratic attitude, without which outstanding accomplishments and the ready recognition of individual Negroes according to merit in Latin and Latin-American societies could never have taken place. One need only recall the Chevalier Saint-Georges; General Dumas and his even greater son, Alexandre Dumas, in France; such pioneer patriots as Plácido, Calixto García, and José Martí in Cuba; Machado de Assis, founder of realism in Brazilian letters, and Mario de Andrade, until recently Brazil's leading contemporary novelist.

It is evident that the Anglo-Saxon code of race is based on a priori prejudice, and really pre-judges the individual on the arbitrary basis of the mass status of his ethnic group. It does make occasional exceptions, often grudgingly and *as* "exceptions." More often, however, it forces the advancing segments of the group back to the level and limitations of the less advanced. This hard code has led to some unforeseen and unintended democratic consequences. By forcing the advance-guard of a minority back upon its people, it eventually forges mass organization for group progress out of the discipline of solidarity. The outstanding individual, in the majority of instances still linked to the common lot, is impressed into group leadership, and as he achieves recognition, becomes a human shuttle threading a binding strand of progress. Should his social conscience relax in the satisfactions of success, discrimination would resaddle him with his moral obligation to the group.

So the Latin code, while it metes out readier justice to the individual, does so at the price of an unhappy divorce of the elite from the masses. On the other hand, the Anglo-Saxon code, seriously handicapping the individual and his immediate chances for success, forces, despite its intentions to the contrary, a bond of group solidarity, and unavoidable responsibility for and toward the group. This is a necessary though painful condition of mass progress. Oddly enough, in this hemisphere, both policies were laid down by slaveowning societies before the abolition of slavery. One saw in the more favorable condition and aspiration of the mulatto a menacing advance that must be firmly blocked by a solid wall of prejudice. The other, for the most part, saw in the differential treatment of the *mestizo* the strategy of the buffer class, and therefore granted him considerably more opportunity and recognition than was allowed the blacks, but always something less than was standard for privileged whites. Neither was really democratic in intention. One policy produced an out-and-out race problem; the other policy contributed to a class problem. One system, the Latin, has vindicated a basic condition of cultural democracy: the open career for talent and relatively unhampered mobility and recognition for rising individual aspiration and achievement. The Anglo-Saxon developments have, however, taught an increasingly important essential of a democratic social order: the responsibility of the elite for the masses.

Instead of gradually liquidating prejudice after emancipation, our American behavior, based on the intransigent, rigid, Anglo-Saxon tradition, has tended to intensify racial tensions as the white majority faced the ever-increasing challenges of minority progress. Yet in spite of this compounded discouragement and opposition, the career of the Negro in the United States since 1863 has shown an epic achievement, only some of which—the cultural and artistic—falls within the scope of this book. Broadly regarded, this achievement is American as well as Negro: the common dynamic of American life and civilization has entered into its making. As already pointed out, the Negro is typically American in his group values and objectives, in his spirit and motivations; perhaps he is more American than several other minority groups, by virtue of his long residence and intimate contacts. Discrimination and undemocratic treatment have often operated as goads and special pressures instead of as the intended discouragement and handicaps. The net outcome has been a gradually increased rate and range of progress. Partly through his own patient endurance and effort, and partly through saving alliances with the forces of moral and social liberalism, the Negro has been able to make phenomenal advances in both material and immaterial culture.

The American dilemma deepens with such continued progress of the Negro minority; its paradoxes increasingly defy concealment as the older justifications of backwardness and incompetence disappear. In the light of the rapid general advance of the whole society, weaknesses stand out the more conspicuously. With slavery's obvious inequalities outlawed and largely overcome, disfranchisement, unequal civil privileges, segregation, and discriminatory treatment loom up as even greater contradictions. The economic and cultural aspects of the inconsistency become equally obvious: the shortsightedness of the effort to maintain economic caste in a highly mobile and open-enterprise society, and the futility, in an essentially composite culture, of a chauvinism that blindly prefers an ethnically flattering fiction. Cultural democracy is an important and inescapable corollary of political and social democracy, and it involves an open door for the acceptance of minority contributions and for the full recognition of the minority contributors.

Under such circumstances the Negro minority retains today, as in the past, its significant and symbolic position at the center of America's struggle for the full development of the tradition of freedom. For the core of the issue is wherever undemocratic inconsistencies exist, and the majority stakes in its progressive solution are fully as great as those of the minority.

We must, finally, take note of the fact that today the critical frontier of racial issues is no longer domestic, but in a vital and pressing sense international. Indeed, in the opinion of all competent observers, the international front of race has been permanently joined to the home front of race, with America's moral leadership completely dependent upon the consistency of our democratic practices with our democratic creed and professions. The United States is already under heavy past-and-present suspicion of inveterate and unrenounced racialism. Any discrepancy—political, social, or cultural—threatens to undermine American prestige and moral authority by alienating the confidence, respect, and collaboration of the warrantably sensitive and skeptical non-white world. With all our national power and present strength, over against the huge two-thirds majority of the human race we are in the long run ourselves a rather hapless minority. It must be conceded, and can no longer be concealed, that racial differentials on any level of group living amount to a self-contradicting double standard of democracy.

In 1860, when democracy's vital frontier was the Mason and Dixon dividing line, fate cast the Negro in the role of a critical test of the domestic consistency of democracy in the national Union; today, with the Atlantic, the Pacific and the Rio Grande as cultural boundaries, the Negro is cast very similarly in an international role, involving American democracy's moral and cultural integrity on a world scale and with world influence and leadership at stake. A review of the cultural status of the Negro and the historical steps in its progressive improvement is without doubt the most accurate way to determine the achieved realizations and further prospects of spiritual and cultural democracy among us.

CHAPTER TWO

The Negro in American Culture

IN A consideration of the Negro folk, we fortunately can leave the risky though necessary level of all-inclusive generalization about "the Negro." At best, such generalization can give us only the barest common denominators, the broadest trends, and the diffuse features characteristic of all composite portraits. The subject of the Negro folk, on the other hand, has flesh-and-bone concreteness, and promises to reveal more of the human reality and texture of Negro life and character. The Negro folk products also reflect most vividly the basic group experience and, as anonymous and unsophisticated mass reactions, possess the substance and flavor of what was the common life of more than three fifths of the whole Negro population during more than two thirds of its group history. These folk expressions, of which unhappily we have only a chance-preserved remnant, give us the generic Negro as nothing else can. Paradoxically enough, because of their deeply original and creative character, American culture is most indebted, above all other folk sources, to this lowly but distinctive level of Negro peasant experience.

Even the life of the ante-bellum Negro had wide contrasts and diversities: it was not confined wholly to the common lot of the plantation slave and field laborer. Completely different and separate, of course, was the life of that very considerable group of free Negroes, who after 1790 constituted over one fifth of the Negro population and by 1860 totaled almost a half-million (488,000). Most of these were safely concentrated in the North, but there were a few on the frontier and in upland settlements. Still fewer were precariously located in the mid-South and in oasis sanctuaries like Charleston, Savannah, Mobile, and New Orleans, where by right of free papers and "passes" they somehow held their status. They clung to this precious and often dearly bought station with desperate middle-class conviction and respectability. Often they were so jealous of their privileges and so fearful of the threat of slavery that they remained stiffly apart from their slave brethren, outwardly indifferent to their predicament. They were, as might be expected, desperate conformists, staunchly conventional and Puritan for the most part, disdainful of the manner, speech, and what were to them the demeaning relaxations of the shouting, boisterous, uninhibited, openhearted Negro peasant. In the North, free Negroes were occasionally engaged in fellowship with liberal whites either in open abolitionist protest or in underground anti-slavery action. But except for such few brave souls, the free Negroes were fully preoccupied in cautious, conservative, conventional living.

There was, next, at the top level of the larger slave society, a small, anomalous segment of household retainers and servitors who lived apart in comfort, symbiotically absorbed in upper-class manners and values. They shared the life, the refinements, and the outlooks of the master class and upheld at a respectful distance the foibles, feuds, and substantial traditions and interests of "their" families. Often, though far from always, they were natural sons and daughters of the masters, and were discreetly conscious of their fathers and half-sisters and half-brothers. They carefully cultivated proper, restrained manners and conservative standards, disdaining the boisterous, carefree ways of the other slaves, whom they regarded as "common field hands." More than they despised these black "pariahs of the big gate" they despised the poor whites, who, as "white trash," became the scapegoats of their own humiliations. Proudly parasitic, these "house Negroes" were culturally sterile, cultivating the airs of "ladies" and "gentlemen," though generally in a bad imitation of the conduct of the masters. From time to time a few, manumitted, became detached to join (usually with a small patrimony) the more useful class of free Negroes. At times, too, this group, with its education by contact, bred such an outstanding talent as that developed by Phillis Wheatley. Yet, inevitably, a Phillis Wheatley was labeled "an exception" and was usually haunted by the superstition that all talents came from white-inherited characteristics. Phillis Wheatley herself, being pure African, did not suffer this embarrassment, but rather was credited as being imitative—of the whites. Typical, then, with this stratum of Negro life, was its perplexity and confusion of "belonging" and "not belonging," alternating moods of pride and boasting with moods of silent shame. How could they have been expected to escape the cynicism and bitterness that illegitimacy and its imposed badge of psychic and social separateness levied on them? Only occasionally was there a full acceptance of being a Negro on the part of one who usually ripened into a crusading, militant Negro, a race-organizer, and a bitter, implacable foe of slavery.

Below this thin upper level there was a thicker mid-class layer of lower servants and artisans, considerably privileged except on those symbolic occasions when slavery exacted its ceremonial rituals. The artisans had necessary exemption from the common lot by virtue of their skills and usefulness; they built and mended, worked and even supervised, like trusties in their institutional prison. In old age, after years of faithful service, they became privileged characters and prize exhibits of slavery's benevolence. In the household, with the exception of the chore underlings, they, too, had status: there were the "Mammy" nurse, the cook, the gardener, and even the most useful supernumerary, the messenger and tattletale, who often doubled as plantation spy. They knew their rank and held it except when they were subject to punishment. They enjoyed open favor of personal intimacy (after etiquette obeisance) and had a natural security of things by right of the appetites to which they catered. The exception was the ill-fated concubine, whom a Puritan culture condemned to an anomalous status.

At the lowest level, and really supporting all on his bent and lash-scarred back, was the Negro peasant. He sank deeper and deeper into the subsoil of plantation slavery as slavery's weight became harsher and heavier. Harried by day in the fields, and only half relaxed in slave quarters except on festive occasions, the masses of Negro slaves toiled, suffered, and, by some miracle of emotional endurance and compensation, survived. As they shared their burdens, their folk living took on the most intimate sort of collective community. From these depths and pressures arose crude folk reactions expressive in an elemental fashion. These folk products have preserved for us the unique quality of the Negro's mass experience.

It must be understood that slavery was not, even on the average plantation, quite so manorial as this; but such was its basic model. Although it ran a realistic gamut from the frontier holding of a single proprietor with one or two slave helpers to the late-period cotton barony with over one thousand slaves and a corps of driver-overseers, the South's "peculiar institution" assumed the characteristic form here indicated wherever prosperity permitted.

Throughout the many generations of mutually dependent living, contacts between black and white, though not so acknowledged, were close and intimate because of the domestic character of the American slave system. Blacks and whites were also actively reciprocal despite a great outer show of social distance and an elaborate etiquette of social untouchability. Southern tradition has never denied the closeness, but has always rejected any notion of reciprocal exchange. It is a fallacy to assume that the overlord influences the peasant, but remains uninfluenced by him. In this particular historical instance, the undeniable intimacies of the Southern scheme of living, reinforced by considerable crossbreeding, forged bonds too vital to be negated by caste custom and etiquette and too humanly contagious not to transcend "official" color prejudice. Ironically enough, the Old South itself and its insistently intimate domestication of the Negro were mainly responsible. And so, even in his lowly condition of servitude, with its imposed condition of cultural unawareness and intellectual illiteracy, the Negro became a potent folk influence. By planting him in the heart of its domestic life, Southern society provided the base for the Negro's clandestine and unforeseen effect upon its own folkways and institutions.

The orthodox version of race contacts in the South assigns to Negroes solely a one-way direction of cultural traffic and influence, on the understandable but hardly warranted assumption that the Negro, deliberately cut off from the sustenance of his native African culture and fed on the crumbs of an adopted one, had no cultural assets with which to make a contribution. With regard to formalized culture, this was indeed true, but folk culture is another sort of social plant. It has an atmospheric mode of growth and propagation. Within little more than the first generation after his arrival, sturdily surviving slavery's rude transplanting, the Negro rapidly assimilated the basic rudiments of a complex and very alien culture: its English language, its Christian religion, and its Anglo-Saxon mores. The nearly complete loss of his original culture and the resultant vacuumlike emptiness undoubtedly speeded the absorption. The Negro, traditionally credited in this respect with only a "most unusual degree of imitativeness," is really to be credited with phenomenal flexibility and adaptive capacity.

This hasty acculturation, crude as it was, is the outstanding feat of the Negro's group career in America. Considering its handicapped start, one may well concede that it is quite without parallel in human history—certainly on such a mass basis. It is even more significant that within another generation the Negro became originally and vigorously productive at the folk level, and that before very long vital influences from Negroes were weakening the barriers of caste and prejudice. By his characteristic humor, emotional temper, mystic superstitions, contagious nonchalance, amiability, and sentimentality—all of which were later to find expression in typical modes of folk art—the Negro observably colored the general temper and folkways of the American South.

The master class, proud and prejudiced, could, however, under no circumstances take the Negro seriously enough to acknowledge any indebtedness. Its members felt committed to reject one who to them was a legal chattel as well as a hapless, childlike dependent. They even resented any Negro influence that could be recognized as such. But the same society that shut its front doors so relentlessly and raised such formidable barrier of caste, naïvely left its psychological rear doors unguarded. Negro influences came creeping, indeed often crowding, in.

Let us consider a typical instance, that of the humble but triumphant invasion of Negro humor. Behind the humor, seemingly so simple and natural, are a very complex pattern and a complicated social history. Frequently masking sorrow, and sometimes impotent resentment, the Negro's laughter was certainly more often contrived and artificial than natural and spontaneous, despite contrary Southern conviction. Grasping with a desperation that an instinct for survival developed, the Negro early learned the humble, effective art of placating his capricious masters. In time, with the masters' hearty and constant encouragement, the Negroes became established as the South's official jesters. We need assume in this interpretation nothing more sophisticated than the mere adroitness of mother wit, nothing more premeditated than the anticipation of ready rewards for ingratiating behavior. Despite the sad fact that it also led to the most ingrained and contrary-to-fact of all the Southern stereotypes—that of the "happy, contented slave" —this protective mimicry of laughter was for generations an almost infallible psychological weapon of appeal and appeasement for the otherwise defenseless Negro. The South itself occasionally suspected this, as its jocular anecdotes of the Negro's "possum-playing" fully attest. But it yielded, preferring not to spoil the fun by questioning it too deeply. The Southern spirit must often have craved not merely amusement, but also contentment and ease of conscience. Without hurt to its pride and arrogance it often achieved shrewd penance in the capricious kindliness and familiarity evoked by the comradeship of laughter.

Because the comic side of the Negro offered no offense or challenge to the South's tradition of the Negro's subordinate status, it richly colored Southern local and regional culture, and eventually that of the whole nation. The improvised plantation entertainment of ragamuffin groups of dancing, singing, jigging, and grinning slaves, staple amusement of the theaterless South, was the genesis of a major form of the American theater: blackface minstrelsy and its later stepchild, vaudeville. Together they dominated the national stage for a period of at least seventy years (1830–1900). Negro minstrelsy was also destined to become one of America's famous native-culture exports during the latter half of that same period. Despite its broad and frequently misrepresentative caricature, minstrelsy, with its basic idioms of song, dance, and humor, patently reflects its Negro folk origins. It also records the far-reaching consequences of the naïve devices of the Negro folk temperament.

What is of particular interest for the moment is the far different fate of another and even more representative aspect of the Negro folk genius. It must not be overlooked that the comic "jig-song and dance" and the serious, almost tragic "spirituals" were plantation contemporaries. The South that gleefully heard the one must at least have overheard the other. However, the religious folk songs, though equally odd and attractive, did not meet a receptive Southern mood: in fact they ran counter to the stock conception of the Negro's character and status. They are barely mentioned in the whole range of literature of the Pre-Civil War South; in its post-bellum letters they receive only the most casual and indifferent notice. Southerners had been listening to plaintive and rhapsodic folk-singing for generations, but because they listened with cavalier condescension and amused bewilderment they could dismiss the music as just the Negro's "way of carrying on." Although now recognized even by the South as one of its most distinctive regional folk products and as among the rare elements of American native culture, the spirituals could not find recognition and proper appreciation for many years.

At the close of the Civil War, a Northerner, spurred by the sensitive interest of Thomas Wentworth Higginson (colonel of one of the black regiments that served heroically on the Union side), explored with sympathetic curiosity the group life of the Negro freedmen in refugee camps. Noticing what he called "these peculiar but haunting slave songs," he took them seriously and thereby made the momentous discovery of the American Negro's now universally recognized musical genius. He was William Allen, and in 1867, he published *Slave Songs of the United States*, a transcribed collection of the melodies he heard. Out of such chance recovery from generation-long neglect and belittlement, these "slave songs," the unique spiritual portrait of the Negro folk temperament, rose to final recognition and universal acclaim as the incomparable "Negro spirituals."

Even in the Allen transcriptions the precious folk products were only half revealed, for Allen was unable to give adequate notation to the unique folk way of singing them. Only in 1879 was proper interpretation given them by the choral singing of the Fisk Jubilee Singers, a Negro university group. The Jubilee Singers themselves, so under the hypnotism of white disparagement of things wholly and distinctively Negro that they hesitated to put the spirituals on their regular programs, at first gave them as experimental encores and only on request. Not until after the revelation of their profound effect upon musically enlightened audiences, American and European, were the spirituals finally launched on their triumphant career of revealing and vindicating the extraordinary folk genius they so clearly reflect.

Here, then, in epitome, is the story of the Negro as art influence, and of the career of the folk elements in American culture. Negro expression, when flattering and obsequiously entertaining to the majority ego, is readily accepted, and becomes extremely popular in a vulgarized, stereotyped form. When more deeply and fully representative, with undiluted idioms, it has invariably been confronted with apathy and indifference and has been faced with a long struggle for acceptance and appreciative recognition. In the minstrel role, for instance, where at best the Negro was only half himself, at the worst a rough caricature, he was instantly popular and acceptable. The spirituals, in which he was seriously self-expressive, met with long-standing disinterest and misunderstanding. In the arts, as in matters political, economic, and social, the Negro advance has been a slow, tortuous journey from slavery toward freedom. Step by step, and from one province to another, Negro genius and talent have plodded a hard road to freer and more representative artistic self-expression.

In many fields the goal of maturity and freedom has now been achieved or nearly achieved; in some areas the Negro artist is on a parity with his white fellow artists. In a few fields, as in music, the dance, and acting, by reason of an unrivaled quality of expressive control, he has staked out areas of distinctive originality and pre-eminence. But on the whole, the Negro's conquest of the more formal and sophisticated arts—fiction, playwriting, literary and art criticism, and the like—has been slow and hazardous, in part because of his limited cultural opportunities and contacts. Faster progress, as might be expected, has been made in those areas where there was an early start in well-developed folk art. This explains very obviously why the Negro was outstanding in vocal and choral music earlier than he was successful with instrumental music; again, there was a great skill and preference for improvisation as opposed to formal musical composition. The Negro has, in fact, many generally recognized qualities of special excellence in the arts. His talents, however, are best understood and interpreted as the cumulative effects of folk tradition and group conditioning. This interpretation belies the popular hypothesis that some mysterious "folk traits" or native ethnic endowment are responsible for Negro artistic capabilities and expression. What might be called, for lack of a better term, "folk virtuosities" must be credited to the special character and circumstances of the Negro group experience. The artistic "virtuosities" have been passed on by way of social heritage; they are just that: a heritage, not an endowment.

Among these artistic virtuosities may be mentioned what is often referred to as the "gift of spontaneous harmony." This is really a transmitted musical ear-mastery based on group choral singing, and is very like that of the Welsh or Russian peasants. Similarly to be explained is the Negro musician's instrumental versatility in improvisation and inventive sound and rhythm, lying back of the resourceful impromptu musicianship and extraordinary techniques of jazz. Like the phenomenal, unorthodox resources of the gypsy performer, the techniques go back to the ready skills and tricks of the humble folk musician. Other outstanding Negro artistic "gifts" include an unusual fluency of oral expression, both forceful rhetoric and spectacular imagery. The Negro has, also, a marked, almost intuitive, skill in mimicry, pantomime, and dramatic projection. Above all, he has a virtuoso facility in rhythm, both formal and spontaneous, which is the taproot of his notable aptitude in dance and body-control. These, and others to be examined later in greater detail, are indeed characteristic Negro folk qualities, but they have no need of the trite, pseudoscientific explanations so frequently given of them. On the contrary, they suffer from such unscientific and unrealistic implications.

The few but significant African cultural survivals and carryovers in American Negro life have likewise been too magically conceived as transmissions by heredity. They also have a realistic social explanation. Their supposed innate character is disproved by their relative or complete absence among Negroes in localities where, as in the northern and western United States, the environment favorable for their survival is lacking. The converse proof is the greater prevalence and intensity of such traits in areas like the Caribbean and Brazil, where native African culture was not so ruthlessly broken down, where the racial concentration was denser, and where, most important of all, the more lenient attitudes of Latin culture did not suppress Africanisms as "horribly" venal and pagan.

Negro folk influences have generally exerted themselves with more immediate and lasting effect in the zone of the more tolerant Latin culture, though even there in degrees varying according to local cirucumstances. In those areas characteristic African patterns in folklore, music, and ritualistic folk customs still survive recognizably intact. For the same reason, as after-effect of the French tradition in New Orleans, we still find in Louisiana strong survivals both of musical idioms and of such ritualistic customs as "voodoo." On the other hand, broadly speaking, within the radius of the rigid, less tolerant Anglo-Saxon zone (which characteristically reinforced its racial prejudice with cultural disdain) Negro cultural influence, though by no means negligible, is much more indirect, Here, in most cases, the African elements survive only fragmentarily.

There are, however, surviving Africanisms within the borders of Anglo-Saxon communities—the coastal islands of Georgia and the Carolinas and even the vicinity of Charleston, South Carolina, are examples. But these are amply explained—in the case of the islands by their relative isolation and the dense and stable character of their Negro population, in the case of the Charleston region possibly by the cultural differential of its French Huguenot stock, which, though Protestant, was Latin in social attitudes.

With the exception of New Orleans, the United States lacks almost completely the interesting mixed or "creole" cultures so typical of Latin-American contacts with the Negro and, for that matter, with the Indian peoples also. Although biologically the mulatto is conspicuously present in our society, that parallel phenomenon, which Manuel Gonzales so aptly calls the "mulatto culture," is just as conspicuously absent. In marked contrast also with the many *patois* language mergers to the south of us, language crossing has rarely occurred in the United States, again with the exception of New Orleans Creole. Carolina "Gullah," which at one time promised to spread as a Negro pidgin English, is now only an exceptional reservoir of African linguistic survivals with no cultural outlet or influence. The chauvinism and exclusiveness of the Anglo-Saxon code of culture, mainly responsible for this, are deeply ingrained and characteristic. Its aftereffects, resulting in the late maturing and delayed influence not only of the Negro, but also of other minority-group cultures, have thus considerably affected American art and letters. Until comparatively recently this rigid snobbishness has kept the upper levels of American culture "pure," but also, as many are now willing to admit, thin and anemic. Meanwhile, at all other less-guarded levels, as our anthropologists have been discovering, the inevitable osmosis of culture contact has been taking place constantly.

For the double reason of such inhospitable attitudes and the lack of any vitally intact ancestral culture, the American Negro's folk products have had to be fashioned almost wholly from forms and ingredients borrowed from the majority culture. This has had advantages and disadvantages. The compensating advantage has been that, without substantial loss of racial character, Negro folk expression is also characteristically American and, when adopted, has circulated as indigenous to the national culture. Unlike the products of Creole and *patois* culture, it is not felt to be alien or exotic, but is sensed as just another emotional dialect of a common heritage and tradition. Even when the Negro producer has himself not received comparable acceptance, his creations have often been widely and openheartedly accepted. Some indeed, like minstrelsy and jazz, have been so completely and congenially shared that they have taken on national representativeness, and when exported have become known as "American," and not particularly as American Negro, products. After all, this is in accord with our type of composite and democratic culture, especially when, as is now more frequently the case, the Negro artist is being acknowledged and credited along with his own creative productions.

There is the disadvantage: that of being subject, as hybrids of one degree or another, to endless vulgarized exploitation. Jazz and ragtime are obvious examples. As another, the folk sagas of Uncle Remus and others have been watered down to tawdry sentiment and pale banality, their fine folk speech and imagery effaced by insipid, badly transcribed dialect. In spite of all this, the admixture of the Negro temperament and its folk idioms has usually produced something recognizably characteristic by virtue of a distinctive emotional stamp and flavor. In rare cases like the spirituals, the subtle folk alchemy has transformed the borrowed materials into an end-product so uniquely intimate and typical as almost—but not completely—to defy imitation. Even the spirituals have not been entirely exempt from attempted imitation, although fortunately a synthetic spiritual usually rings counterfeit after the first few phrases. More typically, however, the creative Negro folk fusions have fallen, for better or worse, into the public artistic domain. Most notable in this last instance are the style and patterns of ragtime and jazz, which for at least two generations have dominated popular American music and our stage and popular dance. Associated with them has been that contagious succession of new and compelling dance idioms which have enjoyed similar vogue. Only slightly less influential have been the matchless folk balladry of the "blues" and the popularity of many of the secular work songs and folk-tale ballads. Some of them, like *John Henry,* are Negro originals; others, like *Casey Jones* and *Frankie and Johnny,* are remodeled from general American folklore and often have greater power and wider currency than their originals.

The more the cultural rather than the sociological approach

to the Negro is emphasized, the more apparent it becomes that the folk products of the American Negro are imperishably fine, and that they constitute a national artistic asset of the first rank. They have survived precariously; much has been lost. Modern research, especially the folk-music-archives project of the Library of Congress, has retrieved a noteworthy remnant. But Uncle Remus and the spirituals are enough to establish the high quality of the unadulterated product. The folk-story background was recovered by such discerning Southern writers as Thomas Cable and Joel Chandler Harris. But modern scholarship has yet to delete the sentimental additions that glossed over the real "folkiness" of the originals. Grateful as we must be to Harris for his timely preservation of the most organic body of Negro folk tale American literature possesses, we cannot help wishing that he had been a more careful and less improvising amanuensis for the mid-Georgia Negro peasant whom he knew and liked so well. For when the contemporary folklorist arrived on the scene with his scientific attitudes and skills, Uncle Remus and his kind had all but vanished.

The heritage of the religious and secular folk song and dance was saved by the Negroes themselves, beginning, as we have already seen, with the work of the Fisk Jubilee Singers. Their effort, dating from 1878, has culminated since 1900 in the work of an outstanding succession of such Negro musicians as Harry T. Burleigh, Nathaniel Dett, Rosamond and James Weldon Johnson, John Work, Jr., Roland Hayes, and Hall Johnson, all of whom have labored to preserve and promote the folk music. Some have done it through careful transcriptions of Negro folk song; others have created elaborate formal composition based on folk themes. Through the creative work of the musicians and in increasingly competent musicology, critically interpreting this most important folk phase of American music, we are now in a position to appraise its genuine worth. Rated as finely representative of its historical source and setting, this folk treasure is regarded as even more precious in its potential value as material for fresh artistic reworking. Consequently, contemporary musicians and folklorists, Negro and white, are turning back more and more to early Negro folk music. For the Negro musician it has served as a special asset, especially since the onset in the 1920's of the "New Negro" movement, which established as a basic objective the artist's return to Negro folk materials.

This claim to being the most important body of American folk music is well supported by comparison with the competitor traditions: the so-called "hillbilly" tunes, dances, and ballads of the "mountain whites," the "cowboy" songs and ballads of the ranch country, and the less-known but richly potential

Spanish-Indian folk materials of the Southwest border. Without minimizing any of these, one may easily concede that none is comparable in either range of artistry or scope of influence to the many-sided, perennially influential Negro tradition. The balladry of the mountain culture is of great value and interest, particularly as a fine survival of old Scotch-Irish and English lore and folkways, but its musical and dance idioms are, in comparison with Negro idioms, mediocre and monotonously shallow. By right of kinship and racial affinity, however, the mountain culture should have been the preference of the South. But the Southern patricians looked down on the "poor whites" and disdained their culture. Only in the upland retreats away from the pressures of this condescension did the Appalachian culture become assertive enough to flourish, and even there it was inbred and somewhat anemic.

Paradoxically, then, the South, by culturally rejecting the "poor whites" and patriarchically accepting the Negro (on its own terms, which included keeping the Negro "in his place"), paved the way for Negro folkways to become the peasant culture of nearly three fourths of its geographic area. The plantation system dominated the entire lowland agrarian region and, with its semifeudal regime and the relation of the Negro masses to it, provided the closest approximation in American social history to the conditions and social climate of peasantry. The United States has never possessed a true peasant class: the geographic and the class mobility of almost all elements of the population precluded the slow compounding of one generation on the other. Even the Negro, whose masses did live for generations in a static, stratified way, shared, to a reduced degree, the typical American experience and privilege of place and class mobility. After emancipation, he underwent wave after wave of migration, intersectional to the North and Midwest, intrasectional from the plantations and farms to the Southern cities. But certainly during slavery, and in many of the more rural areas of the South thereafter, it was the Negro's hard lot to remain static from one generation to the next and thus to approximate a peasant class. This social experience, if analyzed in some detail, can explain both the peculiar character and the unusual strength of the Negro folk influence.

This fate, which was and to some extent still is the Negro's basic ordeal and handicap, had one lone compensation. The immobility, reinforced by the psychological weight of prejudice, developed an unusual degree of group solidarity, tended to preserve the characteristic folk values, and intensified the Negro's traditional modes of expression. Out of rejection and oppression there evolved emotional distinctiveness; out of persecution and suffering there evolved unique compensatory ways of making life livable. Until recently, then, caste prejudice has considerably insulated the Negro folkways from the powerful standardizing processes of general American living. With the aboriginal Indian folkways pushed to the periphery of American society and concentrated on reservations (which did not occur in Central and South America), the Negro folk offerings stand out in the rather colorless amalgam of the general population as among the most distinctive spiritual elements in American culture.

By virtue of these folk qualities and their artistic manifestations, the foundations of which were well laid before the end of slavery, the Negro has made America considerably his cultural debtor. For here in the United States there has been no exception to the historical rule that the roots of a national culture are in its soil and its peasantry. Accordingly, some of the most characteristic features of American culture are derivatives of the folk life and spirit of this darker tenth of the population. This claim, first made in 1922 by James Weldon Johnson in his famous preface to *The Book of American Negro Poetry*, has never been challenged seriously. The inventory of this humble but influential contribution is impressive: the spirituals, Uncle Remus, a whole strain of distinctive humor, some of the most typical varieties of Southern folk balladry, a major form and tradition of the American theater (the minstrel and vaudeville), and practically all of the most characteristic idioms of modern American popular music and dance. Many of these idioms, of course, have been blended with elements from the majority culture, sometimes for the better, sometimes for the worse; but their Negro origin and distinctive uniqueness are now universally acknowledged. This adds up to a patterning of a substantial part of the native American art forms and to an unusually large share in molding and sustaining the entertainment life of the whole nation. Strange trick of destiny this, that the group of the population most subject to oppression and its sorrows should furnish so large a share of the population's joy and relaxation!

These contributions stretch out, of course, over a wide span of time and a variety of social conditions, but divide naturally into two phases. The first is a true folk period of slavery, the second a post-slavery period in which, in addition to continued folk production, creative artists, Negro and white, have engaged in extensive elaboration and reworking of the folk materials. Only a small, precious remnant of the first phase survives: much more was undoubtedly produced and then irretrievably lost. Nevertheless, the scant fragments of Uncle Remus, the spirituals, and a few older-generation seculars give us a revealing portrait of the ante-bellum Negro and his composite folk temperament.

The post-slavery crop, much more extensive and varied, as well as more adulterated, gives us the important picture of the interaction of Negro folk idioms and materials with the rest of American culture. Indeed, as we approach our own times, we discover Negro influences operating simultaneously on three cultural levels: the folk, the popular, and the formally artistic. Production still continues in very reduced volume on the folk level, while influences like ragtime music and jazz expand importantly in the popular arts, and still other strains of influence work constructively on the sophisticated levels of formal American music, art, and literature—a rare cultural phenomenon indeed. Research in remote, undisturbed areas has unearthed creative folk artistry still active, producing contemporary religious and secular folk balladry only slightly different from the spirituals and blues that are their traditional prototypes. Though in imminent danger from an advancing technological civilization, the folk well-springs are not yet quite exhausted. After nearly a generation of most profitable and creative use, the artistic potentials of Negro materials in popular and formal American art seem still considerable and promising.

The most deeply characteristic folk qualities, which even today are sources of artistic strength and appeal, are registered perhaps most clearly in the earliest folk products. Of course, we find in them only a dated portrait of the ante-bellum Negro and his outlook, but they nonetheless supply a key to later phases of Negro creative expression. For the Negro experience during slavery, and to a modified degree ever since, has involved abnormal degrees of emotional stress and strain, and has evoked deep, elemental, though far from primitive, reactions. Not all of these have been somber and tragic: indeed, as we have seen, some have been exuberantly lighthearted and joyful. But all of them in some aspect or other have been compensatory. Alongside that serious, mystical, and other-worldly catharsis of religious escape and ecstasy, there existed, quite as usefully for successful survival, the emotional exhausts of laughter, ridicule, and even mockery, of which Uncle Remus is such a good example. Indeed, there would be much more of this comic relief of satire and laughter on record if Negro folk humor could have had an inside instead of an outside reporting. But the scheming, relentless "Br'er Fox" and the patient, cunningly resourceful "Br'er Rabbit" remain to tell a sly, meaningful allegory and to display the crafty comic consolation they once afforded.

The spirituals naturally reflect the most serious and intimate aspects of the slave Negro. Under the crucible-like pressures of slavery, with semiliterate but deep absorption of the essentials of Christianity, the slave Negro found with remarkable intuition and insight his two main life-sustaining aspirations: the hope of salvation and the hope of freedom. This was a creative reaction of the first magnitude, for it did much to save his spirit from breaking. It was also a triumph of folk art. From the episodes and imagery of the Bible, the Negro imaginatively reconstructed his own versions in musical and poetic patterns both highly original and of great emotional vitality. The borrowed materials were transformed to new fervor and a deepened mysticism, stemming very unexpectedly from a naïve and literal acceptance of Bible truths and a translation of them into the homeliest, most vividly concrete sort of imagery. Sober evangelical hymns became rhapsodic chants, and the traditional Bible lore came alive again in such new colloquial phrases as the "deep river that chills the body but not the soul," "De morning star was a witness, too," "Dese bones gwine to rise again," "Bright sparkles in de churchyard give light unto de tomb," and "My Lord is so high you can't get over Him,/He's so low you can't get under Him,/You gotta come in an' through de Lamb."

At the same time, from Old Testament sources, the slaves' imagination singled out the episodes relevant to their own condition, and used Jewish parallels to nourish their own hopes of physical freedom and to chide shrewdly and challenge their masters with their own beliefs. There was social point as well as religious faith to such exhortations as "Go down, Moses, tell ole Pharaoh to set my people free" and "Didn't my Lord deliver Daniel and why not every man?" "Steal away to Jesus" was sometimes a plea for revival conversion, at others, a password for camp-meeting assemblies, and, it is said, occasionally an encouraging signal for slave fugitives. Rescued from the disesteem of slavery and properly appraised, these first-crop folk creations fully justify James Weldon Johnson's estimate: "The Uncle Remus stories constitute the greatest body of folklore America has produced, and the spirituals are its greatest single body of folk-song." Although reactions to the Negro's own specific situation and experience, they are so profoundly intense as to become significantly universal; there are no finer expressions than these Negro folk utterances of the belief in freedom and immortality or of the emotional essences of Christianity native to the American soil. A brilliant ex-slave, Frederick Douglass, aptly called slavery "the graveyard of the mind," but happily it did not turn out to be the tomb of the Negro spirit.

CHAPTER THREE

The Early Folk Gifts: Music, Dance, Folklore

THE EARLY Negro folk gifts of music, dance, and folklore had a much stronger influence or impact on Southern whites than was generally conceded. This is understandable, because white Southerners were notably articulate about the implications of a true democracy, but were dedicated to the rigid perpetuation of a society whose foundation rested upon slavery. Yet, because plantations—indeed, the plantation tradition itself—precluded access to theaters or music halls, plantation dwellers lacked formal entertainment. In time, the overt manifestations of the slaves' adjustments and reactions to slavery became the only steady form of "entertainment" for Southern plantation whites. The Negro slave, for innumerable reasons, cultivated, through the medium of folk tales, music, and dance—and the various ramifications of each—what might be termed an emotional or psychic catharsis for his utter frustration and often bitter sense of personal and group futility as he pondered on his humiliating and hopeless condition as a slave. As a matter of sheer survival, both physical and spiritual, it was essential that the Negro slave develop some source of release for the resentments and frustrations that human bondage created. These releases acquired diversified forms and qualities. Yet, in the main, there was a sufficient amount of instinctive adroitness for each "release"—whether it was in terms of profoundly serious religious expression or of sly and ingratiating wit—to keep the white owners assured that nothing more significant than native religious fervor (which they disdained) or native capacity for buffoonery (which they regarded with amused condescension) was involved. In the final analysis, both extremes were tolerated not only as Negro folk expressions, but also as the only available sources of entertainment.

The Early Folk Gifts: Music, Dance, Folklore 39

Although the whites were less amenable or susceptible to the deeply moving pathos of the spirituals than they were to the Negro secular music, they at least did not ban the former; despite themselves, they were influenced by the deep piety of the spirituals. Actually, the fact that Negroes were by nature spontaneously musical and rhythmic confirmed the Southern whites' studiously cultivated conviction that the Negro was less than civilized, being pagan-primitive in his essential nature, and therefore needing the benevolent protection that slavery accorded him. Outrageous as this thesis is to modern sensibilities, it must be recalled that early colonial America was tuneful only in church. But even church music, in early colonial times and later, was neither spontaneous nor original. The best explanation is that early America was mostly Anglo-Saxon (more so than present-day America), which meant a weak musical heritage, a very plain musical taste, and a Puritan bias against music as a symbol of sin and the devil and a threat to work, seriousness, and moral restraint. So early America could sing only in church, in praise of God; in the daily routine of life, she hummed or whistled simple songs or kept silent. There was open and obvious joy in music only where French or Spanish influence touched American life (as in Louisiana and Southern California) or, later, where German immigrants, with their traditional background of music, settled in considerable numbers. The beginnings of American opera occurred at New Orleans, and our great orchestras and their cultivation of serious classical music are to be traced in most instances to German influences. It is doubtful that America would have heard much great or original music without these foreign minority influences.

If American civilization had absorbed instead of exterminating the American Indian, his music would have been the folk music of this country. It could well have been, for it was a very noble and simple music full of the spirit of the wind, woods, and water, as serious American musicians have discovered too late. It fell to the lot of the Negro, whom slavery domesticated, to furnish our most original and influential folk music and to lay the foundations for native American music. Certain strains of Irish and Old English folk music have lingered in our mountain country and the backwoods, and are still important as musical sources; but the Negro's music has gradually dominated the field.

There are three strains in the music of the Negro. One is his folk music, produced without formal musical training or intention by the greatest and most fundamental of all musical forces—emotional creation. In the Negro's case, this creative force was deep suffering and the spiritual compensation of intense religious emotion and ecstasy. This rich vein of emotional expression has yielded not only the "spirituals," but also the most characteristic Negro musical idiom. It is an idiom sad but not somber, tragic but ecstatic, intense but buoyant.

The Negro's love of gaiety and humor and his periodic rejection of the intense sorrow and seriousness that slavery brought him inspired the second strain of Negro folk music—light, mock-sentimental, full of pagan humor and sharp irony. Very little pure folk music of this lighter strain remains: in highly diluted form, imitatively exploited by both white and Negro musicians, it has become the principal source and ingredient of American popular music. Indeed, both strains of Negro folk music have been crudely imitated, the tragic and heroic elements too frequently reduced to the sentimental, the comic and ironic elements reduced to burlesque or farce. There is no truer test of what is genuinely folk quality in Negro music than a contrast of the melodramatic sentimentality of a manufactured spiritual like *De Glory Road* and the heroic simplicity of *Go Down Moses* or *My Lord, What a Mornin'*. Or again, the contrast of the slapstick comedy of *It ain't Goin' Rain No More* with the true folk humor of *Oh, didn't It Rain*.

The third strain is a strictly formal or concert type of music, properly styled Negro only when obviously derived from folk-music idioms or strongly influenced by them. Music in the universal mode without trace of folk idiom and influence earns cultural credit for the race when composed by Negro musicians and is properly mentioned in this or any other similar account, but is in no proper sense styled "Negro music." "Classical jazz," however, whether written by white or Negro musicians, is properly labeled "Negro music" because it is basically Negro in derivation and inspiration. Classical jazz is an important part of typical or national American music, and must be evaluated as one of the Negro's major cultural contributions.

Humanity's musical experience has taught us that the roots of all great music lie in folk music, to which musical geniuses invariably turn for source material and inspiration. Much classical music is folk music at second or third remove from the original folk source. Yet folk elements do not necessarily make folk music. Only when pure and in the form originally used by the people themselves do they yield true folk music. When folk elements are stereotyped and imitated, we have popular music with a folk flavor, from *Yankee Doodle* to *Old Folks at Home*. When developed and blended with the technique of formal music, these elements, no longer content with the simple forms of the folk or sentimental ballad, yield

The Early Folk Gifts: Music, Dance, Folklore 41

classical music of folk origin. Examples are Dett's *Juba Dance* or a concert arrangement of a "spiritual." When so thoroughly blended as to be recognized only through technical analysis, folk music has become completely universalized and has made its final contribution, as the German chorale in a Bach instrumental chorale or a Polish folk dance in a Chopin polonaise. Similarly, the melodic forms of Italian opera come from provincial folk songs. A song originally at home in the mountain valleys of the Caucasus or the lonely northern steppes or the half-Asiatic towns of Russian Georgia would finally wind up in the composition of the great Russian musicians of St. Petersburg and Moscow. When the folk songs of the Negro of the Georgia plantations, the Carolina rice fields, or the Mississippi bayous emerge as spirituals and blues in concert halls, or as ingredients in the symphonies of such white European composers as Dvořák, Delius, and Milhaud, or such Negro composers as William A. Dawson, Nathaniel Dett, and William Grant Still, Negro folk songs are following the traditional course.

An invariable question is: "Is folk idiom racial or national?" It is both, with a difference of degree only. What we call racial is only an intensified variety of the elements we call national. Likewise, if we call the Negro especially musical, he is so only in degree. As we approach the peasant stocks of the Irish, Italian, German, and Russian nations, we see they all have their wellsprings of folk music. The Negro in America furnished the subsoil of our national music because he supplied the peasant class.

Another early folk gift of the American Negro was rhythm. Master also of pitch and harmony, as are all folk-singing people, the Negro excelled in his mastery of rhythm. Of the many reasons advanced for this unrivaled skill, the most likely is the fact that the Negro has had such long contact with the dance. Dancing, for the Negro, has always been a spontaneous and normal mode of expression, rather than an artificial and formalized one. The Negro dancer improvises not only in solos, but frequently in group dancing. Although Negro dancing is seemingly a matter of foot movements, the rhythm always begins from within as a body vibration, and throughout the whole dance the body vibrates sympathetically. The Negro dancer's capacity to elaborate upon a basic rhythm by changing, doubling, and skipping beats bewilders those less expert in rhythmic patterns and designs. Along with this, the Negro dance has the features, characteristic of Russian, Polish, and other Slavic folk dances, of sudden changes of pace and daring climaxes of tempo. These subtle ways of varying the simplest rhythmic patterns constitute the secret of their unusual and basic musical ability. Many think the Negro rhythm inimitable in its naturalness, its lack of self-consciousness, and its freedom and technical assurance.

When Negroes were first imported into North America as slaves, they brought with them the religious and ritualistic dances of their African tribal culture. Over a period of time, with the Negro's adoption of Christian beliefs and dogma, the African forms were modified—in some instances absorbed by the dominant culture, and in others assimilated. Katherine Dunham, in her essay "The Negro Dance," points out that England (and obviously America) is more prone than, say, France, to impose its own culture on a minority. To quote her: ". . . the integrity of African culture and the sanctity of African religious tradition persists to a greater extent in, for example, Haiti and Martinique than in Jamaica or Trinidad." She concedes, however, that, although "a direct retention of African forms in North America is certainly the exception rather than the rule," there is unmistakable evidence of assimilation of African religious expression into Christian ideology. She cites hand-clapping, foot-stamping, the "confession" and "conversion," the jumping and leaping that typify many church rituals as direct carry-overs from African tribal ritual. It might be noted that churches given to such practices are not limited to rural areas. In many large cities, as well as in small towns, so-called "store-front" churches perpetuate this blend of African and Anglo-Saxon religious expression. Only recently in a mountain town in West Virginia I had occasion to visit such a church. The meeting was in a tiny one-room building; only seven or eight persons were present. Each rose in turn to confess his sins or to "testify" to some startling religious experience or revelation. Generally beginning in a low monotone, the speakers invariably worked themselves into a terrifying frenzy—in three instances collapsing on the floor. They cried, sobbed, moaned, and often became absolutely rigid.

By and large, however, African religious rituals became less dominant because of their incompatibility with basic Christian ideology and ritual. As the Negro church became more conventional and conservative, the tribal legacy diminished.

Insofar as the dance is concerned, "the transition from tribal to folk culture expressed itself in three ways," Miss Dunham notes. She points out: "1. the use of African ritual patterns for the expression of Christian ideolog ; 2. the degeneration of religious ritual patterns by virtue of the degeneration of the ideology which sustained them into secular use; and 3. the combination of secular African patterns with the secular patterns of whatever European nation happened to

The Early Folk Gifts: Music, Dance, Folklore 43

dominate the territory." Here in America, the "Juba" dance is a good example of a secular. The late Thomas Talley describes it in *Negro Folk Rhymes* as a dance involving a large number of participants of whom only one or two perform at one time. The dancers perform inside a large circle and are expected not only to punctuate the rhyme with improvised steps, but also "to execute some graceful dance in such a manner that their feet would beat a tattoo on the ground answering to every word, and sometimes to every syllable of the rhyme being repeated by those in the circle." The folk dance rhyme *Juba*, obviously highly rhythmic, starts:

> *Juba dis, an' Juba dat,*
> *Juba skin dat Yaller Cat. Juba! Juba!*
>
> *Juba jump an' Juba sing.*
> *Juba cut dat Pigeon's Wing. Juba! Juba!*

Other secular dances demand that the performer act out the words. *Jump Jim Crow* demands:

> *Git fus upon yo' heel,*
> *An' den upon yo' toes;*
> *An' ebry time you tu'n 'round,*
> *You jump Jim Crow.*
>
> *Now fall upon yo' knees,*
> *Jump up an' bow low;*
> *An' ebry time you tu'n 'round,*
> *You jump Jim Crow.*
>
> *Put yo' han's upon yo' hips,*
> *Bow low to yo' beau;*
> *An' ebry time you tu'n 'round,*
> *You jump Jim Crow.*

The large group maintains constant hand-clapping and foot-tapping, and dances singly or in pairs. Talley's explanation, which seems plausible, is that the foot-tapping is a substitute for the drum beats of African orchestras. African war songs and others are sung against the background of native drum orchestras. There being no drums in America, foot-tapping was instituted.

A further gift of the Negro folk is that of folklore. Joel Chandler Harris, with his Uncle Remus stories, established a vogue for Negro folk tales which has persisted until the present day. Harris, as critics pretty generally agree, handled Negro dialect well. He constructed classic animal stories based on Negro fables, many of which have parallels in Africa and the Caribbean.

Critics, however, are rather severe on the Uncle Remus stories. With justification, Arthur Fauset denies the tales true folklore status because the narrator plays a too-important role, and thus "this type of story ceases to be a folk tale and becomes in reality a product of the imagination of the author." Fauset suggests that the narrator interprets the Negro folk instead of recounting a tale from the conventionally dispassionate or unobtrusive point of view of the folk narrator. Sterling Brown has referred to "Uncle Remus" as a walking apologist for slavery. Certain stereotypes speedily developed: the "good Negro" was the docile, contented one; the "bad Negro" was the malcontent, the aspiring *type* (not person). Domestic loyalty of the Negroes, paternalistic condescension by the whites, and the happy and benevolent relationship between the two dominated the Harris tales. A succession of imitators produced volumes of folk tales. With varying degrees of success they attempted to create Negro dialects, to defend ante-bellum traditions, to dramatize Negro superstitions, and to stress the colorful and the exotic. Today, as we shall see later, the entire approach to and interpretation of folklore are completely different.

Related to folk music, the dance, and folklore was early Negro minstrelsy. It was not primarily music: the early minstrel was no lyric troubadour, but an improvising clown. Music was part of his show, but his prime responsibility was to perform ridiculous antics and eccentric dancing. Plantation minstrelsy existed for generations, but it was not presented professionally until the 1830's. James Weldon Johnson tells us: "Every plantation had its talented band that could crack jokes, and sing and dance to the accompaniment of the banjo and the 'bones'—the bones being the actual ribs of sheep or other small animal, cut the proper length, scraped clean and bleached in the sun. When the planter wished to entertain his guests, he needed only to call his troupe of black minstrels." At times these bands became semiprofessional and traveled around a circuit, but the limitations of chattel slavery set definite bounds to this.

An account of minstrelsy's professional history is given in the chapter on drama. Here we are concerned with the fact that minstrelsy was originally a folk offering limited to plantation families and their guests. Because the minstrels were meant to entertain, the elements of Negro life and character traditionally and conventionally regarded as typical were emphasized and elaborated. The happy, carefree, ingenious, sly,

The Early Folk Gifts: Music, Dance, Folklore

comic aspects of the Negro character dominated. The slave knew what the masters wished to see and believe. The slaveowners, seeing their own concepts of slave character reaffirmed by the cavortings of the slaves, could reassure guests as to the wisdom of slavery, and themselves be reassured.

To what extent can the early Negro folk gifts be related to the African background? To what extent have the folk gifts been modified or distorted by American components? Many American Negro folk tales are based upon African legends, but the original legends have been examined, studied, or credited too rarely. According to Arthur Fauset, the amount and quality of the folklore that the American Negro inherited from Africa "rivals . . . that of any people on the face of the globe, and is not confined to stories of the Uncle Remus type, but includes a variety of story forms, legends, saga cycles, songs, proverbs, and fantastic, almost mythical, material." Only in the comparatively recent past have writers applied more scientific techniques to the matter of collecting and transcribing folklore. The work of such present-day writers as Guy Johnson, Julia Peterkin, and Zora Neale Hurston (to name but three out of many) has done a great deal to establish the folk tale in legitimate perspective. In contrast with post-Civil War collections, present-day ones reflect not the bias for slavery or the stereotyped Negroes, but the wide, natural range of Negro character and sensibility. Humor, irony, tragedy, pathos, exuberance—these qualities make Negro folk tales come alive and take on universal appeal. Yet, even now, the study of Negro folklore is not receiving sufficient serious attention—particularly in terms of the African ancestry. However, Negro folklore and legends, the "tall tales" and anecdotes, have become a recognized part of American folk culture.

The relationship of American Negro folk music, poetry, and the dance to Africa is more difficult to determine. The American Negro's emphasis on these arts was in striking contrast to the African's predominant concern for the arts of decoration and design. There are, of course, the remarkable carry-over of the rhythmic gift and an emotional inheritance of deep-seated aesthetic endowment. But when the African was transplanted to America, more than a change of art forms and cultural patterns resulted. There was a reversal of emotional temper and attitude. The spirit of African expression, by and large, is disciplined, sophisticated, laconic, and fatalistic. The emotional temper of the American Negro has been exactly the opposite. What has often been thought of as primitive in the American Negro—his naïveté, his sentimentalism, his exuberance, and his improvising spontaneity—is not characteristically African. Nor can these qualities be explained as an ancestral heritage. They are the result of the African Negro's peculiar experience in America, with its emotional upheavals, ordeals, and sufferings.

Increasingly, however, there is evidence of the influence of what might be called the Gulf Stream of African musical influence. It has followed the African wherever he has gone. The nearer the source, the more evident the influence. Strongest in the South, the Carolina coast islands, Haiti, the Bahamas, the eastern provinces of Cuba, Vera Cruz, and Yucatán, it is less strong in Brazil, the Spanish West Indies, the Creole area of America, and lower Spain. It is reflected but faintly in the American Southwest and in sophisticated Mexican and Argentine music; yet it is strong enough to be detected even there. It turns up unmistakably in a Southwestern ballad like *The St. James Infirmary Blues*, in the *Brazilian Quartet* by Heitor Villa-Lobos, in the carioca of Trinidad, the beguine of Guadeloupe, and the Argentine tango.

Even when the stream divides between two different cultures, as in the case of the basic triple rhythm characteristic of Creole, Caribbean, and Negro South American music and the two-four, four-four rhythm with displaced beat characteristic of North American Negro music, we can, if we trace back far enough, find them side by side in Africa. Similarly, the distinction still made by many critics between the Afro-American and the African music generally fades out at the source. It has been said that the harmonic element in American Negro music is "an acquired element due to the religious music of the Anglo-Saxons." Constant Lambert insists that harmony does not exist in primitive African music, and that its presence in Afro-American music is a sign of Anglo-Saxon influence. But Ballanta Taylor, an African musician, insists that a comparison of American Negro spirituals with West African folk song revealed that both are sung in harmony. All other folk songs except those of Hungary are in unison. If this is so, the strangeness of African musical patterns has led the European critics astray. A characteristic Negro harmony, latent in the complex antiphonal music of Africa, needs only simplification to become obvious. But the actual connecting link among all styles and varieties of Negro music is rhythm which, though everywhere distinctive enough to be recognized, reaches, in Africa, a peak of development admittedly unsurpassed.

The matter of African survivals in American Negro folk art and the extent to which this native art was tempered by Anglo-Saxon custom and tradition can probably never be conclusively resolved. It is certainly an established fact, however,

The Early Folk Gifts: Music, Dance, Folklore 47

that no group of people transported permanently from one culture to another can fail to absorb and be influenced by the dominant culture or the environmental factors of the new situation. The men of the New England theocracy, for example, were not for long Englishmen in a new world; they quickly acquired a new "identity" created and tempered by the conditions of the New World. Because of the peculiar impact of frontier conditions, the early frontiersmen of the West acquired new "identities," developing different objectives in every area of life from religion to making a living. Obviously, then, American Negroes reacted to and were influenced by their new surroundings. The adoption of Christianity alone would account for a large measure of cultural transformation. But the Negro, relegated to peasant status, and thus destined to be the folk "carrier," retained a latent cultural identity with Africa. It is to be assumed that this was not always a conscious retention—certainly not after the earliest generations had died. The major and obvious exceptions, of course, are the few remaining areas where a sustained homogeneity of Negroes prevails—the coastal islands off Georgia and South Carolina, for example, as observed earlier.

The question is often posed as to whether or not the Negro's cultural identity will eventually be lost. I think that it is clear that the Negro, with his folk gifts, has contributed substantially to American culture. As has been noted, the ultimate destiny of any folk art is to mature to a point at which it has universal rather than folk or regional meaningfulness. This does not by any means detract from either the identity or the worth of the basic folk contribution.

The whole matter of Africanisms and African survivals has been a historical dilemma that for generations has troubled the Negro mind and spirit and divided Negro thought. There has been a conflict between deep-seated emotional pride of race and equally deep-seated intellectual shame of and distaste for race. This dilemma we recognize immediately as the aftereffect of slavery, which rudely cut Negroes off from their ancestral African culture and taught them to ignore or despise their racial past. Haiti, with its proud tradition of self-emancipation and nearly one hundred and fifty years of political independence, has been less the victim of this psychological aftermath of slavery than any other American area with people of African descent. Nevertheless, we must note that generally speaking—and even sometimes in Haiti—Africa and things African have been misunderstood and disparaged for lack of proper evaluation of their cultural significance. By and large the Negroes have been at a loss to implement their pride of race, to give it proper force and authority, or to supply it with intelligent directives. Long after the physical ills and handicaps of slavery ceased, the psychological stigma persisted. It has conditioned in many groups of African Negro ancestry a negative rather than a positive regard for their racial past and their cultural roots and origins. Some have contended that even if this past was worth while, it is now too late to salvage and reconstruct it; others, even more under the influence of what has aptly been called the "myth of the Negro past," have regarded that past as of little or no cultural value. This has been tragic; both contentions are wrong; in time both must definitely be refuted.

All of the constituent American stocks except the American Indian (and maybe even the American Indian, according to contemporary anthropological findings) are transplanted groups who, by adoption and assimilation, have become what might be termed "hybrids" of culture. The European-American has not found it necessary or desirable to renounce his European cultural heritage. The European, in turn, did not find it profitable to repudiate either his pagan or his barbarian past. Both persist in his cultural tradition, particularly as a heritage of art and folklore which yields constant spiritual dividends. Whether this background is Scandinavian, Slavic, Teutonic, Anglo-Saxon, Celtic, or Latin, it has remained a vital and precious inheritance. Neither the superiorities of the American Negro's adopted religion nor those of his newly acquired civilization warranted the heavy price of repudiating or minimizing the African background.

Fortunately, present-day scholarship is opening up a normal, wholesome perspective of the American Negro's African past. The reconstruction of the Negro's group history, though racially motivated, has been objective and above reproach as far as scholarship is concerned. Two Negro scholars, W. E. B. DuBois and the late Carter Woodson, pioneered in this and insisted on the special importance of restoring the African background. Younger scholars have taken up the study in greater detail; also, the new materials and techniques of anthropology have substantially aided the movement. One need only mention such names as Melville J. Herskovits, Morton Kahn, George Simpson, Harold Courlander, Zora Hurston, Maurice Delafosse, and Price Mars to realize that the reconstruction of the African past is one of happy collaboration among scholars of different races and nations. Oddly enough, some of the best clues have come from the comparative study of African survivals in the New World. In spite of the wide dispersion of the slave trade and the many different strains of cultural assimilation to which Negro groups have been subject, there are traceable survivals. Observations made by anthropologists in

West Africa, South and Central America, and the southern United States, when pieced together, will eventually give us an over-all picture of what was basic in the ancestral African culture rather than just detailed minutiae of isolated tribal folkways. Eventually there will be available the outlines of a common-denominator culture that may reliably be considered typically African.

As suggested earlier, scholars have traced the outlines of such African common denominators in music and folklore. There remain yet to be disentangled many more complex institutional heritages, especially those of social and spiritual significance, which closer scrutiny of African survivals and comparison of them with the ancestral cultures will doubtless reveal. For we know that such deeply rooted traits survive even as rude and radical a transplanting as slavery. Not even loss of language or radical change of religion or ways of living can completely blot out what once existed in a people's cultural bloodstream. A characteristic posture, a typical musical idiom or folk belief, a curiously persistent social attitude or temperamental reaction, a stubbornly recurring bit of ritual—here they are—scattered up and down from the Georgia seacoast islands to Pernambuco, from Dahomey and Guinea to the hills of Haiti and the villages of the Bahamas. Here is evidence of the tenacious hold of folkways upon a people who have lost even primary contact with their languages, history, all their original culture patterns.

Of general interest and importance to laymen is the radically changed approach characteristic of this new scholarship, an approach which, in spite of differences over specific issues, represents scientific opinion. Although recognizing typical and unique Negro and African traits and characteristics, scholars have abandoned the pseudoscientific belief (which still unfortunately dominates lay opinion) that there are special and peculiar innate racial traits.

Wherever such characteristics are believed to exist, they must be explained, the new scholarship insists, in terms of definite historical causes and specific sociological conditions, or of cultural influences that can eventually be traced by careful research and analysis. We thus no longer have (at least as scientifically tolerated) those unsound, misleading, and often humiliating interpretations by special hypothesis or as cases of racial exception. We know that no such special explanations exist except in the mind of the unscientific observer, and that they are invalid except for biased racialists. On this point, one must condemn and renounce again the pro-Negro as well as the anti-Negro racialist: neither serves the cause of truth and ultimate social understanding. Hasty generalizations, favorable or unfavorable, are out of keeping with the scientific method; there is no gain in replacing old stereotypes with new ones, or ancient prejudices by flimsy, equally unscientific countergeneralizations. Both errors must be relegated to the past, and interpretations must be substituted which explain the traits and behavior of one racial group by the same factors and forces that would explain the traits and behavior of any other under similar conditions and circumstances. The groundwork of the analysis that is revealing for us so much that is new in the sociology of the Negro peasant was laid down by William I. Thomas and Florian Znaniecki in their pioneer study, *The Polish Peasant in America*. Much of the new anthropology by which we are gaining insight into African and Negro culture stems from the revolutionary approach and monumental work of Franz Boas: many of the leading exponents in this field are his pupils and disciples.

Of course, the phenomena of cultural contact and interaction occur for specific reasons far removed from the moral plane. However, as objectively studied and correctly interpreted, they give small comfort and no justification to conventional notions of culture, with their false assumptions of power, prestige, and racial exclusiveness. The modern view is that cultural influence is always a two-way process, proceeding not only from the top down, but sometimes also from the bottom up. Master influences slave; slave in some respects influences master. Where divergent groups are in contact, their influence is reciprocal whether the differences are of race, class, or nationality. Our new science of culture has the net effect of repudiating doctrines of racism and race superiority and of giving intellectual and moral support to a democratic theory of human society.

CHAPTER FOUR

Negro Music and Dance: Formal Recognition and Reconstruction

ONLY since 1900 have the depth and true folk character of the spirituals been gradually discovered and recognized. Generally conceded the most characteristic product of Negro genius to date, the spirituals rank among the classical folk expressions because of their moving simplicity, their characteristic originality, and their universal appeal. Although the product of the slave era and the religious fervor of the plantation religion, they have outlived the generation and conditions that produced them. One of the proofs of their immortality lies in the abuses they have survived. Having lived through the contempt of the slaveowners, they survived in spite of never having been written down or formally composed. Although they evolved from hymns, they were driven out of church worship by the conventions of respectability and the repressions of Puritanism as the Negro church became more "sophisticated." After enduring the neglect and disdain of "second-generation respectability," they have had to survive successive waves of false popularization—first the corruption of sentimental balladry, then a period of concert polishing, and finally the stage of being ragged or jazzed.

One of the great services of W. E. B. DuBois, in his unforgettable chapter on "The Sorrow Songs," was to give the spirituals serious and proper interpretation as the slave's instinctive distillation of sorrow and spiritual triumph over it in religious ecstasy and hope. It was realized increasingly that the spirituals, though ostensibly naïve and simple, are intrinsically profound. Underneath broken words, childlike imagery, and peasant simplicity lie an epic intensity and a tragic depth of religious emotion for which the only equal seems to be the spiritual experience of the Jews, the only analogue the Psalms. The spirituals stand as one of the great classic expressions of religious emotion and Christian moods and attitudes.

After Dr. DuBois's memorable interpretation, Henry Krehbiel, one of the leading music critics of his generation, gave the spirituals serious and adequate musical analysis and interpretation in his *Afro-American Folk Songs*. Thereafter, spirituals increasingly came into their own and were recognized not only as unique folk music, but also as the main strand in American folk song. No stronger evidence of this can be cited than the fact that in 1894 they received the highest possible recognition, being used as the thematic material for symphonic music by Antonin Dvořák. Dvořák, with other folk themes, chose spirituals to represent American atmosphere in his symphony *From the New World*. Since then the spirituals and even secular Negro folk melodies and their harmonic style have been regarded by most musicians as the purest and most valuable musical strain in America.

Second only to the spirituals is the secular or nonreligious folk music of Negro peasant origin. It, too, for generations was neglected and despised. Until recently people violently enthusiastic about secular folk music in foreign countries have looked down on comparable native American music. Thus, much of it has died unrecorded. Now the musical folklorist is trying desperately to preserve its last remnants and to reconstruct the older primitive versions from the somewhat "fancy" popularizations still dominant. For some years now, it has been the fashion to collect Negro folk and work songs; the "blues," of course, have achieved eminent respectability.

The secular theme material is far more fragmentary than the material for the spirituals. But because the material is a combination of folk poetry and folk music, words and music are more closely related than in the spirituals. This is no doubt because the seculars were more direct improvisation than the spirituals, which in essence and thought were influenced by the evangelical hymns after which they were originally modeled. Some Negro seculars were dialect versions of ballads current in colonial days. Many of the "mountain ballads," now equally prized after generations of neglect, can be found in parallel Negro and white versions: *Frankie and Johnny* is a case in point. In the main, however, Negro ballads are very "racy" and thoroughly original. They deal, for example, with unrequited love, with risky and daredevil adventure. The Negro love themes are almost invariably treated more ironically and less sentimentally than their white analogues. Whatever the theme, whether it be the sob or the laugh, the plea or the threat, a cry of despair or revenge, of defeat or triumph, the mood is registered in pithy and vivid phrases. Joe Turner says: "Ef yo' don't believe Ah'm leavin', jes count de days Ah'm gone"; the deserted girl ironically wails: "Ticket agent, ease your window down, De man I love done lef' dis town"; "Twa'n't for power an' fo' store-bought hair, De man Ah love wouldn't a-gone nowhere." More poetically we hear this lament:

> We wreck our love boats on the shoals,
> And in the wreckage of desire,
> We sigh for things like Noah's dove
> To fly away from wingless love.

For every dozen labor and work songs and folk ballads still preserved, we have, unfortunately, only one genuine folk tune. Most of the folklorists interested in this material were not skilled musicians and could transcribe only the words. Yet here was first-rate music. It grew up as part of the workaday rhythms of daily toil, with genuine, unsophisticated moods, with irresistible swing, and with elemental philosophy. A classic of this type is *John Henry*, which exists in scores of versions. The levee songs are another important variety. As will be noted later, the "blues" are not a part of this original folk saga, but a later product of the same folk spirit.

Negro folk secular music is regional. Roughly, there are six zones or provinces, each with its characteristic musical idiom. They are:

1. Virginia and the Upper South
    Melodic—earliest to gain favor, heavily influenced by Irish and English folk ballads and dances. This is the school that gave us Jim Bland and *Carry Me Back to Ole Virginny*.
2. The Creole South
    Mixed tradition—melodic—influenced by Spanish, French, and Cuban idioms; "lullaby" and Negro version of French folk ballad typical. Examples: *Petite Ma'mselle, M'sieu Banjo*.
3. The Seaboard Lower South
    A more racy strain of folk balladry; product of the Carolinas and Georgia—realistic, less sentimental: road songs, pickin'-songs, shouts, game songs, blues, ballads. Examples: *John Henry, Casey Jones*.
4. The Mississippi Strain
    Levee and delta music, racy, sentimental, the "tap-

root" of jazz. Examples: *Joe Turner, Memphis Blues, Gulf Coast Blues.*

5. The Southwest

The Kansas, Oklahoma, Missouri strain; heavy influence of the cowboy and Western ballad style—*St. James Infirmary Blues.* Negroid, not pure Negro-parallel versions.

6. The Mountain Music

Parallel Negro versions of hill ballads; Kentucky and Virginia highlands; Negroid. Examples: *Frankie and Johnny, Careless Love.*

The first four groups are more typically racial and important. The upper South influenced the music of the first and second ages of minstrelsy and also gave us, for the most part, the spirituals. Jazz, by common knowledge, developed from the Mississippi strain. Although a complete geography of Negro folk music has yet to be worked out, the music of each region has its own characteristic flavor and musical idiom.

John Henry is supposed to be the parent of the Negro ballads, just as *Joe Turner* is of the "blues." The work-song type is composed of several short, repeated lines with pauses intervening for the stroke of a pick or hammer, and is usually sung by a group.

> *John Henry said to his captain,*
> *Well—a man ain't nuthin' but a man,*
> *And before I'll let your steam drill beat me down*
> *I'll die wid' my hammer in my hand.*
> *I'll die wid' my hammer in my hand.*

Guy Johnson says: "John Henry is the Negro's greatest folk character. . . . The songs, of a narrative-ballad type, sung most frequently as a solo with banjo or guitar accompaniment, are the heart of the legend which has sprung up around him. . . . No description of the harmonic and rhythmic beauties of the Negro work song can do the subject justice. The concerted movements, the grunts emerging at each stroke of pick or hammer, the off pitch, slurring, sliding attacks made upon the tones, the unsteady harmonic patterns, these have to be seen and heard in order to be understood."

The "blues" form has an epigrammatic flavor and a folk quality peculiar to itself. The dominant blues mood is lament, beginning in a sentimental expression of grief or hard luck, sometimes ending on an intensification of the same mood, sometimes turned to ironical self-ridicule or fatalistic resignation. Irony and disillusionment are frequent motifs.

> *Gwine lay my head right on de railroad track,*
> *Gwine lay my head right on de railroad track,*
> *Cause my baby, she won't take me back.*
>
> *Gwine lay my head right on de railroad track,*
> *Gwine lay my head right on de railroad track,*
> *If de train come 'long, gwine snatch it back.*

or

> *Boll-weevil, where you been so long?*
> *Boll-weevil, where you been so long?*
> *You stole my cotton, now you wants my cohn!*

The musical rhythm and harmony of the blues are as characteristic and simple as their verse form and idiom of thought. The tunes are built around a succession of three common chords: the tonic triad, the subdominant triad, and the dominant seventh. The form is admirably adapted to impromptu singing and versifying. The repetition of the second line gives emphasis and a chance for improvised variation, leaving a wait in which to think up the last line and, later, to improvise and vary the rhythm before returning to the regular pattern of the original theme. This original is the original "break"—the narrow cradle of the improvised rhythm and eccentric intervals from which our jazz was born.

Before discussing jazz we must direct our attention to its predecessor, "rag," which followed the decline in popularity and appeal of minstrelsy. In 1891, a group of veteran minstrels produced *The Creole Show*, which, though something of a refurbished minstrel show, broke the "blackface" tradition by featuring a chorus of attractive well-costumed Negro girls who both sang and danced well. The show played a whole season at the Chicago World's Fair in 1893. There, oddly enough, a strain of genuine Negro music that was to revolutionize American music had come up from Memphis and the Mississippi. W. C. Handy had gone to the World's Fair with Mahaly's Minstrels, seeking a fortune they did not find. Handy's was to be a future he could not possibly have dreamed of.

For a time these two forces, destined ultimately to fuse, went their separate ways. Eventually, however, undiluted folk music and dance were to merge with the stage talent of vaudeville and Negro musical comedy. *The Creole Show* was followed in 1895 by *The Octoroons*, presented by John Isham, a Negro manager who knew and believed in the possibilities of Negro talent. The following year he presented

Oriental America, the first all-colored show to play Broadway. Into it he put Sidney Woodward, a concert tenor; J. Rosamond Johnson, the composer; and William Elkins, an expert director of serious Negro choirs. There were others of an order of talent and training not recognized before by the burlesque and variety stage. It might be said that Negro musical comedy made its way by luring its audience with comedy farce and then conquering it with music. This was eminently true of the next success, *Black Patti's Troubadours,* written and scored by the talented Bob Cole. As its star attraction it offered Madame Sissieretta Jones, one of the great sopranos of her generation. Already internationally known, the "Black Patti" interrupted her concert career for the show, which ran several years throughout the country. She made no other concessions to vaudeville, however, singing her operatic and concert repertory, the ensemble numbers supported by first-rate Negro stage choruses.

While ragtime's audience was being captured, ragtime itself was in the making. "Rag" made its earliest appearance in the mid-nineties in the guise of a "coon song." The "coon song" was a relic of the worst minstrel days: slapstick farces about "razors, chickens, watermelons, ham-bones, flannel shirts, and camp-meetings." The appeal was not in what was said, but in the rhythm and swing. Either the public was understandably tired of the sentimental waltz ballads so plentiful in the nineties or the new Negro rhythm was genuinely compelling. Whatever the reason, such astute entertainers of the nineties as George M. Cohan, May Irwin, and Marie Harris knew that the new "black" music had a future. They devised new rhythm to songs like May Irwin's *Hot Tamale Alley* and the popular *Ta-ra-ra Boom de Ay*. Meanwhile Negro comedians were countering with *Smokey Mokes* and *I Don't Care if You Never Comes Back*. At about this time Negro composers and songwriters picked up the baton and gave America its first experience of genuine Negro tempo. Wrote Isaac Goldberg: "The earlier ragtime, for all its debt to white writers and the white performers, was definitely and refreshingly black. The rule of the white upon the pseudo-Negro stage was virtually over. The Negro upon the vaudeville and musical stage was achieving a certain revindication." In 1898 Bob Cole presented his *A Trip to Coon-Town,* labeled by one authority "the first Negro show to make a complete break from the minstrel pattern; the first that was not a mere potpourri, the first to be written with continuity and to have a cast of characters working out a plot . . . the first Negro musical comedy."

Out of this success grew the partnership of Bob Cole and

Billy Johnson and, later, the more famous combination of musical-comedy talent: Bob Cole, James Weldon Johnson, and J. Rosamond Johnson. Negro songwriters and composers now began to appear as if by magic. Will Marion Cook composed the famous *Dark Town Is Out Tonight*, Al Johns his *Go Way Back and Sit Down*. Will Accoe, Tom Perrin, and many others were rapidly turning out "rag" tunes. Will Marion Cook was, with Bob Cole, the guiding genius of the rag movement. A thorough musician, trained in the violin and harmony here and abroad, Cook saw the serious potentialities of Negro ragtime music. As early as 1897 he wrote the score for the next great musical success, *Clorindy: The Origin of the Cake-Walk*, with the collaboration of Paul Laurence Dunbar in the lyrics. *Clorindy*, ahead of its time, hinted at the symphonic development of Negro syncopation and harmony which was not to be fully achieved for another ten or fifteen years. The American ear was just being accustomed to the Negro tempo; its subtleties were missed in the consternation over the new fast pace and swing of "raggin'" tunes.

While Negro performers and songsters were pioneering on the stage, white pioneers were staking the fortunes of ragtime in Tin Pan Alley. Many Negro performers were too close to the new tempo to sense its originality and financial potentials. They often gave the canny Tin Pan Alley composers invaluable "leads" by letting them "set" their music. Ernest Hogan's *All Coons Look Alike to Me* was set to a "rag accompaniment" by a certain Max Hoffman. One of the first musical notations of "rag" appeared in D. A. Lewis's setting (1896) of Bert Williams's *Oh, I Don't Know, You're Not So Warm*. Rag was reduced to a technique of piano writing and thus made a popular-song vogue. Soon America would be trying to imitate this syncopation swing. Ben Harney, credited with being the first white composer to transcribe ragtime for the piano, published his *Ragtime Instructor* in 1897. Goldberg says: "Harney had served as accompanist to a Negro and had toured the West and the Middle West long before he came East to start the rage of ragtime in Gotham." What passed for ragtime was not the full rhythmic and harmonic idiom of the real "rag" as used, for example, by Will Marion Cook and the Negro musical-comedy arrangers, with chorus and orchestra at their disposal, but the thin, superficial, eccentric rhythm as it could be imitated on the piano or in the necessarily simplified "accompaniments" of popular sheet music of the day. Still, a few artists like Scott Joplin wrote real rag in such compositions as his *Maple Leaf Rag* and *Palm Leaf Rag*. Kerry Mills's *Georgia Camp Meeting*, *Rastus on Parade*, and

Whistlin' Rufus set a pace that was to captivate the entire country and culminate in that instrumental classic of matured ragtime—Irving Berlin's *Alexander's Ragtime Band*. Two outside forces of great significance combined to reinforce the contagious singing and dancing of the Negro performers and the salesmanship of Tin Pan Alley. The first was the sudden vogue of the cakewalk as a fashionable dance; the second the hectic enthusiasm for the Spanish-American War music enhanced by the introduction of ragtime tempo. The most popular marching song was *There'll Be a Hot Time in the Old Town Tonight*, which was hybrid ragtime. It was one of America's favorites until the faster tempo of *Alexander's Ragtime Band* topped it in popularity.

There is much conflicting legend about *There'll Be a Hot Time in the Old Town Tonight*, but all stories agree in at least one particular—it is a polished version of a less polite Negro cabaret song and dance from St. Louis. George M. Cohan called it a dressed-up version of a tune popular in St. Louis. He insisted that the original tune was popular in an all-colored resort in the Missouri city and that it was brought East by old theatrical troupers. The importance of this is not documentation of the Negro source of a tune, but rather proof that rag, like jazz, is a product of the Mississippi region, of Memphis and St. Louis particularly. The music followed a circuitous route, spreading to Cincinnati and Chicago, and then to New York.

To the commercial successes of the ragtime era some serious musical contributions can be added. Will Marion Cook's *Mandy Lou, Exhortation, Rain Song*, and *Swing Along, Children* are examples. Rosamond Johnson's *Since You Went Away* and *Li'l Gal* are others; Cole and Johnson's musical operettas *Trip to Coon-Town* and *The Shoofly Regiment* are further samples.

The ragtime era continued the minstrel tradition of a band, but with a difference. The leader became a conductor, not a clowning drum major. In the Negro musical shows real musicians were the arrangers and the conductors of the orchestras, and their conception of instrumentation and playing began to affect dance music as well as dancing itself. The peculiar combinations of instruments known to the jazz age had not yet made their appearance, but the best leaders insisted—when they were not restrained—on characteristic Negro harmony and swing. Handy, "Father of the Blues," in the mid-nineties had to do operatic selections and fancy cornet variations in florid concert style (and as a thorough musician could do them) when he really wanted to organize a Negro band to his own liking. Not until 1903 did he get a chance.

Will Marion Cook had an equally difficult time as he protested against the minstrel tradition on the one hand and the imitation of florid classics on the other. Not until 1905 did Cook get his chance when he obtained the "Memphis Students" for their appearance that year in Proctor's Theatre in New York. This organization was the first truly genuine Negro playing unit; like the original Jubilee Singers, it blazed a trail to Europe its first season and was overwhelmingly successful in its demonstration of "the new music." The name "Memphis" was well chosen; it was the early tribute of those who knew the true folk source of this musical style. The band was composed of twenty of the best musicans who had gravitated to New York from everywhere, though it is doubtful if any were from Memphis. It was a folk orchestra like the gypsy or balalaika groups. They used their own characteristic combinations of instruments, chiefly banjos, mandolins, guitars, saxophones, trumpets, trombones, a violin, a double bass, and drums. Will Dixon was the conductor, but the genius of Will Marion Cook dominated the group. In less than ten years he was to organize his own "American Syncopated Orchestra," which really initiated symphonic jazz.

In New York between 1905 and 1912 or 1915, four Negro conductors and arrangers of real genius raised Negro music out of a broken, musically illiterate dialect and made it a national and international music with its own peculiar idioms of harmony, instrumentation, and playing. These men saw the future of Negro music; they had the courage to be original. They had swift vindications; in less than ten years Europe knew that musically something new had come out of America. These men were Ford Dabney, James Reese Europe, Will Marion Cook, and W. C. Handy. Dabney revolutionized the Negro dance orchestra and started the musical fortunes of Florenz Ziegfeld when he was experimenting with roofgarden productions. Jim Europe, a member of the "Memphis Students," alternated with Cook as musical director of the Cole and Johnson shows, and organized the famous Clef Club Orchestra. Europe was later to make Negro music the preferred rhythm in the new dance vogue started by Vernon and Irene Castle. As will be noted later, Irene Castle gave Europe full credit for the fox trot, which she labeled the most popular dance of the day. Cook not only gave Negro music its first serious orchestral works, but with his "Syncopated Orchestra" surprised and converted audiences in London, Paris, and Berlin in 1919-20. Handy, it is well known, championed the despised Mississippi folk music between 1909 and 1912 and created the "blues."

In May 1912, three Negro conductors led a syncopated

orchestra (today we would say jazz orchestra) of one hundred and twenty-five Negro musicians in a "Concert of Negro Music." The concert was at Carnegie Hall; the audience included some of New York's most sophisticated music-lovers; the atmosphere resembled that of any concert of "classical music." The compositions were conducted by their own composers or arrangers. Perhaps the transformation was too sudden; many did not recognize this folk music in "full dress." Some thought it was incongruous (some of it was), but those who recall only the epoch-making concert of "Classical Jazz" by Paul Whiteman in 1924 or a similar concert by Vincent Lopez the same year should be reminded of the historically more significant concert by The Clef Club in May 1912. At that time ragtime matured fully and the age of jazz really began.

Isaac Goldberg suggests, following no less an authority than W. C. Handy, that the spirituals, ragtime, and jazz form one continuous sequence of Negro music. Says he: "Handy, the recognized pioneer of the 'blues,' insists that ragtime, essentially, is nothing more than a pepped-up secular version of the Negro spirituals. He recalls how in the old minstrel days they rendered such haunting exhortations as 'Git on Board, Little Chillun.' To sing it in the traditional fashion of the earnest if ecstatic spiritual was too tame. So sung faster to the accompaniment of eccentric hand-clapping, and gestures, it becomes the 'spiritual' disintegrating, breaking up into its ragtime successor. . . ." (In fact, in the camp-meeting style of jubilation, the dividing line between the spiritual and ragtime almost completely breaks down.) "Today," he continues, "hearing Handy jazz up the invitation to a ride on the heavenly railroad, one would exclaim, 'Why, he's simply jazzing it.' In Handy's minstrel days they called it 'jubing,' from the word 'jubilee.' "

Ragtime, then, is to be discovered deeply entrenched beneath the ecstasy and rhythms of the more jubilant songs to the Lord, just as in the slower-paced spirituals one hears the mood, though not the peculiar pattern, of the "blues." If we recall how jazz grew out of the improvised break interval of the blues, this theory becomes even more plausible. For then we have approximately the same contrast in the religious music between the stately spiritual chorale and the jubilant spiritual camp-meeting shout that we have in the secular music between the slow-swaying melancholy blues and the skipping rag and fast-moving jazz. The extreme contrast within the Hungarian czardas is another case in point and, clearly, a close analogy. As Goldberg later says: "Ragtime, then, is, in part, the pagan release of the Negro from his addiction to holiness, and his rhythms brought to us something of that —deliverance.... The spirituals translate the Bible; ragtime translates the other six days of the week."

In spite of the obvious development of ragtime and jazz from Negro sources and the pioneer artistry of Negro dancers and musicians, the question frequently comes up: "How Negro is jazz after all?" No one will deny that the elements of ragtime and jazz can be found elsewhere in the world, not only in other folk music, but as a device of syncopation in some of the most classical music, that of Beethoven, for example. But jazz and ragtime are nonetheless distinctively Negro. Original jazz is more than syncopation and close eccentric harmony: it has a distinctive intensity of mood and a peculiar style of technical performance. These can be imitated, but their original pattern was Negro. Inborn with the folk Negro, this is a quality detected in a stevedore's swing, a preacher's cadenced sermon, a bootblack's flick, or the "amen" from a corner of a church.

But this can be said only of the early jazz, which was not only the most racial, but musically the most powerful. To sense the difference instantly one has only to contrast, for example, one of the early blues, like Bessie Smith's old version of the *Gulf Coast Blues*, with any contemporary blues. Another classic in point is W. C. Handy's *The Memphis Blues*, the first jazz classic. Handy began experimenting with the blues form in 1909 after having watched the earliest jazz-makers, the itinerant piano-players who moved through the Mississippi area improvising music which, as J. A. Rogers puts it, reproduced the sentiments and moods of the dock laborers, railroad gangs, and simple folk. Until 1897 his concern was exclusively with classical music, but when, during that year, he discovered the appeal of real "down home" music, he initiated a serious search for folk music. The *Joe Turner Blues*, an early lesson in the folk idiom, led to his adopting it as the novelty feature of the Pythian Band that he organized in Memphis. In 1909, still in Memphis, Handy composed his third blues, *Mr. Crump,* which helped elect the city official of that name. No one of the three was accepted for publication, and eventually Handy brought out *The Memphis Blues* independently. But sales were poor, and Handy sold the rights to the composition to a white promoter for one hundred dollars. In a garbled version, in which the rhythm was simplified and words were added, it was republished in New York and earned a fortune for the copyright owners. Handy, refused permission by the owner to use *The Memphis Blues* in his own *Blues Anthology* thirteen years later, was thus "Father of the

Blues," though disinherited from his rightful recognition and rewards.

"The success of the 'Memphis Blues,'" Abbe Niles wrote in his preface to the *Blues Anthology,* "resulted very shortly first in the borrowing of the magic word, and then, of the jazz idea and the 'blue note.' The 'blue note' is in official music the invention of W. C. Handy to devise a musical notation for representing the typical Negro voice slur or 'break' and its characteristic treatment of the tonic third. Stereotyped as the introduction of the minor third into melodies based on the prevailing major, this interpolated minor third has become the famous 'blue note.' Later the harmony of such a suspended third or seventh was introduced as the concluding harmony instead of the major tonic in compositions of the later period of sophisticated jazz. A similar treatment of the seventh note is the secondary 'blue note' and has been extensively used. It was responsible for the device of ending up a tune on a diminished seventh chord as in Gershwin's opera, '135th Street,' and later the added sophistication of the 'chord of the ninth.'"

Another cradle element of jazz was in Handy's blues. It was the habañera or tango rhythm, first used by that composer in the original *Memphis Blues.* The justification for the use of the tango rhythm as characteristically Negro, and its popularity among Negroes become very plausible when we recall that this is originally an African rhythm (the native word for it is "tangana") and that it probably became Spanish through the Moors. This is corroborated by the fact that this same tango rhythm is basic in the purest and oldest strains of Afro-Cuban music, the folk music of Mexico, in Brazil, where the Negro influence has been dominant, and in Negro dances of even the Bahamas and Barbados.

In addition to jazz rhythm and harmony, jazz improvisation emerged from the blues. It grew out of the improvised musical "filling in" of the gap between the short measure of the blues and the longer eight-bar line, the break interval in the original folk form of the three-line blues. Such filling in and compounding of the basic rhythm are characteristic of Negro music from Africa to South Carolina, from the unaccompanied hand-clapping of the street-corner "hoe-down" to the interpolations and shouts in Negro church revivals. Handy's own theory of jazz is that it is, in essence, "spontaneous deviation from the musical score," in other words, an impromptu musical embroidery woven around and into the musical tune and the regular harmony. This means short, daring, and inspired music. When this style was incorporated into orchestral music, a new sort of instrumental music was born out of the folk jazz. Thus jazz is a towering and elaborate superstructure built upon the basic foundation of the blues. The controversy as to whether jazz is a new type of music or another method of playing music can be resolved by this fact, because it shows the difference between superficial jazz and the really solid type. The one is merely a series of musical tricks by which any tune can be ragged or jazzed. The other is an organic combination of jazz rhythm, harmony, and creative improvisation.

Superficial jazz is the cheap product of Tin Pan Alley; many classical compositions have been subjected to trick and surface popularization. Beethoven, Verdi, Mozart, and Tchaikovsky have all been subjected to exploitation by unscrupulous commercial composers who reduce them to a banal form "for the masses." Nevertheless, it is only half true to say, as Gilbert Seldes does: "There is no such thing as jazz music; jazz is a method of playing music." Eccentric tone distortion and rhythmic antics are only one side of jazz, the more superficial side. What is deeper and more important is the mood out of which it is generated and the instinctive gift for doing it spontaneously. No really Negro musical group worries about what the other musicians are going to do; they are just as likely to vary and embroider at will and whimsy as to follow a score. No one approaching the issue from the side of experience rather than that of academic debate could be in doubt about the racial color and feeling of jazz. Niles observes: "Up to this time, every other type of orchestra had played as best it could what was set before it in black and white. Successive and competitive improvisation was unknown and heresy." Louis Armstrong, in his *Swing That Music*, says that "to become a front rank 'swing player' a musician must learn to read expertly and be just as able to play to score as any 'regular' musician. Then he must never forget for one minute of his life that the true spirit of swing lies in free playing and that he must always keep his own musical feeling free. He must try to originate and not just imitate. And if he is a well-trained musician in the first place, he will be able to express his own musical ideas as they come to him with more versatility, more richness, and more body. . . . To be a real swing artist, he must be a composer as well as a player."

For the process of composing by group improvisation, the jazz musician must have a whole chain of musical expertness, a sure musical ear, an instinctive feeling for harmony, the courage and gift to improvise and interpolate, and a canny sense of the total effect. This free style, which Negro musicians introduced into playing, really has generations of experience behind it. It is derived from the voice tricks and vocal habits of Negro choral singing. Out of the voice slur and quaver between the flat and the natural came the whole jazz cadenza and all the jazz tone devices. Out of the use of a single sustained voice tone as a suspension note for chorus changes of harmony came the now elaborate jazz harmonic style. It is interesting to note that the African has this same fluid, shifting musical scale, even more subtle than the scale shifts of American Negro folk music. In fact, it seems that many American Negro musical traits are the original African ones modified by the more regular pattern of European music. These basic racial idioms are more apparent in the simpler, earlier forms of jazz, and more in the vocal than in the instrumental pieces. As Sterling Brown has rightly said: "There is rich material on hand for a revaluation of the Negro folk. Out of penitentiaries, in the deep South, John and Alan Lomax have brought the musical memories of singers with names such as Iron Head, Clear Rock, and Lightning. From what is more truly folk culture these men and others like John Hammond, Willis James, and John Work have brought hidden singers and songs." Whenever Negro folk music is evaluated or revaluated, the old cheap Okeh and Columbia records of The Memphis Students, the McKinney Cotton Pickers, The Chicago Rhythm Kings, The Dixieland Orchestra, and the early blues singers—Bessie, Clara, and Mamie Smith, and Ma Rainey—will prove to be priceless materials, not only, as Sterling Brown implies, to round out the true picture of Negro folk music, but also to show how jazz was created.

With the full vogue of the jazz age, the traditional characteristic Negro instruments—the guitar, the fiddle, and the banjo—were pushed into the background of the jazz orchestra by the saxophones, trumpets, trombones, and clarinets. Only the bass fiddle and the drums survived, but with a changed technique. One reason for the saxophone's dominance was its ability to simulate voice harmony. Fletcher Henderson in New York and Will Stewart of Chicago early demonstrated the mellow, songlike possibilities of the saxophone. These possibilities could not have been realized except for the astonishing revelations of new techniques of playing the wind and brass instruments which came from the pioneer jazz players. "Sweet jazz" developed from the saxophone; what subsequently became known as "hot" jazz stemmed from the trombone and trumpet. Jim Europe and Will Vodery were influential in consolidating these new instrumental setups and timbres in the balanced orchestras. Europe's 15th Regiment Band astounded European musicians, who could not believe that the musicians did not use special instruments totally different from their own. Not until the Negro artists played on instruments borrowed from their hosts were the latter convinced. Their display of agility and variability of tone, combined with their use of odd intervals and widened range were, indeed, a distinct innovation. Of course, some of these jazz effects will never rise above the level of mere musical tricks that are amusing, fascinating, or arresting. Others, however, are musical in a truly masterful way. The jazz revolution was technical, the forerunner of the new harmony. No limit has ever been set on the amazing variety of modern instrumental combinations and their new effects whose possibilities jazz players demonstrated.

With the jazz vogue, melody, technically, slipped into second place. The sentimentality of the earlier period was quickly abandoned in favor of the vernacular and realistic new style. The new tempo, admittedly representative of the increasingly hectic pace of the times, challenged white arrangers and composers. Among important white pioneers in jazz were men like Lewis Muir, Ben Harney, and Scott Joplin. Among later phenomenal jazz performers were Leon "Bix" Beiderbecke, Jack Teagarden, Frank Teschmaker, Rademan (the originator of the "trombone laugh"), Eddie Lang, Gene Krupa, Jess Stacy, Joe Venuti, and Benny Goodman. It is remarkable to recall how quickly the new style developed its own virtuosos, whom the expert critics of jazz know by their individual tone and style. There is no more interesting feature of this movement than the way in which the white musicians studied jazz. Often they would sit long hours in Negro cabarets, listening patiently to the Negro originators; later they would feebly imitate them. In time the white musicians not only rivaled their Negro competitors musically, but dominated the commerce of jazz.

Only when we trace jazz to its humble roots can we comprehend the succession of styles which has given us the various schools of jazz or understand why the critics prefer early "pure" jazz to the concocted, artificial variety. Part of the early history is well traced in George W. Lee's *Beale Street: Where the Blues Began,* in which there is an account of the Memphis beginnings. The history of the equally important New Orleans school is vividly told by Louis Armstrong in *Swing That Music.* The Memphis strain goes back to just after the Civil War. It began with an orchestra directed by West Dukes, who was followed by Jim Turner, and Handy. At the same time, Charles Bynum, reputed to have been the first to play blues orchestrally, was the leading bandmaster on Beale Street. In succession came Alex Green, Charles Holmes, Robert Henry, and Will Stewart. This succession will not impress the reader until he learns how, by a system of apprenticeship, this tradition has come steadily down from one musical generation to the next as a young member of one band branches out to found his own orchestra and develop his individual style. Two examples are William Grant Still, one of the outstanding Negro composers in symphonic forms, and Jimmy Lunceford, an expert in jazz orchestration, both of whom are indebted to a Beale Street apprenticeship. Considerably later, the powerful New Orleans strain started up the river on the famous old stern-wheeler excursion boats. LaRocca's Dixie Land Orchestra, Keppard's Creole Band, Perez's Band, Kid Ory's Jazz Orchestra, and King Oliver's Band were all of the New Orleans school.

According to George Lee, Will Stewart was largely responsible for transplanting the blues to Chicago, just as Handy transplanted them to New York. Thus, after leaving its humble sources—on the delta, on the levee, and in the Memphis saloons—jazz divided into two streams. Chicago became the center for the rowdy, hectic, swaggering style known as "hot jazz," while New York became notable for "sweet jazz," the cosmopolitan style that stressed melody and flowing harmony. Later came the development of the sophisticated hybrid style known as "classical jazz." Curiously enough, most of the outstanding white jazz musicians were disciples of the Chicago school; Beiderbecke, Teschmaker, and the Stacys learned jazz in the Chicago cabarets. The New York school was polished and urbane, from the early days of Ford Dabney, Will Marion Cook, Jim Europe, and Fletcher Henderson. This was fortunate, for these were the men who carried jazz to Europe, and their smoother, more mellow jazz was the first to become world famous and have international influence.

European musicians, on the lookout for a new style in music, seized upon jazz, and a mixed style of music developed. Composers like Jaromir Weinberger, Darius Milhaud, Kurt Weill, and Ernst Křenek are responsible for what is known as continental classical jazz. Considerably later, of course, were the American jazz classicists—Aaron Copland, Louis Gruenberg, John Alden Carpenter, and George Gershwin. Ultimately "hot jazz" reached New York and, in turn, Europe. With the European enthusiasm for Duke Ellington and Louis Armstrong, a second wave of jazz popularity overwhelmed European audiences.

Jazz, in spite of its varying levels of excellence, mediocrity, and outright worthlessness, has made some important contributions to music and art. More than that, jazz must always be regarded as an important factor in interpreting the spirit of our time. There are several explanations for this. George

Antheil stresses jazz as a gift of "primitive joy and vigor." "Negro music," he says, "appeared suddenly [in Europe] after the greatest war of all time . . . it came upon a bankrupt spirituality. To have continued with Slavic mysticism (Russian music was the great vogue when the World War broke out) would in 1918 have induced us all to commit suicide. We needed the roar of the lion to remind us that life had been going on for a while . . . we needed the stalwart shoulders of the younger race to hold the cart awhile until we had gotten the wheel back on. . . . The Negro taught us to . . . come back to the elementary principles of self-preservation."

There is also the theory of emotional escape, seemingly contradicting this first theory of emotional rejuvenation. Jazz, according to those who support the second theory, was a marvelous antidote to twentieth-century boredom and nervous tension—a subtle combination of narcotic and stimulant. An "opium" for the mind, a tonic for the feelings, echoing the quick, nervous pace of modern civilization, jazz was regarded as something of a cultural guard.

The term "jazz classic" is disturbing to some who feel that only traditional music may rightly be labeled "classic." It is helpful to concede that the important distinction to be made is not between jazz and classical music, but among the good, mediocre, and bad of both varieties. In spite of the fact that much jazz composition is worthless or cheaply imitative, many compositions and versions of compositions may justly be styled "jazz classics." One version of a song or dance tune may be cheap, trite, and stereotyped; another version may be distinguished, original, and highly musical. It depends upon who "arranges" or recomposes it, and also upon who plays it. Some clownish version of *It don't Mean a Thing*, some crooner's wail of *Stormy Weather* will be musically worthless, while an Ethel Waters or a Duke Ellington version must be rated a "jazz classic" because of technical musicianship and typically racial or "pure" style.

Classical jazz has been convincingly praised by many outstanding orthodox musicians. "Jazz," said Serge Koussevitzky, "is an important contribution to modern musical literature. It has an epochal significance—it is not superficial; it is fundamental. Jazz comes from the soil, where all music has its beginnings." Leopold Stokowski says, more pointedly: "Jazz has come to stay because it is an expression of the times, of the breathless, energetic, super active times in which we are living—it is useless to fight against it. . . . America's contribution to the music of the past will have the same revivifying effect as the injection of new, and in the larger sense, vulgar blood into dying aristocracy. Music will then be vulgarized in the best sense of the word, and will enter more and more into the daily lives of the people. . . . The Negro musicians of America are playing a great part in this change. They have an open mind and an unbiased outlook. They are not hampered by conventions and traditions, and with their new ideas, their constant experiment, they are causing new blood to flow in the veins of music. The jazz players make their instruments do entirely new things, things finished musicians are taught to avoid. They are path finders into new realms."

These two critics, as well as others who have praised jazz, are judging only the two worth-while types of jazz. The first is that which rises from the level of ordinary popular music (usually in the limited dance and song ballad forms) and achieves creative musical excellence. This we may call the "jazz classic." The other is that type of music which successfully transposes the elements of folk music—in this case, jazz idioms—to the more sophisticated and traditional musical forms. This second type is "classical jazz." Both types are examples of the serious possibilities of the Negro's music and have been vital contributions to the music of our time.

The outstanding creator of jazz classics is Duke Ellington. Constant Lambert, a composer who used jazz idioms in his own works, once wrote of Ellington: "Ellington is . . . a real composer, the first jazz composer of distinction, and the first Negro composer of distinction. . . . I know of nothing in Ravel so dexterous in treatment as the varied solos in the middle of the ebullient 'Hot and Bothered' and nothing in Stravinsky more dynamic than the final section. The combination of themes at this moment is one of the most ingenious pieces of writing in modern music. It is not a question either of setting two rhythmic patterns working against each other in the mathematical Aaron Copland manner—it is genuine melodic and rhythmic counterpoint which, to use an old fashioned phrase, 'fits perfectly.' . . . He has crystallized the popular music of our time and set up a standard by which we may judge not only other jazz composers, but also those high-brow composers, whether American or European, who indulge in what is roughly known as 'symphonic jazz.'"

Although this is extravagant praise, it has been echoed by most of the competent European critics and composers, all of whom agree that Ellington is not only one of the exponents of pure jazz, but is also a pioneer composer of jazz classics. His compositions, R. D. Darrell reminds us, "gravitate naturally toward two types, the strongly rhythmed pure dance pieces ('Birmingham Breakdown,' 'Jubilee Stomp,' 'New Orleans Hoe Down') or the slower-paced lyrical pieces with less forcefully rhythmed dance bass ('Mood Indigo,' 'Take

It Easy,' 'Awful Sad'). Occasionally the two are combined with tremendous effectiveness, as in the 'East St. Louis Toodle-O,' 'Old Man Blues,' or 'Rocking in Rhythm.' The most striking characteristic of all his works, and the one that stamps them as ineradicably his own, is the individuality and unity of style that weld composition, orchestration, and performance into one inseparable whole. . . . Within an Ellington composition there is a similar unity of style of the essential musical elements of melody, rhythm, harmony, color, and form."

Actually, what R. D. Darrell says in tribute to Ellington could be said, to a degree at least, of other composers and arrangers. Don Redman, Benny Carter, and Sy Oliver, for example, were all great composers and arrangers. Like Ellington, they were subject to Darrell's word of caution: "He [Ellington] may betray his uniqueness for popularity, be brought down to the level of orthodox dance music, lose his secure footing and intellectual grasp. . . ." This was a sound reminder to both Negro and white musicians. For Ellington it was not necessary; he still maintains a top position in jazz circles. His consistently excellent band of musicians, his brilliant arrangements, and his long list of musical successes, such as *Solitude*, which won him an ASCAP prize, *Mood Indigo*, *Portrait of Bert Williams*, and *Sophisticated Lady*, have kept him there.

Prior to the real onset of classical jazz many composers had been seeking a typical idiom for American music. Their search led them in two directions—toward American Indian and American Negro themes. The first highly successful use of such thematic material was, as has previously been noted, by Dvořák, who was destined to make a contribution to the development of native American music as vital as the discovery of American Negro folk songs. He investigated Indian, Negro, and other native materials, but in *From the New World* the Negro elements dominate. It is true that this highly composite work also reveals both Indian themes and Dvořák's Bohemian style; it is equally true that except in the celebrated slow movement and the main theme of the scherzo, the Negro elements are much diluted. However, in the largo of the symphony, we sense the true atmosphere of a Negro spiritual. In the scherzo, Dvořák was close to jazz because he took his rhythms and tone intervals from the shout type of Negro dance. The record shows that Dvořák's guide and consultant was Harry T. Burleigh, then a graduate student at the National Conservatory in Brooklyn.

Once the Negro material had been so triumphantly vindicated, many native composers turned to it also for serious inspiration. Ernest Kroeger wrote *Humoresque Negre* (1899); George Chadwick wrote *Jubilee*, No. 1 of his *Four Symphonic Sketches* (1895); Henry Hadley called the third movement of his *Symphony Number 4* "South" (1902); Henry Gilbert wrote his *Comedy Overture on a Negro Theme* in 1907, to be followed by a *Negro Rhapsody* eight years later. John Powell, who later tried to discredit the originality of Negro music, used Negro themes throughout his earlier work in his *Suite, "In the South" (Negro Elegy), Suite Virginesque,* and *Negro Rhapsody*. Rubin Goldmark wrote *A Negro Rhapsody*, and E. Burlingame Hill wrote numerous studies on Negro rhythms, notably a *Scherzo* and a *Jazz Study for Two Pianos*. This was still the pre-jazz era.

Then came the second phase of the influence of Negro folk music on the classicists—the jazz vogue. As early as 1917 Hiram Motherwell had proposed a classical jazz concert program which would include traditional spirituals (*You May Bury Me in the East, Play on Your Harp Little David,* etc.), and songs by Will Marion Cook, W. C. Handy, Irving Berlin, and Jerome Kern. Said Motherwell: "To me ragtime brings a type of musical experience which I can find in no other music. ... I love the delicacy of its inner rhythms and the largeness of its rhythmic sweeps. I like to think that it is the perfect expression of the American city, with its restless bustle and motions, its multitude of unrelated details, and its underlying rhythmic progress toward a vague Somewhere. . . . I firmly believe that a ragtime program, well organized and sung, would be delightful and stimulating to the best audience the community could muster. . . ."

In 1924, Paul Whiteman gave his first concert of "classical jazz," with selections of orchestral complexity and classical form by Zez Confrey, Jerome Kern, Ferde Grofe, Berlin, and Gershwin, whose *Rhapsody in Blue* was the climax and sensation of the concert. By 1926, Whiteman had published his critical analysis *Jazz* and Henry Osgood his *So This Is Jazz;* Abbe Niles, with the collaboration of W. C. Handy, had written *Blues: An Anthology,* with the famous preface on Negro folk music. Darius Milhaud made two visits to America to study the new music and wrote enthusiastically of it. Calling it the "music of the age," he was further inspired a short time later to write an African Ballet, *The Creation of the World*. His enthusiasm introduced jazz to the experimental younger French musicians.

Thereafter came Weill's *Mahagonny*, a semi-jazz opera, Křenek's jazz opera (once produced at the Metropolitan) *Jonny spielt auf,* the blues movement in Ravel's *Violin and Piano Sonata,* and Constant Lambert's *Rio Grande*. Europe's

Negro Music and Dance

most original composers thus paid tribute; Ravel, Stravinsky, and Milhaud all made formal acknowledgment to their conviction that jazz is linked with what is typically modern in music.

Meanwhile the younger Negro musicians were creating impromptu and often anonymous jazz pieces that could have won them both fame and money if they had worked more deliberately and carefully. There were one or two exceptions: Edmund Jenkins had the training and the foresight to write *Charlestonia: A Negro Rhapsody for Full Orchestra,* which was played in Brussels and Paris in 1924. William Grant Still began presenting his serious compositions on the programs of the League of Composers. Thus New York heard, in 1927, Still's *From the Land of Dreams,* and two years later *Levee Land,* a suite for voice and orchestra, *Africa: A Symphonic Poem,* and parts of the now completed *Afro-American Symphony*. The last and other works in classical form have been presented often under the patronage of Howard Hanson, of the Eastman School of Music, Rochester, where seldom a year passes without a new work by Still on the annual festival program.

On the whole, however, the Negro musicians of the first jazz decade were too close to jazz to see its future. Until the day of the composer-conductor in jazz, around 1927, many a fine bit of creative composition was cloaked and put down as an "arrangement." Yet out of these humble ranks the most gifted and original American composers, Negro and white, have come. The list is worth noting, even rapidly: Porter Grainger, Spencer Williams, Clarence Williams, Will Vodery, Lovie Austin, Jim Europe, Rosamond Johnson, Fletcher Henderson, Duke Ellington, Don Redman, Benny Carter, Louis Russell, Sy Oliver, Jimmy Lunceford, Reginald Forsythe, Jenkins, and Still. Their musical significance becomes all the more obvious when we mention some of their white colleagues, all of whom served a jazz apprenticeship: Frank Black, Ferde Grofe, Adolph Deutsch, Hoagy Carmichael, Irving Berlin, Jerome Kern, Richard Rodgers, Cole Porter, and George Gershwin.

George Gershwin must be given credit for pioneering in "symphonic jazz," but even he did not fully succeed in his effort to lift jazz to the level and form of the classics. Often it has been too evident where the jazz idiom leaves off and the superimposed classic form begins. For example, discerning critics detect too much Liszt in the *Rhapsody in Blue* and too much Puccini in *Porgy and Bess*. Gershwin's success—that is, his ability to blend the elements—increased with time, and doubtless had he not died so early he would have created even finer music. The vitality and imaginativeness of Gershwin's music combined with its originality went a long way to offset his technical faults.

The most musically satisfactory composers of this "super-jazz," American as well as European, have treated jazz in terms of its basic factors—rhythm patterns and kaleidoscopic harmonic sequences. One of the best and earliest compositions of this type was Aaron Copland's *Piano Concerto*. John Alden Carpenter's pioneer work in classical jazz was similarly linked with the strictest classical tradition. In the meantime, Paul Whiteman, guided by Gershwin and Grofé, was exploiting and popularizing jazz tone-color, harmony, and rhythm in the larger forms. This was no small service. Whiteman had converted the American public to the seriousness of jazz and had confirmed Dvořák's prophecy that future American music would draw some of its substance from Negro sources. Classical jazz achieved new eminence with Gruenberg's *Daniel Jazz* and his setting of James Weldon Johnson's *Creation*. His opera *Emperor Jones* opened the way for Frank Harling's *Deep River*, and Gershwin's *Porgy and Bess*. Later classical jazz clearly displays a style more firmly fused and closer to the original Negro idioms. Dana Suesse's *Jazz Nocturne* and *Concerto in Three Rhythms* and Otto Cesana's *Negro Heaven* are excellent cases in point. Lamar Stringfield's *Parade* and his symphonic ballet *The Legend of John Henry* give further support to the claim that the second phase of classical jazz was not dominated by timid or artificial hybrids. Rather, genuine developments of the international idioms of jazz itself now were being projected into the newer music.

However, a great deal remained then and remains now to be done to develop a sound, substantial body of American music. One has a right to expect a large share of growth from the Negro composer. The death of Edmund Jenkins just a few days before his *Rhapsody Number 2* was scheduled for performance in Paris was a tragic loss to our racial and national art. As a child, Jenkins had been a member of his father's Charleston (South Carolina) Orphanage Band and had acquired a hold on Negro idioms and jazz accent that persisted after years abroad following his graduation from the London Royal College of Music. No compositions of maturity and genius equal to his came along from Negro sources until the works of William Grant Still and William Dawson appeared. With the successful presentation, in the thirties, of symphonies by each of these composers, based on folk themes, the hope for symphonic music in Negro idiom was revived. In 1935, ten years after his enthusiastic championing of the serious possibilities of jazz, Leopold Stokowski was able to present William Dawson's *Negro Folk Symphony* with the Philadelphia Orchestra. This work is somewhat romantic, but its orchestration of themes from Negro spirituals, though broad and dramatic, is completely unorthodox.

Also in 1935, William Grant Still's *Afro-American Symphony* had its New York *première* with the Philharmonic. Much of Still's work, especially his *Sahdji: An African Ballet* and *Ebon Chronicle,* is ultra-modern, too sophisticated for the uninitiated. The symphony, however, has moving simplicity and directness of musical speech. Its folk theme is treated in contrasted moods, with corresponding rhythms, making for a combined symphony and tone-poem of Negro experience. It is less programistic than Dawson's symphony, and gains by its nearer approach to pure music.

An interesting third composer is Florence Price, a Chicago musician whose *Symphony in E Minor* was presented several times by the Chicago Symphony Orchestra under the direction of Frederick Stock, with whom, also, Mrs. Price played her *Piano Concerto.* In the straight classical idiom and form, Mrs. Price's work vindicates the Negro's right, at choice, to pursue the broad road of classicism rather than the narrower, more hazardous (but often more rewarding) path of racialism.

The Negro's admitted excellence in song has not been an unmixed blessing. It has diverted interest from other forms of musical expression, limiting musical opportunity because of the general impression that it was the Negro's special field. Thus, there was too much emphasis on the interpretative aspect of musical art. Gradually this one-sidedness was corrected. Until comparatively recent years, the public invariably expected the Negro to sing and dance, exclusively in the popular vein. In fact, prejudices seriously handicapped the Negro musically even when his special musical aptitude was conceded. Serious Negro musicians were frequently inclined to ignore their folk music because of the insistent claim that this was their lone musical province. The sensitive, ambitious, and well-trained artist saw in this, with some warrant, the threat of a musical ghetto. Often his violent reaction led him to the extreme of completely ignoring his own rich heritage. For a painful period there was a feud between Negro musicians who championed "the classics" and those who defended the folk forms. The latter for a long time were in the minority. Singers of an older generation, when asked to sing spirituals, likelier than not would refuse on the ground that they did not particularly care for them. The newer singers are more likely to answer that they respect and like *all* great music, including spirituals.

This healthy reversal of attitude must be credited to a

group of master singers, most of whom came from New York. All had formal conservatory background and a deep faith in the dignity of Negro folk music. Two of them, J. Rosamond Johnson and Will Marion Cook, projected a Negro conservatory of music. The third, Harry T. Burleigh, dignified and popularized the spirituals by winning a place for them in the general repertory of the concert stage. Mr. Burleigh not only sang the spirituals, but also prepared excellent and moving arrangements of them. Many of his arrangements have become standard concert favorites. During more than forty years Burleigh not only prepared these concert arrangements of spirituals, most of them for solo voice, but also composed at least a hundred original songs. Of the latter, *Jean, Little Mother of Mine,* and *Just You* are particularly well known.

Clarence Cameron White, a concert violinist and composer, was also deeply concerned with perpetuating the Negro idiom through the use of spirituals. He, too, arranged many and incorporated them into much of his work. His *Bandana Sketches* are based on four Negro spirituals: *Nobody Knows the Trouble I've Seen, I'm Troubled in Mind, No More Auction Block,* and *Sometimes I Feel Like a Motherless Child.* Other titles reveal their folk-idiomatic background: *Slave Song, Levee Song, From the Cotton Fields.* His opera *Ouanga* is based on Haitian themes. The story is that of Haiti's hero, Dessalines. Because of the violence of his career, there is ample justification for powerful rhythms in the score. Yet, according to the critics, many of the arias had good lyrical quality and the music was "attractive and evocative." "For this work," wrote Carter Harmon in *The New York Times* (October 28, 1950), "he drew on Haitian songs and rhythms. . . . One scene developed a fine, sardonic lilt when one set of dancers paced a minuet and another, dressed as witch doctors and other grotesque figures, mimicked them in the background. Best of all was the first scene of the third act, where the pagan ritual was aptly rendered in sound. . . ." Other critics referred to "the sophisticated score" and the "fine choral writing," and Arthur Farwell commented that "too much cannot be said of the beauty and masterfulness of the orchestration."

Nathaniel Dett firmly believed in extensive use of the folk idiom, and though he experimented with other media, his most important works were based on Negro spirituals. *The Ordering of Moses* reflects a fine blend of traditional forms "to fit the needs of a new expression on large scale." All voices, according to Leonard Ballou, "must have a wide range; conductors must be skilled in executing intricate rhythmic patterns—the warp and woof of the 'Negro idiom.' " During the forties this opera was performed in Pittsburgh by the National Negro Opera Company. In 1951 it was performed in Carnegie Hall and recorded by the Voice of America.

On the current scene three Negro composers and several white ones are among those who use native American themes. John Work, a long-time professor at Fisk University, is composer, arranger, and critic of, as well as authority on, folk music. His arrangements of spirituals are noted for their simplicity. Too frequently excessive sentimentality and undue technical adornments spoil true folk songs, but Mr. Work's arrangements never reveal these flaws. He has made a host of arrangements of spirituals and has composed many original ones. In addition, he has composed songs free of the racial idiom (*To a Mona Lisa* and *Soliloquy,* for example), piano pieces, and *The Singers,* a cantata that won first prize in a competition sponsored by the Fellowship of American Composers (1946).

Another Negro composer on the contemporary scene is Howard Swanson. His first symphonic success was his *Short Symphony,* first performed in 1950 by the New York Philharmonic-Symphony Society; the following year it was played during the Edinburgh Festival. In February 1951, Bernard Greenhouse, cellist, played Swanson's *Suite for Cello and Piano* (Anthony Makas was the pianist) in Town Hall. In May 1951, Helen Thigpen sang a number of Swanson's songs and a *New York Times* reviewer rated the songs over a group by Aaron Copland being presented at the same time. New York critics have said that Swanson "is considerate [with his songs] of the human voice," that his work "is refined . . . sophisticated of line and harmony in a way not at all common among American music writers."

Ulysses Kay is a third contemporary Negro composer. A former student of Paul Hindemith, he is modern in terms of what *Time's* music critic called "listenable fashion." Obviously this term challenges opposing critics, some of whom insist the music is too "listenable." His background music for *The Quiet One* was quiet indeed, if not banal. His symphonic score *Of New Horizons,* which the Tucson orchestra played in 1954 under his direction, is far more important and won him good critical notices. His *Suite for Orchestra* won for him the 1946–7 American Composers' Alliance contest; his *Sinfonia in E* has been performed by the Rochester Eastman Orchestra; and his two *Meditations* for organ have been performed by E. Power Biggs, and broadcast.

Three outstanding white composers of today, Samuel Barber, Aaron Copland, and Roy Harris have used Negro themes. Barber in his *Excursions* (1946) developed Americanisms, and therefore incorporated a blues passage and numerous regional folk idioms. Roy Harris's fugue in his *Third Symphony* is pure folk idiom. Aaron Copland, who had done so much to popularize modern American music, makes rich use of Negro and other folk idioms.

There is now no deep divide between our folk music and the main stream of music. The critical transition between a half-understood dialect and a compelling variety of world speech has been successfully made. But great effort and native genius are still needed because Negro music, in gaining universal vogue and prestige, must not lose its characteristic and unique qualities. Russian, Hungarian, and Bohemian composers were confronted with this problem within the last century. They widened the localisms of their native music to a universal speech; they were careful, in breaking the dialect, to reflect the characteristic folk spirit and preserve its unique flavor. What Glinka and his successors did for Russian music, Liszt and Brahms for Hungarian music, and Dvořák and Smetana for Czech music, can and must be done for Negro music.

The contributions of Isaac Albéniz and Manuel de Falla to modern Spanish music reinforce the point. By utilizing native themes, harmonies, and rhythms in formal compositions, they produced distinctive modern music. In addition, they revived interest in the traditional music of their native land.

Eventually the art music and the folk music of this country must be fused into a vital, superior form. Howard Swanson has begun this fusion. His universal appeal through technique rather than substance, his fusion of the folk spirit with traditional procedures, have brought him to an unprecedented eminence. But more must be done. Neither America nor the Negro can be content to have a single exception, or even just a few exceptions, to the statement: "Jazz is America's outstanding contribution to world music."

Interestingly enough, *The New York Times* for Sunday, November 6, 1955, carried a headline on its front page reading: "United States Has Secret Sonic Weapon—Jazz." Excerpts from the article, a special to *The New York Times* by Felix Belair, Jr., from Geneva, follow:

GENEVA, Nov. 5.—America's secret weapon is a blue note in a minor key. Right now its most effective ambassador is Louis (Satchmo) Armstrong. A telling propaganda line is the hopped up tempo of a Dixieland band heard on the Voice of America in far-off Tangier. . . .

All Europe now seems to find American jazz as necessary as the seasons. Yet Europeans don't bounce to the syncopated rhythm of Stan Kenton or Duke Ellington and their bands or the still popular recordings of Benny Goodman's quartet. They can swing and sway with Sammy Kaye, but for the most part they find in jazz a subject for serious study. . . .

They like to ponder the strength of its individuality and speculate on the qualities that differentiate it from the folk music of any other country. Somewhere along the line they get curious about the kind of people that first contrived it.

This is not to suggest that Europe has turned its back on the symphony and classical composition. Far from it. Wilhelm Backhaus was a sellout here last week with Beethoven's Piano Concerto in C minor. But not even Walter Gieseking could have caused the recent Hamburg rioting by those turned away when they pulled in the Standing Room Only sign. . . .

American jazz has now become a universal language. It knows no national boundaries, but everybody knows where it comes from and where to look for more. Individual Americans will continue to pack them in and the reasons for this are clear. . . .

The New York Philharmonic-Symphony, London's Symphony and the Boston Pops are no strangers to any European capital. They are appreciated for their versatility as much as for their faithful renditions of the classics associated with European composers over the centuries. . . .

Quoting this article seemed important, if not imperative, in light of the frequent charge that jazz is outmoded.

Can we do anything more with folk music than merely preserve it? It seems that we can. Often we forget that the roots divide and go deeper. While one strand of our musical heritage leads back to the delta and the plantation, another leads to the Negro elements in the West Indies and Central

America, and still another to Africa. The Negro musician must study African music and perhaps even African culture. Nearer home are the rich fields of West Indian native music and a flourishing school of Afro-Cuban and Brazilian composers fully aware of the possibilities of Negro music—the serious music of Central and South America, but particularly of Cuba, Haiti, and Brazil. One great advantage in these idioms is that they are more strongly racial than American Negro idioms—that is to say, undistorted culturally (American Negro idioms have been distorted by the plantation tradition). These idioms are valuable because of a healthier primitivism.

Concern for the African sources struck the American composer and the American stage, to some degree, in the thirties. We have mentioned White's *Ouanga*. William Grant Still wrote a well-received West Indian ballet, *La Guiablesse,* and an even more elaborate African ballet, *Sahdji,* which was performed at the Rochester Musical Festival in 1932. In addition, in 1934, New Yorkers saw Asadata Dafora Horton's African dance opera, *Kykunkor,* which was thoroughly native in plot, cast, music, dances, and type of orchestra. In fact, the native-drum orchestra was a revelation of new musical possibilities. *Kykunkor* represents the beginning of an entirely new and healthy adaptation of the pure African tradition of ritual dance, costume, and music. After several generations of mere effects, this was refreshing. Much as we owe to the early musicals *Abyssinia* and *In Dahomey,* they were musical comedy dominated by a transposed plantation formula. Inspired by *Kykunkor*'s success, the Federal Theatre Project directors organized an African unit. One of its early productions was an African "dance drama" under the direction of Momodu Johnson, with a cast of seventy, many of whose members were African born. Hampton Institute at the same time had a Creative Dance Unit under the direction of Charles Williams and Charlotte Moton. There the African and American Negro students presented African and other folk dances.

In the modern dance this new interest was reflected in the repertories of Martha Graham, Angna Enters, and Tamiris. Martha Graham's *Magic Chant,* Angna Enters's two Negro motifs for her *American Ballet No. 2,* and Tamiris's interpretative series of Negro spirituals are dance classics. Doris Humphrey and Charles Weidman devised Negro dances of both social significance (*Lynch Town* and *Atavisms: A Dance Series*) and decorative appeal (*Americana*). Before his tragic death, Hewsley Winfield, the young Negro director of the Negro Dance Unit that did the choreography for the Metropolitan Opera performance of *The Emperor Jones,* had attempted to organize a Negro dance group with a concert repertory. Today Katherine Dunham and Pearl Primus have such groups and are well established as concert dancers.

The realization that for many years the Negro dancer could not aspire above the vaudeville level is a sorry one. His accomplishments within such a narrow medium of footwork and acrobatic eccentricity were possible only through sheer genius. What Stella Wiley, Ada Overton, Florence Mills, "Peg Leg" Bates, Pete, Peaches, and Duke, the Berry Brothers, and Bill Robinson could have done in a freer medium with more artistic background can only be imagined.

Now, however, with the gradual but steady breaking down of barriers, talented dancers can aspire to wider opportunities. The use of Negro dancers in productions like *This Is the Army, On the Town, Sing Out, Sweet Land, Call Me Mister,* and *Finian's Rainbow* is heartening. The appointment of Janet Collins to the ballet of the Metropolitan Opera Company was much more so.

In the strictly colloquial field of social dancing, Negro music is unquestionably the underlying motivation. Since the pre-World War I period, the Negro popular idiom has inspired the successive popular-dance vogues. Miller and Lyles, musical-comedy artists, devised the Charleston in 1920. Successively the Turkey Trot (one of a group of "animal dances" including the Bunny Hug, Grizzly Bear, and Kangaroo Hop), the Black Bottom, the Big Apple, and the Lindy Hop reflected trends in jazz and swing music. Tap dancing, of course, was the obvious accompaniment to both "hot" and "sweet" jazz.

The Negro dance and Negro-inspired dances appealed to the French. André Levinson, writing in the *Theatre Arts Monthly* (May 1927), observed:

Negro music having conquered the public, Negro ragtime having become worthy of the most serious consideration, jazz is henceforth admitted into the hierarchy of the arts; and although it has only been a little while since it was the butt of the press and public, the time is at hand when it will provide material for a Doctor's thesis at the Sorbonne.

He then goes on to eulogize the Negro dance, comparing it to a Russian or Scottish folk dance. He admired the direct, audible expression of the rhythm, the staccato, rapid, clear articulation. Mr. Levinson's enthusiastic comments followed his having seen Josephine Baker and Florence Mills dance in Paris. Characterizing the two, respectively, as "an African Eros" and "a black Venus," he further characterized Miss

Baker as "a stream of rhythm" reflecting "impulsive vehemence" and displaying "symmetry of pattern." If Mr. Levinson's exuberant reactions were in any degree typical, one assumes that the new Negro dancing was appealing to Parisians! Actually the innate, unselfconscious freedom that defined the new rhythms captivated and dazzled most European audiences.

Since Bill Robinson there have been a few talented popular dancers. In her *The Negro in the American Theatre,* Edith Isaacs observes: "There have been at least a score of other Negro dancers *almost* as good as Bill Robinson." Mrs. Isaacs points out, however, that some of these dancers combined dancing talent with other talents. She emphasizes particularly the pure talent of Katherine Dunham, Pearl Primus, and Josephine Baker. Of Miss Baker, Mrs. Isaacs says:

> Josephine Baker was not an artist in the sense that Florence Mills was. She was a "natural," with an uncanny power of projecting her personality and her talent.

This pronouncement raises certain questions, as Florence Mills, in terms of at least one critic's definition (Gilbert Seldes's), was herself a "natural." According to Seldes, Florence Mills had "little or nothing to give beyond her presence, her instinctive grace, and her baffling, seductive voice."

Katherine Dunham's anthropological studies have been richly rewarding to dance audiences as well as to the literature of anthropology. Her belief that dance traditions are a strong racial link with the past has led her to study native dances in Trinidad, Haiti, and Martinique. Her findings became the basis for articles as well as for dance concerts. In addition, she has a repertory of native American dances.

The racial mastery of rhythm is the one characteristic that seems never to have been lost. When customs were lost and native cultures cut off in the rude transplanting of slavery, when languages and rituals were forgotten and nature-worship displaced, rhythm memories and rhythmic skill persisted, later to merge with and transform whatever new mode of expression the Negro took on. For just as music can be carried without words, rhythm can be carried without the rest of the music system, so intimate and instinctive is it. From a kernel of rhythm, African music has sprouted in strange lands, sending out offshoots of folk song and folk dance, going through the whole cycle of musical expression as far as the soil of the cultural conditions permitted.

After the initial "sprouting" stage, favorable nurture and

appreciation are needed. Unlike folk music, which is hardy, art music is sensitive. It needs the kind of sound encouragement and sober cultivation that will enable Negro music to enrich even more than it has our racial and national culture.

CHAPTER FIVE

Negro Folk Poetry and Folk Thought

THE SPIRITUALS, the seculars, and the blues, as we have seen, were forerunners of later music—of ragtime, of musical blues, and of jazz, both popular and classical. These forms have another significance: they give us a clear insight into the folk mind and character. The concern for freedom, the anticipation of a better life after death, the conviction of a literal heaven, and the despair at injustice clearly portray slave thought. The seculars and the blues are equally revealing of the Negro folk thought.

The poetry of the spirituals is not to be overrated as poetry; its value lies in the reflection of the intrinsic folk feeling. Frequently, of course, quaint symbolisms and passages of fine imagery appear, as in the much-quoted:

> *I know moonlight, I know starlight*
> *I lay dis body down.*
> *I walk in de graveyard, I walk troo de graveyard*
> *To lay dis body down.*
>
> *I lay in de grave and stretch out my arms,*
> *I lay dis body down.*
> *I go to de judgment in de evenin' of de day*
> *When I lay dis body down,*
> *An' my soul an' yo' soul will meet de day*
> *I lay dis body down.*

Or:

> *Bright sparkles in de churchyard*
> *Give light unto de tomb;*
> *Bright summer, spring's over—*
> *Wet flowers in their bloom.*

> *My mother once, my mother twice,*
> *My mother, she'll rejoice,*
> *In the Heaven once, in the Heaven twice*
> *She'll rejoice.*
> *May the Lord, He will be glad of me*
> *In the Heaven, He'll rejoice.*

The naïveté and faith in the latter passages suggest the medieval tone. Here indeed is a combination of childlike simplicity of thought and strangely consummate artistry of mood which could be paralleled only in the Middle Ages. Fervent expressions of Christian belief, these words suggest the evangelical and Protestant counterparts of tenth- to thirteenth-century naïve Catholicism. There we had quaint versions of Bernard of Clairveaux and St. Francis in the Virgin songs and Saints legends; here we have Bunyan and Wesley translated by the simple, faith-abiding Negro slave. If the analogy seems forced, let us remember that we see the homely colloquialism of the one through the glamorous distance of romance; the other we see through the disillusioning nearness of social stigma.

Emotionally, the spirituals are far from naïve or simple. They reveal a wide range of concerns, although the most serious and "pure" examples are primarily concerned with a better life after death in a literal heaven and with the sorrows and travail of earthly existence. Such slow-moving, stately spirituals as *Deep River, My Lord What a Morning, Nobody Knows the Trouble I've Seen,* and *Were You There?* reveal a depth of both piety and pathos which suggests again medieval ecstasy. It might be noted, too, that although earlier comparison of the spirituals to the Jewish Psalms has been made, the difference lies in the absence of bitterness or vindictiveness in the spirituals.

The humility, the lack of vengefulness revealed in the texts of so many of the spirituals, is understood more fully when it is recalled that the folk Negro, the slave, had an unshaken conviction that Heaven existed in a thoroughly material fashion. Anticipation of rest and joy, of solace and compensation, of complete release from earthly burdens lessened the daily hardships. Heaven was a place of milk and honey, of harps and crowns, of marble streets. Everybody was to wear shoes and robes, crowns and golden ornaments. All this, and more, was to follow the glorious chariot ride.

The spirituals show a remarkable knowledge of the Bible. John Work suggests that the spirituals were the only Bible the slaves had; they were unable, for the most part, to read.

Many Bible stories are fully related, in essential detail at least.

> We read in the Bible and we understan'
> That Samson was the strongest man.
> Samson went out at one time
> And killed about a hundred Philistines.
> Delilah fooled Samson, this we know
> Because the Holy Bible tells us so.
> She shaved off his head just as clean as your han'
> And his strength became as any other man.

Similarly other Bible stories, particularly the more dramatic, and those which conceivably might be construed as having symbolic significance for the Negro slave—his trials, his hopes for eventual freedom—are retold in the spirituals. Moses' burial, the Hebrews in the fiery furnace, David's flight from Saul and his fight with Goliath, and the slaying of Abel are all told through the medium of the spirituals. Newman Ivey White made the point that the details are not always accurate (Cain hit Abel "in de head wid de leg of a table"), but in spite of frequent anachronisms, these songs are appealing because of their obvious sincerity, intensity, warmth, and rich imagery. The following (which suggests Johnson's *The Creation*) is as succinct and vivid an account of the Creation as one could find:

> Lord he thought he'd make a man,
> Mixed a little bit o' dirt and san'.
>
> Thought he make a 'oman too,
> Didn't know zacly what to do.
>
> He took a rib from Adam's side,
> And made Miss Eve fo' to be his bride.
>
> Put 'em in a garden rich and fair,
> Tol' 'em to eat whatever was there.
>
> Of this tree you must not eat,
> If you do you'll have to skeet.

Some of the finest spirituals recounting Bible events are those retelling the Crucifixion. *Were You There?* and *He Never Said a Mumblin' Word* are two of the best. The latter might well be interpreted as reflecting the patient forbearance that the slave himself had to cultivate in order to survive.

Not only the Crucifixion, but also all the related stories—the burial, the rising from the tomb, the lament of Mary—are retold in song.

But all these songs were not concerned with God and Heaven or the Bible. The Devil came in for his share. More scorned than feared, he was the evil force to be eluded, defied, routed, outwitted.

> *Shout! Shout! Satan's about.*
> *Shut yo' do' and keep him out.*
>
> *Ol' Satan's mad and I am glad.*
> *He missed the soul he thought he had.*

As denominational rivalry developed, it was reflected in song. Strong partisanship and rivalry between denominations are revealed by:

> *There's a camp meeting in the wilderness.*
> *I know it's among the Methodists.*
>
> *I'm Baptis' bred and Baptis' bo'n,*
> *And when I'm dead there's a Baptis' gone.*

There are other themes, of course, for there are spirituals that reveal a passionate desire for freedom; there are those that express a weariness with this world; others warn of the penalty of evil and the need for good behavior; still others lament the loss of family ties, mothers, fathers, brothers, sisters. Some are pious, some are superstitious, some are exuberant, others are melancholy. All reveal some facet of a simple, faithful, religious folk sharing the common group experience of slavery.

The seculars reveal a great deal of spontaneous humor and irony. Fortunately, the slaves were frequently able to laugh at themselves and the petty hardships they had to accept.

> *Way down yon'er 'un de Alerbamer way,*
> *De Niggers goes to wo'k at de peep o' de day.*
> *De bed's too short, and de high posts rear;*
> *De Niggers needs a ladder fer to climb up dere.*
>
> *De cord's worn out, and de bed tick's gone.*
> *Niggers' legs hang down fer de chickens t' roost on.*

Or:

> *Chile: I come from out'n slavery,*
> *War de Bull-Whup bust de hide;*
> *Back dar, whar dis gineration*
> *Natchully widdered up an' died!*

With more bitterness we hear this:

> *We raise de wheat,*
> *Dey gib us de corn;*
> *We bake de bread,*
> *Dey gib us de crust;*
> *We sif de meal,*
> *Dey gib us de huss;*
> *We peel de meat,*
> *Dey gib us de skin;*
> *And dat's de way*
> *Dey take us in;*
> *We skim de pot,*
> *Dey gib us de liquor,*
> *And say dat's good enough for nigger.*

The Negro seculars, to be distinguished from the ballads, the blues, and the work songs, are often shrewd appraisals of the slave's daily life and living. A slaveowner forgets her promise of freedom:

> *My ole Mistiss promise me,*
> *W'en she died, she'd set me free.*
> *She lived so long dat 'er head got bal',*
> *And she give out'n de notion a dyin' at all.*
>
> *Ole Mosser lakwise promise me,*
> *W'en he died, he'd set me free.*
> *But ole Mosser go an' make his will*
> *Fer to leave me a-plowin' ole Beck still.*

A slave makes a burial request:

> *W'en I goes to die, you mus'n' bury me deep,*
> *But put Sogrum molasses close by my feet,*
> *Put a pone o' co'n bread way down in my han'.*
> *Gwineter sop up on de way to de Promus' Lan'.*

We know from many slave narratives, as well as from formal historical accounts, that slaves were given a very limited diet, just enough to keep them strong enough to work.

It is not odd, then, to find seculars that talk about getting enough to eat.

> I'se gwine now a-huntin' to ketch a big fat coon.
> Gwineter bring him home, an' bake him, an' eat him wid a spoon.
> Gwineter baste him up wid gravy, an' add some onions too.
> I'se gwineter shet de Niggers out, an' stuff myse'f clean through.
>
> I wants a piece of hoecake; I wants a piece o' bread,
> An I wants a piece o' ash cake: I wants dat big fat coon!
> An' I sho won't git hongry 'fore de middle o' nex' June.

Or:

> Dar ration day come once a week,
> Ole Masser's rich as Gundy;
> But he gives us 'lasses all de week,
> An' buttermilk fer Sund'y.
>
> Ole Masser give me pound o' meat.
> I e't it all on Mond'y;
> Den I e't 'is 'lasses all de week
> An' buttermilk fer Sund'y.
>
> Ole Masser give me a peck o' meal,
> I fed and cotch my tucky;
> But I e't dem 'lasses all de week,
> An' buttermilk fer Sund'y.
>
> Oh laugh an' sing an' don't git tired.
> We's all gwine home, some Mond'y.
> To de honey ponds an' fritter trees;
> An' ev'ry day'll be Sund'y.

The slave wants, when his wife dies, to "git . . . anudder one; a big fat yaller one," revealing that already color caste has taken hold. This is more boldly stated with:

> I wouldn' marry a black gal;
> I'll tell you de reason why:
> When she goes to comb dat head
> De naps'll gin to fly.

I wouldn' marry a black gal;
I'll tell you why I won't:
When she'd oughter wash her face—
Well, I'll jes say she don't.

I wouldn' marry a black gal;
An dis is why I say:
When you has her face around,
It never gits good day.

In amusing contrast to this is the declaration of another slave who wouldn't marry a "black, yellow, *or* white Nigger gal"! A slave declares: "I'd druther be a nigger dan a po white man," suggesting an early and primitive counterchauvinism. Another reveals his cunning. Finding Miss Sallie away for the day, he "slipped in de rockin' chair" and "rocked all day."

Some Negro seculars were dialect versions of ballads current in colonial days. Many of the "mountain ballads," now equally prized after generations of neglect, can be found in parallel Negro and white versions. However, most Negro ballads are thoroughly original. They deal even more often with unrequited love, though many glorify risky and daredevil adventure.

The blues express cynicism, despair, grief, unrequited love.

Money's all gone so far from home,
Money's all gone so far from home,
I just sit here and cry and moan.

When a woman gets the blues she hangs her head
and cries—
When a woman gets the blues she hangs her head
and cries—
When a man gets the blues, he catches a train and
rides.

Yaller gal makes a preacher lay his Bible down,
Yaller gal makes a preacher lay his Bible down,
Good lookin' high brown make him run from town
to town.

Woman without a man like a ship without a sail,
Woman without a man like a ship without a sail,
Ship without a sail like a dog without a tail.

Both the spirituals and the seculars represent something of a musical paradox when we reflect that the former were dedicated to Christian Protestant worship and the latter were the day-by-day musical expressions of Christian people. The pagan elements of early slave music, with its wild abandon, strongly marked rhythms, and alien chants, though early merged with Christian church ritual, were in sharp conflict with austere Puritan church ritual as it was performed until well into the eighteenth century. The New Englanders not only disapproved of music as "sinful," and therefore had neither practice nor talent for church music, but were so totally immune to either rhythm or harmony that even the mild "lining out" that had prevailed as an earlier English practice was, according to accounts, a painful thing to hear. The deacon "set the tune," sang one line of a psalm, and waited while the congregation painstakingly imitated him. As few, including deacons, could read music, the songs were rarely "lined out" exactly the same way, and over a period of time it was difficult to know which tunes went with which psalms. This is aside, however, from our point that Negro music, from its earliest beginnings, never lacked either vigor or an indigenous racial quality. Thus, in its earliest stages of identification with newly embraced Christianity, the religious music of the slaves was contradictory to an essential aspect of Puritan dogma. Although Southern church ritual underwent a liberalizing transformation in the period immediately following the Revolutionary War, it, too, tended to conservatism, though of a less hidebound nature than that of New England. But there is no history of early Southern church music either. Southerners either disregarded slave music or regarded it as proof of the slaves' contentment.

According to George Pullen Jackson, one unusually significant gain is too frequently overlooked or discounted. The yeomen achieved "freedom to worship God according to the dictates of their own conscience." This is dramatized by the fact that just about one hundred years after the Revolution, the combined membership of the Congregational and Anglican Episcopal churches was only one fourteenth of that of all American Protestant denominations, and but one twentieth of American church membership of all faiths. With this new-found freedom and religious autonomy came not only freedom and variation in dogma, ritual, and church polity, but also—because the revolution was of the poor man, the yeoman, the rural man—a music of their own from the hands of the folk. Not only was there a paucity of older music, but what there was was unsuitable for the countless new sects and variants that sprang up among the folk. They made up their own songs, calling them "hymns and spiritual songs," the latter to be distinguished from older psalms. Rapidly songs developed, being compiled and distributed by itinerant ministers throughout the newly freed colonies. The new, independent, individualistic qualities of the songs directly paralleled the essential tenets of the new religious groups. Typical are Joshua Smith's *Divine Hymns or Spiritual Songs,* Elias Smith's *Hymns for the Use of Christians* (the "Christians" were a religious sect), and Abner Jones's *The Melody of the Heart.* In 1805, Smith and Jones collaborated and produced *Hymns, Original and Selected, for the Use of Christians.* From the hymns contained in each we get a fairly clear picture of the rural and folk life of the post-Revolutionary period. There are hymns for Baptist foot-washes, for funerals, weddings, conversion, exhortation; there are hymns for lamenting widows and widowers, for the strong and for the weak, for the sinners of all types. There was a concern for the after life which promised (in heaven) "dazzling robes" and "dress uniforms lined with white and faced with red" or (in hell) "devils . . . a-burning in the fire" while newly arrived sinners "curse that fatal day . . . when [they] exchanged their souls away for vanity and songs." Casualness of grammar and realism of expression found their way into these new songs:

> *See's head all torn with thorns*

and his face:

> *Reeking with sweat and gore!*
> *See His side spout a stream of blood*
> *And water through the wound.*
>
> *His sweet and reverend face*
> *With spittle all profan'd.*

These are examples of religious folk music from the immediate post-Revolutionary years until 1830 or 1840. They were sung throughout the rural area of America, in the main by Baptists. By the 1840's, with the great revivals, inspired largely by William Miller's prediction that the Day of Judgment was imminent (October 1844 was established as the precise time), a new body of music cropped up. Most popular were the so-called "end-of-time" songs. People were exhorted to come to Jesus, get religion, hear the thunder's roar, hear the trumpet sound, see the dead arise, see the world burn, hear the sinners cry, hear the saints shout. Like the millennialists, the Shakers and the Mormons developed a new body of songs to complement their active, if not violent, ritual. The "exercise songs," for example, were just that: they accompanied the dancing and "exercises" of the two unique sects. For what we now know as "revival spirituals" we are indebted to the millennial furore. During the 1840's, collections of them were added to the collections of religious ballads and folk hymns of praise. The early volumes appeared first in the North and then, shortly after, in the South. In the South similar collections were called "slave songs," then "cabin and plantation songs," and finally "spirituals."

This brief reference to white religious folk music is important because so much conflicting testimony, opinion, and research has been introduced to challenge the authenticity of the Negro spiritual. George Jackson essays to prove that neither white nor Negro spirituals were original, but that each borrowed from or improvised upon not only the works of the other, but also upon traditional folk themes brought from the Old World—Britain in particular. Certainly when one examines Jackson's "Tune Comparative List" and the accompanying texts, it is hard to dismiss his thesis. As a case in point, reference is here made to Jackson's spiritual Number 107, the white text of which reads:

Jesus my all to heaven is gone, I'll never turn back no more;
I'll never turn back no more, my Lord, I'll never turn back no more.

This, Jackson tells us, dates to the Georgia *Social Harp* (1853). The parallel Negro version runs:

O just let me get up in the house of God, Just let me get up in the house of God,
Just let me get up in the house of God, and I'll never turn back any more.

Taken from the Fisk *Jubilee Songs* of 1872, this song has been arranged by both Harry Burleigh and Ballanta Taylor.

The striking similarities between white and Negro spirituals as manifest in the entire list are undeniable. Yet, as John Work has remarked, one wonders, even so, if the analysis of only one hundred and fourteen songs out of the hundreds on record does not suggest that the author arbitrarily selected songs to fit his predetermined conclusion. As Sterling Brown has said, enough scholarship has been done to disprove any "romantic theory of completely African origin for the spirituals." It must be conceded, however, that it is equally well established that the Negro spirituals, like their early white counterparts, were frequently spontaneous improvisations that were not, could not have been, recorded. Thus, the unmistakable flavor of the Negro character is the distinguishing feature between the white and Negro spirituals.

What *is* this "unmistakable flavor"? One element of it is, as Dr. DuBois has said, the optimistic faith to which the Negro slave persistently clung in spite of infinite causes prompting him to morbidity, pessimism, or unmitigated despair. DuBois regarded this as an important cultural gift because it enabled the Negro to survive under the hardships of slavery; by the disarming quality of his optimism, the Negro was able to come psychologically very close to the people who were exploiting him. In short, because the Negro was gay, seemingly contented, and invariably properly subservient, he was able to identify himself closely with the master group. Because he was taken into the heart of Southern culture, he left the indelible stamp of his temperament on it.

It is, of course, a little dangerous to talk about a group soul or a group temperament. Yet the net average reaction of a people does suggest a composite psychological portrait. The composite portrait of the Negro under slavery is one of which the Negro has no reason to be ashamed. Rather, he has every reason to be proud. That under the circumstances of slavery the Negro could make *any* contribution to or leave *any* positive mark on Southern cultural history is in itself extraordinary. The gifts at the peasant level—in other words the folk gifts—made by exploited, handicapped, illiterate people are truly remarkable.

In spite of the fact that the spirituals came from the white man's civilization, the Negroes, as they assimilated Christianity, transformed the music in spirit, in idiom, and in symbolic treatment. The composite result is a unique reflection of the Negro. When one considers the powerful expression behind the broken dialect, the distinctive and personal quality is even more evident. There is evident also an extraordinary gift of creative language, a gift difficult to explain because it was revealed by illiterates. If one were to hazard an explanation, it might be this: in the best folk materials all over the world, but especially and peculiarly in the folk reactions of those people who have been emotionally and physically harassed, there is invariably a striking eloquence of expression. Mass suffering and mass sorrow apparently develop a capacity for moving, spiritual reaction. Unmistakably there is this mass reaction in the Negro folk material of the South; unmistakably it can be traced in the folk materials of the Slav, particularly the Russian peasant.

Sensitive and thoughtful artists familiar with the feel of the Negro folk spirit have visited Russia and confirmed this. Each has said that, barring difference of idiom, they sensed in the Russian peasant's dance and music something roughly akin to the folk products of the American Negro. Both have a characteristic group individuality and, despite this, an enlightening generic simplicity.

What was the impact of this folk musical expression upon the white Southerners? For the most part it is neither understood nor deeply valued. To most Southerners this was just a familiar, warm, sentimental expression of Negro emotionalism in which they basked pleasantly and comfortably. Because the music was optimistic and not belligerent or vindictive, it served not only as a balm to white conscience, but also as an escape from deep-seated, well-concealed guilt. The Southerner could not see that even in his real ecstasy the Negro was compensating for what had been taken from him. He did not see that the Negro, even in the secular music, was doing all he could to survive spiritually and to have some freedom of spirit to counteract the frustrating bonds of the slave system. Even second-generation Negroes did not fully appreciate or understand the true significance of the spirituals, their motivation, or their intent.

Although ante-bellum whites did not take with any real seriousness Negro folk thought as reflected in Negro music, both religious and secular, they recognized that the talents of the Negro were of unquestionable entertainment value. Long before minstrelsy, as such, came to the American stage, Negro slave entertainment was an established part of the plantation tradition. In the pre-Civil War days, stage minstrelsy was nothing more than a caricature of Negro life and ways by white performers, and by the 1850's it was the fashion to capitalize on the romantic or idealized version of both plantation and Southern life—an idealization that was to dominate a whole school of writers and apologists in the post-Civil War period.

The works of Stephen Foster epitomize the romantic concept of Southern life that was so appealing and convincing to Southerners and to a number of Northerners. Many of the former, as we have observed, were eager to grasp any rationale to support their conviction that slavery, humane and of incalculable benefit to the primitive Negro, was perpetuated at an actual loss to the owners. Northerners frequently visited the South with predetermined (and unflattering) concepts of slavery, only to be charmed and fascinated by the ostensible ease and gaiety of slave life, the apparently happy and irresponsible nature of the slave. Foster's ballads perpetuated this concept. Himself not a Negro, Foster composed Negro "ballad" after Negro "ballad" inspired by the curious fascination that a romantic and half-mythical South had for him. A native of Pittsburgh, Foster had spent some time in Cincinnati, just across the river from Kentucky, and in addition apparently had had some contact with Negro plantation singing. It is known that he spent time in at least one Kentucky home, that of the Rowan family in Bardstown. He somehow caught enough of the unique flavor of Negro folk thought and song to give vitality to the one and sentimental appeal to the other. The songs he created in the popular and sentimental idiom of the day immediately became popular. His relation to Negro folk song might well be likened to that of Joel Chandler Harris to Negro folklore. Both men modified the original materials just enough to suggest universality without completely destroying the folk flavor. Neither service was an unmixed blessing.

The ballads that Foster wrote in a straight sentimental vein, without Negro elements, are, in the main, completely forgotten. But *Uncle Ned* (1848), *Camptown Races* (1850), *Swanee River* (1851), *My Old Kentucky Home* (1853), and *Old Black Joe* (1860) are well known and will be known as long as American popular music has admirers. The words and the thoughts of these ballads enhanced the sentimental side of slavery; the romantic concept of the plantation was more and more hardened—and accepted. The shallow sentiment and false pathos that dominated Foster's Negro ballads stimulated an unfortunate, often ridiculous glorification of the slave regime. Foster's ballads did more to crystallize the romance of the plantation tradition than all the Southern colonels and novelists put together. It is indeed an ironic tribute to Negro idioms that they inspired a popular balladry that reinforced and helped perpetuate the very system that kept Negroes enslaved.

Some years ago there was a popular song whose first line was: "Is it true what they say about Dixie?" The query, humorous in intent, symbolizes the contemporary revaluation of Negro folk thought and literature whether interpreted or delineated by Negro or by white writers. Both the reconstruction and the reinterpretation of Negro folk literature now reveal that the Foster-Joel Harris picture of the folk Negro was a one-sided, sentimentalized, unrealistic one. Just as the poetry, drama, and fiction of the Negro clung to rigid stereotypes until well into the 1920's, so folk thought and lore remained similarly entrenched until comparatively recent years. Sterling Brown, Alan Lomax, Zora Hurston,

Negro Folk Poetry and Folk Thought

Roark Bradford, Stith Thompson, and a number of other folklorists and anthropologists are conceding that intelligent investigation of American *and* Negro folklore demands a break with sentimental tradition and an alliance with a scientific method of investigation and evaluation that will ultimately make it possible for us to determine the origins and sources of our folk literature and its intrinsic worth to American culture as a whole.[1]

Contemporary folklorists, freed from sentiment and from the compulsion to defend the old tradition, are revealing the Negro folk in terms of very real, diversified experiences—few of which are either romantic or sentimental. The chain gang, the railroad drudgery, the jail experiences, the discouragement and despair at social repression and personal loss—these and countless other human themes universal in appeal color the recent discoveries of modern researchers.

[1] A recent pronouncement apropos Negro folk literature was made by Sterling Brown. In the context of a paper entitled "The New Negro in Literature (1925-1955)" read at the Memorial Service for Alain Locke at Howard University on April 20, 21, and 22, 1955, Brown observed:

At the start of the twenties, the only books available on the folk Negro were the Uncle Remus Tales, a few collections of spirituals, and Talley's *Negro Folk Rhymes*. Today, materials abound. B. A. Botkin's *Lay My Burden Down* (1945), edited from the thousands of ex-slave narratives collected by the Writers' Project, is valuable "folk history," helping to lay the ghosts of the plantation tradition. The vast collection of discs in the Library of Congress Archives, started by the Lomaxes, had discovered unknown songs and singers; among these was the dynamic Leadbelly, who, together with Josh White, brought unadulterated folk music to thousands of Americans. The record companies have responded to the appeal of this music. It is significant that whereas even an artist like Roland Hayes found the recording studios closed to him in his early years, today not only are the voices of Marian Anderson, Dorothy Maynor, and other concert singers everywhere available on records, but staid companies issue long-play volumes of folk singers such as Bessie Smith and Mahalia Jackson with their strong faces gracing the colorful album jackets. Frederic Ramsey's *Music from the South* in ten long-play volumes, from field recordings in areas hitherto untouched, crowns Ramsey's tireless search for the roots of jazz. Together with Charles Smith, Ramsey pioneered in the historical and critical study of jazz; today a long bibliography by many authors shows the wisdom of such pioneering. Most of the above collectors and interpreters are white; Negro collectors of folk material have been rare, but second-generation respectability is declining: J. Mason Brewer has enthusiastically collected yarns; Lorenzo Turner has studied Gullah with scientific linguistic techniques; and William H. Pipes, with sociological interest, has recorded old-time sermons in backwoods churches. The interest in Negro folk expression is not a momentary fad; the collection and interpretation are the work of both white and Negro folklorists, united in respect for material which, no longer set in isolation, is becoming recognized as an integral part of American experience.

CHAPTER SIX

Formal Negro Poetry

THE FIRST two Negro formal writers on record in America were poets: Jupiter Hammon and Phillis Wheatley, both favored slaves from Northern backgrounds. Hammon came from Long Island; Phillis Wheatley lived in Boston. Hammon, whose first publication, *An Evening Thought: Salvation by Christ, and Penitential Cries,* was issued in 1760, continued to write sporadically until 1787. In that year, his last work (his first in prose), *An Address to the Negroes in the State of New York,* achieved popularity because of its ambivalent tone in regard to slavery. Hammon was at best an imitative rhymester, but it is significant that a Negro slave was impelled to write at all. His "The Kind Master and the Dutiful Slave" doubtlessly suggests why he was allowed to write: he was saying the proper thing. Aware of his more talented contemporary, Phillis Wheatley, he wrote twenty-one dedicatory stanzas to her in 1778, revealing at least a measure of race-consciousness.

Phillis Wheatley, in spite of a broader talent and a more powerful personality, also took on the coloration of her patrons and their Boston environment: her role in the educated and humane Wheatley household was that of a favored maid and personal protégée. The Wheatley family not only educated the young woman, but also permitted her to travel in England, where she was warmly received in both literary and court circles. While she was in England in 1773, her first book of poetry was published. The following year, on her return to Boston, she wrote a number of laudatory verses to Washington when he took command of the Continental armies. With minor exceptions, Phillis Wheatley's work was scrupulously modeled after Pope: she invariably used the closed couplet. This was in keeping with the poetic trend predominant among American and English poets of the period, but the sentimentality and piety of Phillis Wheatley's verse, coupled with her vaguely rhetorical racialism, justify

Formal Negro Poetry

the repeated critical appraisal of her work as both imitative and conventional. Already anti-slavery sentiment was crystallizing, and Negro contemporaries of Miss Wheatley were denouncing slavery. Yet, because she had experienced only nominal slavery, the young poetess permitted herself no specific identification with the cause of abolition. Indeed we find her saying: " 'Twas mercy brought me from my pagan land"; later she wrote even more explicitly in "Lines to the Students of Cambridge University":

'Twas not long since I left my native shore—
The land of errors and Egyptian gloom.

Perhaps no more was to be expected of these minds, both of which were groomed in favoritism, yet bound by the limitations of their times and the general misgivings as to Negroes' having intellectual or creative capacities. Their constructive contribution was to give evidence of the intellectual and artistic capacities of the Negro in a time and environment of doubt; this, with a few other talents, they gave.

Somewhat later a Southern Negro, George Horton (1797–1883) wrote enough poetry to buy his freedom. Although he eventually was freed, it was because of the advent of the Union soldiers, not by the sale of his poetry, it might be noted. A few of Horton's poems contained anti-slavery feeling, but they are not to be compared with the anti-slavery poetry of Negro poets like Charles Reason and Elymas Rogers. Rogers is particularly noteworthy for "The Repeal of the Missouri Compromise Considered" (1856), which reveals not only poetic ability, but also a concrete sense of historical reality and social responsibility. Other Negro anti-slavery poets were James Bell, whose "The Day and the War" was dedicated to his friend John Brown; and James Whitfield, a friend of Martin Delaney and of Douglass. In his *America, and Other Poems* Whitfield denounced America's hypocrisy:

Thou boasted land of liberty
It is to thee I raise my song
Thou land of blood, and crime, and wrong . . .

White poets, too, turned their talents to anti-slavery poetry. Longfellow, Lowell, Bryant, Whittier, and Walt Whitman wrote strong indictments of slavery, as well as tributes to Negroes. In his "Commemoration Ode" Lowell does more than moralize:

Bow down, dear Land, for thou hast found release . . .
Bow down in prayer and praise!
No poorer in thy borders but may now
Lift to the juster skies a man's enfranchised brow . . .

Whitman is equally nonsentimental and uncondescending when, in his "Ethiopa Saluting the Colors," he queries:

What is it, fateful woman, so blear, hardly human?
Why wag your head with turban bound, yellow, red and green?
And the things so strange and marvelous you see or have seen?

Again, in his "Song of Myself" Whitman, with familiar universal identification, says:

The hounded slave that flags in the race, leans by the fence, blowing, cover'd with sweat,
The twinges that sting like needles his legs and neck— the murderous buck-shot and the bullets,
All these I feel or am . . .
I do not ask the wounded person how he feels,
I myself become the wounded person.

Whitman and Lowell, because of their more universal perception and approach, created the most artistic and lasting anti-slavery poetry. Or at least it might be said that that of their poetry which was anti-slavery in intent has proved to be the best. But the contributions of Whittier, Longfellow, and Bryant must not be dismissed. Although much of their anti-slavery poetry was something less than first rate, its profound influence on, and appeal to, moral and humane sentiment proved a powerful force in the ideological battle that preceded and, in large measure, dominated the Civil War. Whittier might well have achieved a greater degree of universal recognition as a poet had he not dissipated so much of his time and talent in the anti-slavery cause.

American literature after the Civil War reflects a number of divergent and contradicting points of view, all of which are easily recognized and understood. On the over-all national scale there was a wave of "regional" writing, the forerunner of American realism. In the general context of Southern regional literature, two contradictory tendencies in poetry appear. There developed a "dialect school," which was soon challenged by romantic poets who repudiated dialect completely. Actually, of course, the use of dialect was not peculiar to Negro writers or to writers of the post-war period. Stephen Foster had used it; white minstrel songwriters had used it. After the war, Joel Chandler Harris, Thomas Nelson Page, and an entire school of dialect poets simply continued the pattern. In fact, much of the post-war regional or local-color literature of the South was dialect literature, and its most representative authors were white. The white poet generally credited with being the first to create successful Negro dialect was Irwin Russell. Although his pictures of Negro plantation life both before and after the war are colorful, humorous, and thoroughly entertaining, they follow the idyllic, idealized pattern of ante-bellum apologists. None of the post-war aspirations and struggles of the Negro is revealed; none of the tragedy or suffering of slavery is touched in any of his poetry.

Negro poets, too, had used dialect, but without undue success or wide recognition until the appearance of Paul Laurence Dunbar. Dunbar, though he had never experienced slavery or, for that matter, had any firsthand contact with either the deep South or plantation life, obviously profited from accounts of slavery from his mother, an ex-slave. Although all of Dunbar's folk and dialect poetry is picturesque, often amusing, and frequently idyllic, in the final analysis he also was a part of the apologist tradition; he fails, therefore, ever to take into account the hardships and evils of slavery from the physical, economic, moral, or democratic point of view. Yet he had a tremendous vogue and an immense following as he developed and perpetuated a pattern and style that earned him the title of a "Negro Eugene Field." Acclaimed by William Dean Howells as the lyric spokesman of the Negro peasant, he gave wider and longer currency to the accepted stereotypes. In time, Dunbar was to regret this, as is evidenced not only by direct observation, but also by his pronouncement that his English lyrics, not in dialect, were his better works. Dunbar, however, will be best remembered for his poems about Negro folk life—its children, its holidays, its domestic idylls, its cheerful, optimistic, simple routine. The tuneful creator of "When Malindy Sings," "When de Co'n Pone's Hot," and "Little Brown Baby" is assured of a place in American literature even though he represents the end of one era rather than the beginning of another.

Several Negro poets, though frank imitators of Dunbar, never approximated his popularity. J. Mord Allen, Daniel Webster Davis, and James Edwin Campbell are three major examples; several lesser "preacher poets" made contributions. All of them are to be credited with continuing the familiar plantation tradition; each adhered to the pattern established by

Dunbar. No one of them attempted to inject even a small measure of realism into his poetry: there was obviously an unwritten agreement that nothing conceivably offensive or disconcerting to white Southerners was proper material for Southern regional poetry.

James Weldon Johnson's poetry represents a combination of folk consciousness and intellectualism. His *Fifty Years and Other Poems* contains some outstanding poems, one of which, "Black and Unknown Bards," is often cited as actual explanation of the origin of the spirituals.

> *Oh black and unknown bards of long ago,*
> *How came your lips to touch the sacred fire?*
> *How, in your darkness, did you come to know*
> *The power and beauty of the minstrel's lyre?*
> *Who first from midst his bonds lifted his eyes?*
> *Who first from the still watch, lone and long,*
> *Feeling the ancient faith of prophets rise*
> *Within his dark-kept soul, burst into song?*

Johnson's "Brothers," dealing with the horror and viciousness of lynching, is a thoroughly realistic social-justice poem; Sterling Brown likens it to Markham's "Man with a Hoe." "Go Down Death" is a magnificent folk funeral sermon whose blend of poetic imagery, folk superstition, and verisimilitude is memorable:

> *And God said: Go down, Death, go down,*
> *Go down to Savannah, Georgia,*
> *Down in Yamacraw,*
> *And find Sister Caroline.*
> *She's borne the burden and heat of the day,*
> *She's labored long in my vineyard,*
> *And she's tired—*
> *She's weary—*
> *Go down, Death, and bring her to me.*

Johnson was perfectly competent when it came to dialect poetry, but he eluded the pitfalls of oversentimentality and maintained a light, almost whimsical touch even when expanding such a thought as "Seems lak to me de stars don't shine so bright . . . Sence you went away." Best remembered, perhaps, for his moving "Lift Every Voice and Sing," set to music by his brother, and later adopted as the "Negro National Anthem," Johnson remains firmly established as a competent and stirring poet.

Opposed to the dialect tradition was a frankly romantic one.

There were Negro poets who insisted on the privilege to write as poets freed from racial or regional consciousness. Transcending racial preoccupations, poets like William Stanley Braithwaite, Angelina Grimke, and Georgia Douglas Johnson wrote in pure lyric vein. Braithwaite cultivated the conventional melancholy tone of the late-nineteenth-century romantics, and dwelt on death, dreams, and the wonders of nature. Georgia Johnson protests "I want to die while you love me," and Angelina Grimke, in delicate verse immediately reminiscent of Edna St. Vincent Millay's early lyrics, reflects her awareness of and contact with the imagist school. These poets did not identify themselves with social protest, in spite of living in the context of changing social patterns which challenged the imagination and interest of many white and Negro writers. Had these early lyricists been exceptionally powerful, some justification for their lack of social consciousness would be offered. Poe never attempted to do more than create poems of beauty in emotional, if not sensuous, appeal, and his achievement justified the lack of pure intellectualism in his poetry. But the Negro poets who studiously and self-consciously isolated themselves from racial themes did not measure up to the first-rate lyricists of their generation or to the experimenters and innovators in the newer tradition of "Negro poetry." With varying degrees of merit, these poets were part of a group that bridged the "genteel tradition" and the authentic "new poetry."

The new poetry, early inspired and encouraged by the efforts and actual works of Amy Lowell and her disciples, repudiated the sterile, genteel romantic tradition characteristic of the most popular late-nineteenth-century American poetry. Traditional poetic forms, conventional poetic subject matter, and stereotyped poetic figures were rejected in favor of complete freedom of choice in poetic language and technique. Within less than one decade, from 1914 until 1922, American poets had created such broadly divergent and unprecedented works as "The Congo" and "The Waste Land."

There were immediate forerunners to the "new poetry," however, who were not explicitly part of the official movement itself. Even before 1900, white poets such as Edwin Markham were injecting social protest into their work. Later, in verse, William Vaughn Moody was to decry American imperialism and laud John Hay for his share in preventing the breaking-up of China. W. E. B. DuBois, just after the 1906 Atlanta race riot—a riot of particularly excessive violence and brutality—wrote "Litany at Atlanta." Social inequities, predictions of labor revolts, acknowledgment of Darwinism, bitter protest against mob rule and subjection of human beings to brute violence were poetic themes that stood in marked contrast to those favored before 1912. They pointed the way to poetry's acquiring a new dimension.

If we are to mark 1912 or 1914 as the official date of American poetry's rebirth, we must, as a matter of record and timing, relate the "Negro Renaissance" to it. The Negro's spiritual and literary emancipations coincide exactly. From 1912 until the late twenties there developed a movement that has long been known as the "Negro Renaissance." Here again we have no exclusively minority phenomenon—as we have noted, a general poetic renaissance began in 1912; as we shall observe later, there was a general renaissance in Southern literature from, roughly, 1912 until the thirties, and certain national shifts in temper and theme by novelists took place in the years immediately before and after World War I. The Negro Renaissance, though of extreme importance in itself, can hardly be divorced from the over-all renaissance. The Negro movement is most akin to the entire one in its capitulation to realism. By 1912 not only was realism in an ascendancy never again to be completely overcome, but its corollary, naturalism, which Parrington so carefully defined as "pessimistic realism," a realism tempered with the findings of modern science, was well established in the social and literary consciousness of Americans.

But the Negro Renaissance was more than a reflection of the triumph of realism or naturalism. It was a deliberate cessation by Negro authors of their attempts to influence majority opinion. Negro artists were beginning to outgrow the handicap of allowing didactic emphasis and propagandistic or apologistic motives to stifle their artistry. Partly in disillusion, partly in newly acquired group pride and self-respect, they turned inward to the Negro audience in frankly conceded self-expression. Langston Hughes, one of the "New Negroes," thus phrased this literary declaration of independence:

> We younger Negro artists who create now intend to express our individual dark-skinned selves without fear or shame. If white people are pleased we are glad. If they are not, it doesn't matter. We know we are beautiful. And ugly, too. If colored people are pleased we are glad. If they are not, their displeasure doesn't matter either. We build our temples for tomorrow, strong as we know how, and we stand on the top of the mountain, free within ourselves.

Once again there was a common denominator between the advance-guard elements of the majority and the minority. The anti-slavery collaboration formed a moral alliance; this aesthetic one spelled out a final release from propaganda and its stifling limitations both for Negro materials in American art and literature and for the Negro writer and artist. Without exception, the most important new Southern writers from 1912 until the present have dealt at one time or another with aspects of Negro life and character or Negro-white relationships in the South.

The new Negro poets, like the new Negro writers in other media, reflected a race consciousness divested of the older apology or self-pity. It was a racism at once proud, self-reliant, and challenging. The leading poets were Claude McKay, Jean Toomer, Countee Cullen, Langston Hughes, and Sterling Brown. By 1927 James Weldon Johnson had renounced the traditional dialect, and, with *God's Trombones: Seven Negro Sermons in Verse*, he created what he called "poetry in free verse" that utilized "the truer idioms of the folk imagination." Countee Cullen's "Shroud of Color" reveals a sense of race and a race loyalty, pride, and group confidence that suggest that the Negro was a chosen race.

> *Lord, I will live persuaded by mine own,*
> *I cannot play the recreant to these:*
> *My spirit has come home, that sailed the*
> *doubtful seas.*

In "Song of the Son" Toomer, whose sketches of Georgia in *Cane* (1923) are among the artistic triumphs of the new era, sees slavery in this measured third-generation perspective:

> *Now just before an epoch's sun declines*
> *Thy son, in time I have returned to thee . . .*
> *In time, although the sun is setting on*
> *A long-lit race of slaves, it has not set . . .*
> *Though late, O soil, it is not too late yet*
> *To catch thy plaintive soul, leaving, soon gone . . .*
> *An everlasting song—a singing tree*
> *Caroling softly souls of slavery.*

Instead of Phillis Wheatley's myopic apologies for Africa as "the land of errors and Egyptian gloom," Claude McKay sees the country in dignified retrospective in his sonnet "Africa":

> *The sun sought thy dim bed and brought forth light,*
> *The sciences were sucklings at thy breast;*
> *When all the world was young in pregnant night*
> *Thy slaves toiled at their monumental best.*
> *Thou ancient treasure land, thou modern prize,*

New peoples marvel at thy pyramids!
The years roll on, thy sphinx of riddle-eyes
Watches the mad world with immobile lids.

But the new Negro poets were too realistic to neglect the significant new elements of social protest (and the unequivocal demands that democracy be held to strict and just account) which dominated the thought and writings of both white and Negro liberals. In 1925, Howard Odum and Guy Johnson published *The Negro and His Songs,* one of many books that would supply a more intelligent understanding of the significance of the Negro's contribution to America's music and culture. In the same year, Ellen Glasgow's *Barren Ground* was published—a novel that continued the Glasgow tradition of giving an objective, unbiased account of the South in its successive historic changes beginning with and following the Civil War. Carl Van Vechten's *Nigger Heaven* and DuBose Heyward's *Mamba's Daughters* were published in 1925; both authors were intent on revealing Negro character in human terms rather than in stereotypes. Van Vechten's book described the Harlem urban Negro; Heyward's novel celebrated the folk Negro, the matriarchal tradition, and imposed over all the symbolism of progress haltingly and painstakingly achieved in a democratic society and in a single family. Implicit in these works, which are random samples, is the concept that Negroes represent a wide range of character and personality, of ambition and aspiration, adjustment and isolation. In short, Negroes in American life must be appraised in all their manifold differences just like any other people. Otherwise, democracy, with its promise of a decent concern for the individual, fails. Thus, Negro poets expressed their dissatisfaction with the continuing discrepancy between democratic promise and democratic practice. Countee Cullen voiced his quiet conviction that:

We shall not always plant while others reap
The golden increment of bursting fruit,
Nor always countenance, abject and mute,
That lesser men should hold their brothers cheap, . . .
We were made eternally to weep.

Fenton Johnson's "Tired" is a vivid reflection of the author's personal disillusionment as well as of his identification with the realistic poets who were his contemporaries.

I am tired of work; I am tired of building up
    somebody else's civilization.
Let us take a rest, M'lissy Jane;

Formal Negro Poetry

> *I will go down to the Last Chance Saloon, drink a
>   gallon or two of gin, shoot a game or two of dice
>   and sleep the rest of the night
>   on one of Mike's barrels.*
> *You will let the old shanty go to rot, the white peo-
>   ple's clothes turn to dust, and the Calvary Bap-
>   tist Church sink to the bottomless pit.*
> *You will spend your days forgetting you married me
>   and your nights hunting the warm gin, Ike serves
>   the ladies in the rear of the Last Chance Saloon.*
> *Pluck the stars out of the heavens. The stars mark
>   our destiny. The stars marked my destiny.*
> *I am tired of civilization.*

The harsh defiance of and militant resistance to social injustice were never better expressed than by Claude McKay,
the most vigorous critic of democracy. His thorough contempt
for weakness and his uncompromising insistence that Negroes
perform as men and women rather than as groveling sub-
servients are revealed in these fragments of "White Houses"
and the well-known "If We Must Die."

> *Your door is shut against my tightened face,*
> *And I am sharp as steel with discontent.*
> *But I possess the courage and the grace*
> *To bear my anger proudly and unbent.*
>   (From "White Houses")

> *If we must die, let it not be like hogs*
> *Hunted and penned in an inglorious spot,*
> *While round us bark the mad and hungry dogs,*
> *Making their mock at our accursed lot.*
> *If me must die, O let us nobly die,*
> *So that our precious blood may not be shed in vain . . .*
>   (From "If We Must Die")

In the twenties, white poets, too, began to interpret the
Negro and his problems in a realistic manner. William Rose
Benét's "Harlem," Edwin Arlington Robinson's "Toussaint
L'Ouverture," and Stephen Benét's *John Brown's Body* are
good examples. Vachel Lindsay's "The Congo" had been
published much earlier. "The Congo," whose subtitle is "A
Study of the Negro Race," would not stand up under the
serious scrutiny of an anthropologist or sociologist, but it is
a colorful interpretation of Negro life. The rhythm is free
and thoroughly appropriate for describing the gaiety, abandon, primitivism, and "basic savagery" of the Negro—as

Vachel Lindsay conceived him. An influential single poem for a generation of poets striving to create new poetry and with it to redefine or reinterpret the place of the Negro in American life, "The Congo" has a unique place in modern American poetry. Lindsay's use of rhythm alone, a rhythm unmistakably familiar to any who have heard the sermons of Negro rural preachers, for example, is in itself a remarkable contribution to modern poetry as subsequent attempts to approximate it will suggest. When the poet recounts that:

> A good old Negro in the slums of town
> Preached at a sister for her velvet gown.
> Howled at a brother for his lowdown ways,
> His prowling, guzzling, sneak-thief days,
> Beat on the Bible till he wore it out . . .

anyone familiar with Negro religious folk sermons and with the uninhibited speech and action of the typical folk preacher will credit Lindsay with a warm understanding of one aspect of Negro life.

Before directing our attention to the contributions and significance of two reinterpreters of the Negro folk, let us consider the poet whom Sterling Brown describes as "the most precocious" of the Negro poets of the twenties and early thirties, Countee Cullen. Cullen did not want or expect the fact that he was a Negro writer to accord him a special or distinct critical appreciation. What developed as a dual standard of critical evaluation (a logical, if not an intellectually satisfactory consequence of, among other things, the social doctrine of "separate but equal") was particularly offensive to Cullen. Educated in the best formal tradition and endowed with a wide range of poetic skills, Cullen was equally at ease as a lyricist, an epigrammatist, and a narrative poet. His well-known "Heritage," whose opening lines read:

> What is Africa to me:
> Copper sun or scarlet sea.
> Jungle star or jungle track,
> Strong bronzed men or regal black
> Women from whose loins I sprang
> When the birds of Eden sang?

tells us that he is not unmindful of his identification, be it explicit or symbolic, with Africa. *The Black Christ,* a long poem about lynching, establishes his relationship with the protest poets, while "To John Keats" is completely devoid of any racial elements.

Traditionally, Langston Hughes has been paired with Countee Cullen because they were the outstanding young Negro poets of the Renaissance. Although Cullen was more the traditionalist, Hughes more the unconventional experimenter of the period, the two were linked because of their success and popularity. Today Langston Hughes is frequently paired with Sterling Brown because they have been equally concerned with what might be termed the "revaluation of the Negro folk." Hughes's early work includes poems of Harlem, of Africa, of individual characters whose problems and aspirations appeal to him, and in a few instances of the Negro race as a whole. His "Let America Be America Again," which is obviously patterned after Whitman ("I am the poor white, fooled and pushed apart, I am the Negro bearing slavery's scars; I am the red man driven from the land, I am the immigrant clutching the hope I seek . . ."), combines realistic admission of the temporary defeat of the Negro's hope of sharing in democracy with an optimistic conviction that democracy will fulfill itself. For in his concluding lines, Hughes says:

> *O, yes,*
> *I say it plain,*
> *America never was America to me,*
> *And yet I swear this oath—*
> *America will be!*

Hughes's "Song to a Negro Wash-Woman" and "Mother to Son" are unsurpassed genre pictures of Negro women, mothers whose fortitude is typical of countless Negro mothers responsible for second- and third-generation progress. His characterization of the Negro folk is in marked contrast to the conventionally accepted one, for his Negro folk never whine, never complain. They are stoic, ironic, often pessimistic, but never self-deluded. His "Minstrel Man" warns the observer not to be deceived by externals:

> *Because my mouth*
> *Is wide with laughter*
> *And my throat*
> *Is deep with song,*
> *You do not think*
> *I suffer after*
> *I have held my pain so long.*
>
> *Because my mouth*
> *Is wide with laughter*
> *You do not hear my inner cry;*

> *Because my feet*
> *Are gay with dancing*
> *You do not know*
> *I die.*

The years following the stock-market crash of 1929 were fraught with social changes, social ills, and, in consequence, social protest. Unemployment, racial tensions, and crime, to cite but three major social ills, commanded the attention of politicians, reformers, educators, and poets. The South, as usual, was worse off than any other area in the United States, and, as usual, Southern Negroes bore the brunt of the inequities. Interpersonal tensions were heightened by the competition between poor Negroes and poor whites. The Depression relationship between the Negroes and the white exploiters is tellingly revealed in Sterling Brown's "Old Lem":

> *I talked to Old Lem*
> *And Old Lem said:*
> *They weigh the cotton*
> *They store the corn*
> *We only good enough*
> *To work the rows;*
> *They run the commissary*
> *They keep the books*
> *We gotta be grateful*
> *For being cheated;*
> *Whippersnapper clerks*
> *Call us out of our name*
> *We got to say Mister*
> *To Spindling boys*
> *They make our figgers*
> *Turn somersets*
> *We buck in the middle,*
> *Say 'Thankyuh, sah.'*
> *They don't come by ones*
> *They don't come by twos*
> *But they come by tens.*

In other folk verse Brown ranges from exaggerated humor and satire (reminiscent of Western yarns) to work songs and blues. The "Slim Greer" poems are representative of the humor and satire; "Southern Road," the title poem of Brown's collection, is typical of his work songs. Brown's ballads are possibly his best and most distinctive works because of the comic irony that he employs, but poems like "To Nat Turner" and "Strong Men," though more conventional in theme and structure, are memorable because of the quiet rebuke of the one, the violent rebuke (offset by the promise of ultimate vindication) of the other.

Frank Davis's poetry of social protest is not as finished as that of Sterling Brown, but it is no less incisive in its indictment of "The Cotton South." In his "Snapshots of the Cotton South" Davis condemns the churches, the Southern Tenant Farmers' Union, big planters, and the physical squalor of the poor whites, who, "filled with their pale superiority" over "neighboring blacks," "live in rotting cabins."

Lashing out at the cost in taxes which segregation exacts, he concludes bitterly:

> *There are some who say*
> *Voteless blacks never get*
> *A proportionate return of taxes paid*
> *But since so many*
> *Land in the hoosegow*
> *On copyrighted charges*
> *And the county pays their keep*
> *In stockade, on chain gang,*
> *They really use their share*
> *Of public funds—*
> *The arithmetic and logic*
> *Are indisputable.*

Davis's concluding lines combine protest and challenge:

> *Well, you remakers of America*
> *You apostles of social change*
> *Here is pregnant soil*
> *Here are grass roots of a nation*
> *But the crop they grow is Hate and Poverty.*
> *By themselves they will make no change*
> *Black men lack the guts*
> *Po' whites have not the brains*
> *And the big land owners want Things as They Are.*

His challenge is simple:

> *You disciples of Progress . . .*
> *. . . will you mould this section*
> *So its portrait will fit*
> *In the sunlit hall*
> *Of Ideal America?*

The poetry that followed World War I was largely colored

by protest against social and economic sanctions and, above all, against the continuing denial of basic rights and privileges and opportunities to Negro Americans.

Since the thirties, American Negroes have made rapid social gains. Beginning with the New Deal and continuing until the present, Negro poets have reflected an increasing degree of self-assurance, of what might be termed "racial poise," and of both national and international identity. The equalitarian and nonisolationist coloring of the New Deal's political and social ideology was reflected in the works of several of the outstanding younger Negro poets whose artistic maturing coincided with the decade that witnessed a growing concern for American minority groups and their proper and equitable identification with American society as a whole. These younger poets were freed from the compulsion to justify or explain themselves or their work or to apologize for being Negroes. Education, even at the highest levels, was taken increasingly for granted. With the over-all shifts in economic emphasis that the New Deal sponsored, the economy of the Negro was greatly strengthened and improved. More and more Negroes were being incorporated into the political, professional, and labor world as people of recognized ability whose color was of secondary importance. The millennium had by no means come, but enough had happened and was happening to prompt young Negro poets to urge people to look beyond the superficialities of color and to respect each other as fellow human beings. Thus, we can note the rise of a universalized theme supplementing, but not completely displacing, the poetry of racial mood and substance. A good example is Margaret Walker's "For My People," which concludes:

*For my people standing staring trying to fashion a better way
from confusion, from hypocrisy and misunderstanding,
trying to fashion a world that will hold all the people
all the adams and eves and their countless generations:*

*Let a new earth rise. Let another world be born. Let a
bloody peace be written in the sky. Let a second
generation full of courage issue forth, let a people
loving freedom come to growth, let a beauty full of
healing and a strength of final clenching be the
pulsing in our spirits and our blood. Let the martial
songs be written, let the dirges disappear. Let a
race of men now rise and take control!*

Miss Walker's projection of the racial theme into that of world concern for human rights and dignity distinguishes

Formal Negro Poetry

"For My People" from earlier protest poetry by Negro writers. In similar vein Melvin Tolson concludes his "Dark Symphony" with these lines:

> *Out of abysses of Illiteracy,*
> *Through labyrinths of Lies*
> *Across wastelands of Disease . . .*
> *We advance!*
>
> *Out of dead-ends of Poverty,*
> *Through wildernesses of Superstition,*
> *Across barricades of Jim Crowism . . .*
> *We advance!*
>
> *With the Peoples of the World . . .*
> *We advance!*

Melvin Tolson's later long poem entitled "Libretto for the Republic of Liberia," commissioned for the Liberian Centennial and printed in the July 1951 *Poetry*, is both challenging and significant. Using the ultramodern idiom, including language echoes of the Eliot-Pound tradition, this is a strong repudiation of trite traditionalism. In *Poetry*, the poem evoked a laudatory prose preface from Allen Tate, who called attention to the fact that Negroes should "not limit themselves to provincial mediocrity in which one's feelings about one's difficulties become more important than poetry itself." This is sound advice, as was his remark that by assuming this, "the assumption has made Mr. Tolson not less but more intensely Negro in his apprehension of the world." Such strange lines as these are notable:

> *The ferris wheel*
> *Of race, of caste, of class*
> *Dumped and alped cadavers till the ground*
> *Fogged the Pleiades with Gilan rot.*

This growing concept of human identity as transcending racial identity is expressed, too, in Robert Hayden's "Speech," and here again reference is made to the concluding lines:

> *I have heard the words*
> *They serve like barbed-wire fences*
> *To divide yuh*
> *I have heard the words—*
> *Dirty niggere, poor white trash—*
> *And the same voice spoke them;*
> *Brothers listen well to me,*
> *The same voice spoke them.*

Gwendolyn Brooks, who had the distinction of being the first Negro recipient of a Pulitzer Prize, skillfully combines universal themes with racial overtones as these lines show:

> Grant me that I am human, that I hurt
> That I can cry.
> Not that I now ask alms, in shame gone hollow.
> Nor cringe outside the loud and sumptuous gate.
> Admit me to our mutual estate.
>
> Open my rooms, let in the light and air.
> Reserve my service at the human feast,
> And let the joy continue.

Negro poets of the forties addressed themselves to the problem of war. Race and color, as well as democracy's survival, were implicit issues of World War II. The restatements of democratic principle embodied in the Declaration of Human Rights revitalized the hopes and aspirations of racial and religious minorities at home and abroad. It was inconceivable to the American Negro, after once again he joined in the common cause for saving democracy, that he would be expected to accept less than the kind of human dignity and decent personal accord being fought for and bargained for around the world. In many ways, however, the Negro was doomed to disappointment; once more he realized that victories must be fought for and were not easily granted. Owen Dodson, whose "Conversation on V" relates the racial issue to war, asks:

> Now what is this here Victory?
> It what we get when we fight for it.
> Ought to be Freedom, God do know that.

Miss Brooks, too, in "A Street in Bronzeville," writes about the irony and the brutality of war, its contradiction of human values, and the pitiable unpreparedness of so many of the young soldiers. "No stout lesson showed how to chat with death," observes a soldier in a bar.

Bruce McWright's "Journey to a Parallel," even though merely ironic in mood, stands out as a distinctive statement of the younger generation's war experience. "Sunset Horn," by Myron O'Higgins, does so even more. It is a notably sincere and courageous war poem, which reflects quiet, unrhetorical strength.

> O, we went quickly or a little longer
> And for a space saw caste and categories, creeds and race

Evaporate into the flue of common circumstance.
We sought transcendent meaning for our struggle,
And in that rocking hour, each minute, each narrow second
Fell upon us like a rain of knives,
We grappled here an instant, then singly, or in twos or tens,
  or by bewildered hundreds,
Were pulverized . . . reduced . . . wiped out—
Made uniform and equal!

Raise no vain monuments; bury us down!
Our power is manifest in other glory;
Our flesh in this contested slope of ground.
There is no more but these, a legacy, a grim prediction . . .
One day the rest of you will know the meaning of annihilation
And the hills will rock with voltage;
And the forests burn like a flaming broom;
And the stars explode and drop like cinders on the land.
And these steel cities where no love is—
. . . O in that day
When the tongues confound, and breath is total in the horn
Your Judas eyes, seeking truth at last, will search for us
And borrow ransom from this bowel of violence!

Younger Negro poets writing today include a group of highly cultivated and thoroughly sophisticated intellectuals who, like their white peers, reveal an increasing preoccupation with style and technique. A great variety and a growing mastery of poetic technicalities are revealed in the works of Margaret Walker, Gwendolyn Brooks, Robert Hayden, Myron O'Higgins, Melvin Tolson and M. Carl Holman. This is as it should be, for as Gwendolyn Brooks herself says:

Every Negro poet has "something to say." Simply because he is a Negro; he cannot escape having important things to say. His mere body, for that matter, is an eloquence. His quiet walk down the street is a speech to the people. Is a rebuke, is a plea, is a school,

But no real artist is going to be content with offering raw materials. The Negro poet's most urgent duty, at present, is to polish his technique, his way of presenting his truths and his beauties, that these may be more insinuating and, therefore, more overwhelming.

Gwendolyn Brooks's literary competence bears out this point of view. The ease with which she handles a variety of classical poetic forms and types establishes her as a careful, well-trained, scholarly poet. In addition, she is capable of originality of style and point of view. Her prize-winning *Annie Allen* establishes the universal in the particulars of a modern woman's experiences of love, motherhood, struggle, and frustration. Although to a slight degree turgid and a little contrived, the poems at their best fuse class and race experience into a sardonic, vigorous comment on modern living.

Gwendolyn Brooks symbolizes what must be the objective of Negro poets: to be basically poets, American poets, who at the proper time, and in a proper way can be Negro poets, spokesmen for their innermost experiences.

CHAPTER SEVEN

The Fiction and Polemics of the Anti-Slavery Period

IN 1700, Samuel Sewall, a staunch New England Calvinist, attacked slavery on moral grounds in his pamphlet *The Selling of Joseph*, officially regarded as the first serious *written* anti-slavery propaganda. Much later, after the Philadelphia Friends had instituted certain regulations about slaveholding, New England Friends were ordered to take their slaves to the meetings for instruction. The challenge to slavery by Quaker and nonconformist groups was in large part made by John Woolman, Anthony Benezet, and Dr. Benjamin Rush. These men, all well educated and thoroughly dedicated to the cause of human freedom, set the stage for the abolition movement, the official birth of which occurred in 1775. In that year the first abolition society was organized; within one year Jefferson in his first draft of the Declaration of Independence included a strong appeal (later deleted), based on moral and logical arguments, for the freeing of the Negro slaves.

The first protest by a Negro was published in Baltimore in 1789. The author chose to remain anonymous, as noted earlier, but *Negro Slavery, by Othello: a Free Negro* is a forthright, trenchant, and daring piece of writing.

> When the united colonies revolted from Great Britain, they did it on this principle, "that all men are by nature and of right ought to be free." After a long, successful and glorious struggle for liberty, during which they manifested the firmest attachment to the rights of mankind, can they so soon forget the principles that governed their determination? Can Americans, after the noble contempt they expressed for tyrants, meanly descend to take up the scourge? Blush, ye revolted colo-

nies, for having apostatized from your own principles!
... The importation of slaves into America ought to
be a subject of the deepest regret to every benevolent and
thinking mind. And one of the great defects in the
federal system is the liberty it allows on this head. Venerable in everything else, it is injudicious here; and it is
much to be deplored that a system of so much political
perfection should be stained with anything that does an
outrage to human nature ... So, far from encouraging the importation of slaves, and countenancing that
vile traffic in human flesh, the members of the late Constitutional Convention should have seized the opportunity of prohibiting forever this cruel species of reprobated villainy. That they did not do so will forever
diminish the luster of their other proceedings, so highly
extolled and so justly distinguished for their intrinsic
value.

This historic first protest was followed by a succession of others. Lemuel Haynes, Peter Williams, and David Walker had all made strong arguments against slavery before 1831, when the first Convention of the Free Men of Color met in Philadelphia. The powerful attacks of these and other writers show that if slavery molded the emotional and folk life of the Negro, the anti-slavery struggle developed his intellect and spurred him to disciplined, articulate expression.

The foundation for these and other protests by Negroes was laid by the leaders of innumerable slave revolts, accounts of which were suppressed as much as possible, and leaders of which were invariably denigrated both by slavery's proponents and by Negroes bent on appeasing the white majority. It is tragically ironic that men like Nat Turner and Denmark Vesey, whose slave revolts, though abortive, did so much to create a climate of justifiable unrest, have never been accorded a proper place in history. As Myrdal puts it succinctly, these men laid the foundation not only for Negro protest, but also "for the 'realistic' theory of race relations." Myrdal writes in *An American Dilemma*:

This theory is favored by southern white liberals and is accepted by the great majority of accommodating southern Negro leaders; it holds that everything which stirs up the resistance of the whites will deteriorate the Negroes' status, and that reforms must be pushed quietly and in such ways that the whites hardly notice them before they are accomplished facts comfortably sunk in a new status quo.

American Negroes, in attempting to integrate themselves into American Society, have had to pay the price of forgetting their historical heroes and martyrs.

Myrdal then refers to an observation by Charles Johnson, in *Growing Up in the Black Belt:*

> ... Denmark Vesey, a Negro who resisted slavery and led an insurrection in the effort to throw off the oppression, is a type which contradicts the assumption that Negroes are innately docile as a race and were content with slavery. In a sense, Vesey represents the spirit of independence for which the founding fathers of America are praised—an insurrection is merely an unsuccessful revolution. But Denmark Vesey is a symbol of a spirit too violent to be acceptable to the white community. There are no Negro schools named for him, and it would be extremely poor taste and bad judgment for the Negroes to take any pride in his courage and philosophy. There is, indeed, little chance for Negro youth to know anything about him at all.

Under the zealous instruction of the abolitionists, Negro leaders, some well educated, others self-taught fugitive slaves, learned almost equally well the arts of public speech and platform debate. There began a rare collaboration, which in little more than forty years divided American public opinion and shook the firmly entrenched institution of slavery. Beginning in 1818 with John Russworm, editor of the first Negro newspaper, *Freedom's Journal,* a vigorous group of Negro writers and orators including Martin Delaney, Ringgold Ward, Henry Highland Garnet, and William Wells Brown developed. The admitted giant of them all was Frederick Douglass, ex-slave, journalist, and orator.

As time goes on, the career and character of Frederick Douglass take on more and more the stature and significance of the epical. In terms of the race experience his was, beyond doubt, the symbolic career. On the one hand he typified the common lot; on the other he was a striking and inspiring example of outstanding achievement. The basic pattern of this symbolic career is that of the chattel slave become freeman, with the heroic accent of self-emancipation and eventual participation in the over-all struggle for the Negro. Also, there is a dramatic universal appeal in a personal history of achievement against odds, especially when the hero becomes not only an acknowledged minority leader, but also a well-known figure in American life as a whole. Douglass very modestly explained away his career as being a fortuitous combination of chance and history, but a full reading of his *Autobiography* convinces the reader that in mind and character Douglass was fully capable of shaping the course of his life.

Although Douglass had a long, many-sided career as a public servant, he is best remembered for his close identification with the anti-slavery cause. Long a staunch friend and colleague of William Lloyd Garrison, Douglass parted company with the fiery editor of *The Liberator* only when he launched a paper of his own, *The North Star*.

Douglas expressed himself in bold, uncompromising words that rarely failed to stir his audiences. As Myrdal points out, Douglass and his contemporaries—Sojourner Truth, Samuel Cornish, Harriet Tubman, William Still, John Langston, and others—"unlike the slave insurgents . . . set the future pattern on which Negroes based their protest." This new pattern "consisted of nonviolent legal activities in accord with the democratic principles of the American creed and the Christian religion." Douglass's July 4, 1852 speech reflected this attitude:

> What to the American slave is our 4th of July? I answer: a day that reveals to him, more than all other days of the year, the gross injustice and cruelty to which he is the constant victim. To him your celebration is a sham; your boasted liberty, an unholy licence; your national greatness, swelling vanity; your sounds of rejoicing are empty and heartless; your denunciation of tyrants, brass fronted impudence; your shouts of liberty and equality, hollow mockery; your prayers and hymns, your sermons and thanksgivings, with all your religious parade and solemnity, are, to him, more bombast, fraud, deception, impiety, and hypocrisy—a thin veil to cover up crimes which would disgrace a nation of slaves. . . .
>
> You boast of your love of liberty, your superior civilization, and your pure Christianity, while the twin political powers of the nation (as embodied in the two political parties) is solemnly pledged to support and perpetuate the enslavement of three million of your countrymen. You hurl your anathemas at the crown-headed tyrants of Russia and Austria and pride yourselves on your democratic institutions, while you yourselves consent to be the mere tools and bodyguards of the tyrants of Virginia and Carolina. You invite to your shores fugitives of oppression from abroad, honor them with banquets, greet them with ovations, cheer them, toast them, salute them, protect them, and pour out your money to them like water; but the fugitives from

your own land you advertise, hunt, arrest, shoot, and kill. You glory in your refinement and education, yet you maintain a system as barbarous and dreadful as ever stained the character of a nation—a system begun in avarice, supported in pride, and perpetuated in cruelty. You shed tears over fallen Hungary, and make the sad story of her wrongs the theme of your poets, statesmen, and orators, till your gallant sons are ready to fly to arms to vindicate her cause against the oppressor; but in regard to the ten thousand wrongs of the American slave, you would enforce the strictest silence, and would hail him as an enemy of the nation who dares to make these wrongs the subject of public discourse!

Douglass was able to generalize the issues of the Negro cause and to see them as basic principles of human freedom everywhere. He accordingly took sides with the land and labor reformers in England and Ireland. Similarly, he became one of the first public advocates of women's rights and suffrage; he attended the first Woman's Rights Convention and became the lifelong friend of Elizabeth Cady Stanton and Susan B. Anthony. He clearly saw the land-reform objectives of the Free Soil Party, whose first convention he attended in 1852, and was not merely attracted to it by its more obvious bearing in blocking the extension of slave territory. His advocacy of civil-rights legislation and free public education again shows that he was far in advance of any narrowly racialist stand.

Much of Douglass's writing suggests the timeless wisdom of a real sage. "No people," he says "to whom liberty is given, can hold it as firmly and wear it as grandly as those who wrench their liberty from the iron hand of the tyrant." Or again: "My hope for the future of my race is further supported by the rapid decline of an emotional, shouting, thoughtless religion. Scarcely in any direction can there be found a less favorable field for mind or morals than where such a religion prevails."

Another narrative of outstanding individual achievement and group service, Booker T. Washington's *Up from Slavery*, has long held pre-eminence in popular attention and favor. Its author, himself a biographer of Douglass, suggested at least one important reason for this. Washington referred to Douglass's career as falling "almost wholly within the first period of the struggle in which the race problem has involved the people of this country—the period of revolution and liberation." Continuing, he said: "That period is now closed; we are at present in the period of construction and readjustment." So different did it seem to Washington in 1906 that he could regret "that many of the animosities engendered by the conflicts and controversies of half a century ago still survive to confuse the councils of those who are seeking to live in the present and future rather than in the past." Washington further expressed the hope that nothing in Douglass's life narrative should "serve to revive or keep alive the bitterness of those controversies of which it gives the history." In saying this, Washington did more than reveal the dominant philosophy of his own program of conciliation and compromise; he reflected the dominant psychology of a whole American generation of materialism and reaction which dimmed the fervor of real American idealism as it had been exemplified in the careers of Douglass and the other heroes of the slavery crisis. Washington's period, in turn, has closed. The principles of Douglass and of those who supported him, principles of uncompromising justice and equality, emerge from their social eclipse all the more vital and inescapable in our time.

Negro abolitionists developed such high levels of skill and competence in speaking and writing on behalf of abolition that they were readily credited with being not only as effective as the leading white abolitionists—Lovejoy, Garrison, Theodore Weld, Charles Sumner, Henry Ward Beecher, and Wendell Phillips—but also as valiant collaborators in the struggle for the freedom of their own people. Besides serving as traveling lecturers and abolitionist organizers in the North and Midwest, and occasionally as secret agents of the "Underground Railroad" for the rescue of slave fugitives, many of the more talented Negro abolitionists were sent abroad on extensive tours of England, Scotland, Ireland, and Wales. William Wells Brown remained in Europe on one mission for five years. Douglass became very popular with audiences in England, making several tours of the country. The presence of such men before foreign audiences and at international anti-slavery conferences had a powerful effect in making abolition an international theme.

One of the unique and effective contributions of the Negro to the liberation struggle was the "slave narrative," of which several hundred examples survive. Sterling Brown, Arthur Davis, and Ulysses Lee, in an introduction to their section on biography in *The Negro Caravan,* an anthology of writing by American Negroes (New York, Dryden Press, 1941), said: "There were three classes of such [slave] narratives: the fictionalized, the dictated and edited, and the genuine autobiographies." They cited numerous examples of each type. Marion Wilson Starling, in *The Slave Narrative, Its Place in*

American Literary History—a doctoral dissertation presented to the Graduate School of New York University in 1949—suggested two broad divisions in different terms. Before 1836, he said, the accounts were of and about individual slaves, chiefly of their adventurous escapes to freedom. After 1836, the accounts were chiefly either group narratives or more formalized and studied autobiographical stories. He said that between 1703 and 1944, 6,006 autobiographical records by ex-slaves had been written or recorded. He commented that they had been drawn "from anti-slavery periodicals, court records, uncatalogued library depositions, and unpublished manuscripts." Continuing, he rightly observed that "they provide a valuable supplement to the history of the rise and fall of slavery in the United States, revealing the human equation behind the 'chattel principle' that hastened the end of that policy, in the face of the new social order."

The Library of Congress co-operated with the Federal Writers' Project in assembling slave narratives from many states. It now has at least fifteen volumes, slave narratives from Alabama, Arkansas, Florida, Georgia, Indiana, Kansas, Kentucky, Missouri, North Carolina, Ohio, Oklahoma, South Carolina, Tennessee, Texas, Virginia, and West Virginia. Together they constitute a folk history of American slavery. Unique in the series is *The Negro in Virginia,* originally sponsored by the Federal Writers' Project, but (according to Roscoe E. Lewis) completed "under the administration of the Virginia Writers' Project, whose State supervisor . . . ably and sympathetically edited the manuscript." Lewis, a Negro, was supervisor of an all-Negro unit in the statewide writers' project. The book, for which Lewis took so much responsibility, was referred to by his publisher thus: "The history of the Negro in Virginia is in many respects the history of the Negro in America. It was to Virginia that the first African natives were brought; and here also, more than two hundred years later, their freedom was assured at Appomattox Courthouse. Much of the culture of the American Negro is derived from sources in Virginia just as the roots of many Negro families were first nourished in Virginia."

Another source of slave narratives is Fisk University's *Social Science Source Document Number 2*. Published in 1945 by the Social Science Institute, Nashville, Tennessee, the volume is in two sections. The first section deals with the religious-conversion experiences of Negro ex-slaves. The second part (also known as *God Struck Me Dead*) consists, according to the foreword by Charles Johnson, of autobiographical accounts of Negro ex-slaves "written down exactly as they were obtained except for minor modifications of dialectic peculiarities of some of the informants, to facilitate readability." Some of the titles are very revealing: "Slave Who Joined the Yanks," "Slavery Was 'Hell Without Fires,'" "Times Got Worse After the War."

Long before the middle of the nineteenth century, white writers had been using the Negro-slavery theme in an entire school of fiction. Interest in the exotic "noble savage" dated from Aphra Behn's *Oroonoko* in the seventeenth century. Many white American writers of the late eighteenth and early nineteenth centuries were (1) fascinated by the exoticism of the "savage blacks" or (2) morally outraged by slavery. The one group perpetuated the romantic stereotype; the other—by far the larger—was responsible for a large output of anti-slavery prose. Harriet Martineau, Maria Chapman, Abigail Field Mott, and Richard Allen, among others, described the evils of slavery. Mrs. Mott's *Biographical Sketches and Interesting Anecdotes of Color* is typical of the well-meaning, somewhat colorless accounts by white authors. There was, however, intense sincerity of purpose among these persistent foes of slavery. The fact that books were written for children on the anti-slavery theme is in itself proof of this. *Slave Narrative Sketches for Children* and the *Anti-Slavery Alphabet* are good examples of healthy propaganda for youthful minds.

Before the best of the Negro autobiographies there were dozens of dictated and edited narratives. Nearly three hundred appeared in *The Liberator* alone during the paper's existence. They all took on a certain familiar literary coloration, and the accounts, therefore, cannot be credited with any particular literary distinction; they were unquestionably valuable as propaganda, and the fact that they were repetitious in theme and point of view was an asset. *The Narrative of James Williams* is not only an example of the dictated type of slave narrative, but—as was discovered after its "dictation" by Williams to John Whittier—a fiction. Before its withdrawal as fraudulent, the Williams "Narrative" enjoyed three printings, and its popularity and effectiveness at once convinced the anti-slavery supporters that authentic accounts would be much more useful to their cause than fictionalized narratives by white writers.

Increasingly, dictated narratives and independently written accounts of slavery by ex-slaves themselves were published. *The Narrative of the Sufferings of Lewis and Milton Clarke* is one of the best known of the dictated type; Josiah Henson's *Truth Stranger than Fiction* is, with the exception of Douglass's autobiography, perhaps the best known of the original life accounts. Together with Douglass's story, it is credited with being a source of both inspiration and information for Mrs. Stowe's *Uncle Tom's Cabin*. Henson's narrative, it might be noted, was not published until some years after *Uncle Tom's Cabin* had been printed, but Henson had told Mrs. Stowe of his experiences.

As abolition literature, Harriet Beecher Stowe's two novels, *Uncle Tom's Cabin* and *Dred,* stand in a distinctly independent category. Mrs. Stowe was impelled to write these novels not only by immediate compulsions of anti-slave sentiment, which her associations and immediate personal experiences sharpened, but also by the highest moral convictions stemming from her personal religious nature. A staunch Calvinist, she was literally horrified by what she knew and had seen of slavery. During the years when her father was president of Lane Theological Seminary, she had lived in Cincinnati, a border city separated only by the Ohio River from the slave state of Kentucky. She had seen runaway slaves in Cincinnati; indeed she had seen her father help many of the fugitives escape along the "Underground Railroad." Mrs. Stowe had spent a brief period of time in Kentucky and had seen something of slavery itself. Like most anti-slavery crusaders, she crammed her first novel with heroic and melodramatic action that weakened its artistry, but without question intensified its propagandistic value. In spite of exaggeration, the novel, like the best of the slave narratives, had a human authenticity that was irresistible. No single piece of Southern propaganda could offset or contradict this powerful narrative—certainly none ever was able to refute the claims of Mrs. Stowe.

Uncle Tom's Cabin exemplifies the dilemma of more than two generations of writing about the Negro. As a moral issue and as a controversy, both pro- and anti-slavery thinking reflected everything in moralistic antithesis: sharp blacks and whites, no shadings. Mrs. Stowe herself apparently recognized the artistic failings of her first novel, for in *Dred,* the second, she attempted a more carefully drawn and convincingly balanced picture. Artistically and from the point of view of craftsmanship, it was superior. The popular appeal and the sentimental melodrama of the first book, however, swamped it and dimmed its success. Both the defenders and the opponents of slavery were caught in a polemical trap; an incubus of undiluted moralism (on either side) and polemics settled down on the pre-war phase of American literature. A brief reference to ante-bellum Southern literature will confirm this.

As the controversy over slavery hardened and tightened,

the whole tone of Southern fiction changed. The easygoing rustic atmosphere of such earlier novels as those by John P. Kennedy and William G. Simms was displaced by tense, fictionalized versions of the official pro-slavery argument in action, character, and speech. With his *Swallow Barn,* Kennedy created what was to be a long tradition in Southern literature. What are now familiar and sterile concepts of Negroes and Negro character dominate the book: the slaves were happy and contented and sang all day; their children were happy and contented and romped all day; prosperity for the Negro was in proportion to that of his master, for slaves had gardens and time to tend them. As a matter of fact, Kennedy goes so far as to say that slavery was actually a burden to the white owners, but that because Negroes were by nature naïve and incapable of self-support, the institution had to be perpetuated as a protection for the transplanted barbarians.

Simms incorporated Negro characters into his novels of Southern frontier life. Sympathetic to slavery, he offered no indictment of the system. His roster of Negro characters (all of whom played minor roles) reflects a wider range of types than was usual with writers of the period, but Simms never overstepped conventional boundaries to create a Negro character who, as an individual, reflected the personal degradation of slavery or legitimately aspired to freedom as a human being.

The point is that though these early writers—Kennedy, Simms, and such Virginia writers as W. A. Carruthers and John Esten Cooke—sustained the sentimental and unrealistic plantation tradition, they were not seeking self-justification. Writing in the romantic tradition of the ante-bellum years, at a time when romanticism was moving toward its national climax, the Southern romantics were portraying the idyllic life of the agrarian South, in which the Negro slave was a colorful native background figure. In the years immediately following *Uncle Tom's Cabin* and immediately preceding the opening of the war, the tone of Southern fiction shifted to frank propaganda. Nor was the shift peculiar to the South or to Southern white writers. The search for self-justification rather than truth put a blight upon Negro and Northern writers as well. Negro writers saw themselves and their materials in terms of self-pity or overdeveloped vindication. Northern writers were indifferent, sentimentally indulgents or patronizing.

Marion Starling has said that the slave narratives, though often of "sub-literary" quality, contained the "nucleus of the creative thinking of an oppressed race" and bore a "relationship to the slave novels of 1850." He cites fourteen pro-slavery novels in the 1850's, including the rewritten *Swallow Barn* by Kennedy, the original version of which is credited with having initiated the "plantation tradition" in American fiction. The classic description and analysis of that tradition is Francis Gaines's *The Southern Plantation*.

Within three years of *Uncle Tom's Cabin*, Southern writers had produced a dozen or more pro-slavery novels in a frantic effort to refute Mrs. Stowe, and to document the justifications of slavery. Sterling Brown, in his *Negro in American Fiction*, records that there were fourteen Southern "answers" to Mrs. Stowe, all in a propagandistic vein that completely negated any possible literary artistry—as is evidenced by the fact that not one is remembered today. Reading them now, one wonders that they could possibly have been taken seriously, even by the people who wrote them. The old stereotypes are present, but extended and exaggerated to the point of ridiculousness. Good slaves were not only happy in slavery, but were indignant at the prospect of any freedom save freedom from sin; bad Negroes stupid enough to crave earthly freedom were punished by being set free; the Bible was interpreted as not merely giving sanction to, but as actually demanding that the "sons of Ham" be held in slavery. The comforts, if not luxuries, of slave dwellings were portrayed. Even the most compelling argument of the abolitionists, that slavery divided families and separated mothers from children, was loftily refuted by one writer, who insisted that the white mistresses showed more concern for and lavished more care on the slave children than did the slave mothers. In short, late ante-bellum apologist literature disclaimed all the evils of slavery and credited the meddling Yankee abolitionists with attempting to destroy an idyllic and humane social institution perpetuated by the goodness and compassion of Southern men and women who had rescued the hapless Africans from a state of primitivism and introduced them to a Christian and benevolent way of life.

The theme of miscegenation, which the Southern propagandists studiously avoided, dominated the first novel of a Negro writer, William Wells Brown. *Clotel* is as melodramatic and unequivocally propagandistic as its contemporaries. The novel, whose subtitle was *The President's Daughter* (in later editions Clotel was identified as a congressman's daughter), is a discursive tale in which the near-white Clotel, her mother, and her aunt live through a succession of unbelievably melodramatic and improbable experiences. No overt argument is made for or against miscegenation, and

Clotel's experiences are related not to character, but to the coincidence or irony of her color. In a stilted and pointedly didactic vein Frank W. Webb, in 1857, published *The Garies and Their Friends,* a novel dealing with two families, one all colored, the other "mixed." Here again the problems of the mixed family are superficially attributed to color alone. Color prejudice can and does present obvious social problems, but it is a stacking of the cards to attribute domestic happiness to homogeneity of racial background and to deny the possibility of happiness solely because of a racial difference. Such oversimplification of personal relationships reflects no concern for individual character.

White writers, too, turned their attention to anti-slavery fiction. It cannot be said that they were any less immune to exaggeration and to stereotyped symbols than the apologists for slavery. They exaggerated the piety of the Negro, embellished the concept of the "tragic octoroon," dwelt on the sadism and almost savage fury of the overseers. On the other hand, their preoccupation with broken families, overwork, and enforced physical alliances between masters and slave women had validity.

W. W. Smith's *The Planter's Victim* and Emily Pierson's *Jamie, the Fugitive* are examples of this anti-slavery fiction, but these novels and their authors, and others in similar vein, like the pro-slavery novels and novelists were stifled by didacticism. Only Herman Melville and Mark Twain were able to create really convincing and thoroughly developed Negro characters. Melville's Negro sailors in *Moby Dick,* as well as his vigorous anti-slavery protest in *Mardi,* at once reveal the author's evaluation of the Negro and the Negro-slave problem as something more than a subject for propagandistic controversy or didactic moralizing. Concerned with Negroes as people, Melville was one of the few authors not to make an arbitrary defense of the North and an equally arbitrary denunciation of the South. But he was unequivocal in his evaluation of slavery, which he labeled "a blot, foul as the crater-pool of hell." Mark Twain's Jim, in *Huckleberry Finn,* like Melville's sailors, is much more valuable than the sentimental and exaggerated moralizing that characterized the bulk of anti-slavery fiction.

At the close of the Civil War, the moral enthusiasm of the North was nearly spent. With the Negro occupied by the practical emergencies of emancipation and reconstruction, the South developed another, more successful literary pattern. Shortly after 1875, reconstruction fiction began to appear in the form of adroit glorification of the ante-bellum regime. There was little counterstatement from the North with the notable exception of Albion Tourgee's *A Fool's Errand* and *Bricks Without Straw*, desperate attempts to tell the truth about the obstructionist tactics and Klan terrorism rampant in the South from 1880 on. A former officer in the Union army, Tourgee stayed on in the South after the war. His novels are based on his actual experiences and observations. *A Fool's Errand* is a somber, realistic account of the hatred and scorn that colored North-South relationships after the war. Teachers, politicians, judges, any and all reconstructionists were subjected to insult. Negroes were completely shut out of community life, in spite of their obvious desire to be identified with it. Tourgee's Negro characters are sympathetically drawn, convincing individuals of varying capacities and aspirations. *Bricks Without Straw* challenges the country at large to help the South restore itself to some measure of social and economic stability. The leading Negro character is energetic, ambitious, independent, and, as a former Union soldier, determined to share in the benefits of freedom.

Tourgee's novels and their honest efforts to create an awareness and understanding of the basic problems were overshadowed by the local-color vogue typified by the works of Thomas Nelson Page and Joel Chandler Harris. Unrealistic and exaggerated as this first post-bellum fiction was, it was at least "genteel"; a few years later a thoroughly sinister element dominated Southern fiction. Page and Harris persuaded a majority of their readers that the romantic version of the pre-war South was essentially true. In spite of injustice to the Negro, the dominant motive was to assuage the South's pride and to achieve emotional compensation for the "lost cause." Thus Page, in his *In Ole Virginia*, established a pattern and a vogue that are still beguiling. The old Negro, who reverently and nostalgically recalls the old days, spins a lengthy account of gracious living, of master-slave devotion and reciprocal loyalty, of affectionate byplay between slave and master, and, above all, of the contentment of the Negroes with slavery.

In *Red Rock*, a full-length novel, Page goes further. Although he continues to eulogize the old-time faithful slave, he viciously attacks both Northern Reconstructionists and Negroes who presume to show independence or to act like men. In the preface to *Red Rock*, he laments the good old days before the war, days and nights so blessed that even the moonlight was richer and brighter!

Joel Chandler Harris, though never vitriolic, was nevertheless both an apologist for the plantation tradition and a local-colorist with all the implied limitations. Harris must be praised, however, for having made a thorough study of Negro folklore. From a Negro slave he learned a great deal about the animal fables that for years had been favorites of the Negroes. Altered and embellished by Harris, the stories are told in excellent Negro dialect by Uncle Remus, whom Harris created as the Negro narrator for his folk tales. *Uncle Remus: His Songs and Sayings* and its successor, *Nights with Uncle Remus,* are American classics. Uncle Remus himself is lovable; his humor, his apparently inexhaustible fund of practical information, his knowledge and love of animals and their ways make him a folk hero. Harris's careful transcription of Negro dialect and his portrayal of the warm relationship between the Negro folk philosopher and the little white boy of seemingly insatiable curiosity combine to make these stories excellent examples of Negro folk tales. Later Harris was to use Uncle Remus as a medium for projecting social propaganda. In later Uncle Remus stories, that is, he has the Negro voicing the opinions and sentiments of the apologists for the Old South. These stories are strained and artificial when compared with the earlier ones; they lack the qualities of sincerity and conviction so notable in the animal fables or in Uncle Remus's own experiences with and ideas on a variety of such generally interesting topics as courtship, religion, food, and holidays. But in the main, Harris rendered as much poetic justice to the Negro as an orthodox Southerner could.

George W. Cable, an ardent local-colorist, told decidedly more of the truth about the Negro than was popular in his day. In his *Madame Delphine,* and especially in *The Grandissimes,* he created Negro characters with unprecedented sympathy and understanding. In the latter he introduced two half-brothers, the illegitimate Honoré upholding the family's worthier traits and tradition, the legitimate Honoré exhibiting its worst. In *Madame Delphine* he related the tragic stories of the octoroon women who at best could anticipate the patronage of a white aristocrat in lieu of marriage. What Cable had to say about New Orleans and its Creole society in his fiction, coupled with his forthright observations on the Negro and the South in his essays (collected in *The Silent South*), made him extremely unpopular in Louisiana. In the late eighties he moved to New England. He made a lasting contribution to American literature as a first-rate local-colorist—his novels of Louisiana are classic examples of regional literature. It is even more important for present purposes that, in creating authentic pictures of old Louisiana, Cable used Negro characters effectively because he accorded them truthful and sympathetic analysis as either background or major figures.

Later Reconstruction fiction was openly vindictive and plainly anti-Negro in tone. By 1900, Negroes were rapidly acquiring education and some economic stability. They were also beginning to understand more fully what their rights were, and in spite both of lack of legal protection (by 1894 all Reconstruction legislation had been removed from Federal statutes), and of reaffirmation of the doctrine of white supremacy, were making attempts to secure them. To "keep the Negro in his place" white Southerners resorted to lynching, to the bolstering of the Ku Klux Klan, and to the promulgation of the old arguments of racial inferiority, arguments buttressed now not only by the Bible, but also by the "findings of science." Darwinism may have offended the fundamentalist concept of life's beginnings, but it provided a perfect justification for denying rights and privileges to the Negro. The Negro was promptly recognized as being somewhat above the status of the apes in the scale of evolution, but considerably below the highly developed position of the white man.

In 1900, *The Negro a Beast* was published, and a school of hate fiction was inaugurated. The best known writer of hate fiction, known also as Ku Klux Klan fiction, was Thomas Dixon, a minister. His *The Leopard's Spots* and *The Clansman* were vicious diatribes against Negroes, who were portrayed as depraved, sex-mad lawbreakers whom education had ruined and who had to be suppressed unless the South wanted to risk becoming a mulatto region. Other writers followed the pattern, praised the Ku Klux Klan for protecting white womanhood, praised docile, reactionary Negroes for their loyalty, decried the bestiality of the Negro males, and insisted that the ambition of most of them was to consort with white women. Portraiture of Negroes descended, said William Stanley Braithwaite, "from caricature to libel," in these novels.

In 1895, Booker T. Washington had appeared with his dynamic program of self-help and practical education. With *Up from Slavery* and its theme of Southern appeasement, he was destined to head what became the inevitably popular "school of conciliation." W. E. B. DuBois followed a little later as leader of an initially small equal-rights movement. His *Souls of Black Folk* (1903) became, as the movement grew, the bible of the militant school of protest. Negro writing followed two parallel trends, with Dunbar and Charles W. Chestnutt as their respective proponents. Paul Laurence Dunbar's *Sport of the Gods* is the only one of the four novels he wrote in which there is an obvious effort to escape the sentimental commonplaces of the folk and peasant tradition that colored his earlier novels. In the earlier books he had used white characters and bourgeois themes; in *Sport of the Gods* he used Negro characters, and created a good situation in terms of social injustice and a first portrayal of the urban Negro in Harlem.

The less popular Chestnutt, however, stood for the coming age. His ambitious and progressive aim was to counter the influence of the Thomas Nelson Page school of fiction and reveal a more balanced and accurate picture of Negro life in the South. A native North Carolinian, he knew the South intimately. Modeling his short-story style after Cable's, Chestnutt achieved considerable recognition. He wrote uncompromisingly and impartially, sparing neither whites nor Negroes, Southerners nor Northerners. Himself a quadroon, he ruthlessly satirized the mulatto color line within the race and sought to liquidate all double-standard values. Miscegenation and mob violence were his main themes, as indeed they were for most of the period's fiction about Negroes. With Chestnutt's handling there is the difference of careful, sober documentation and an even balancing of the situation, whether comic, melodramatic, or tragic. Not at all sympathetic to the sentimental interpretations of Southern life, Chestnutt stands as an early realist, the first Negro novelist to handle social themes artistically.

As long, however, as romantic attitudes were in vogue, no amount of counterstatement—Chestnutt's, DuBois's, or anyone's—could arrest the tide of the conventional stereotyping. Realism was to be the eventual antidote, but before its firm entrenchment in the early twenties, a period of what might be called "pseudorealism" brought fresh misinterpretations of the Negro. The last serious majority misconception or stereotype, that of blood atavism and inherent Negro primitivism, emerged in countless popular-magazine stories and articles. Well-intentioned writers for more than a decade deluged readers with pseudoscientific interpretations that still linger on or recur with their false biology of the potent "black drop" of blood. "The Black Drop" is the actual title of a story on the subject by Margaret Deland.

By and large, the Negro as subject matter achieved artistic freedom and stature only as American literature itself moved into the period of realism. Among the earliest instances of formal realistic treatment of Negroes were Stephen Crane's *The Monster*, Upton Sinclair's *The Jungle*, and Theodore Dreiser's *Nigger Jeff*. None of them is a pleasant characterization, but each at least presents full-length social and psychological truths about their respective settings—a Negro in a small Midwest town, Negro strikebreakers in the Chicago stockyards, and a Southern lynching.

Most significantly for Southern literature, realism invaded the Old Dominion through Ellen Glasgow—tentatively in *The Miller of Old Church* (1911), then full-force in 1925 in her epoch-making *Barren Ground,* which put carefully observed "poor whites," as well as Negroes, on the same canvas with the Virginia aristocracy and bourgeoisie. W. J. Cash rightly assesses this as "the first real novel as opposed to romances the South has brought forth, certainly the first wholly genuine picture of the people who make up and always had made up the body of the South." When realism triumphantly crossed the Potomac, the legendary South was finally on the defensive.

CHAPTER EIGHT

The Negro
in Modern American Fiction

SINCE 1920, the Negro in American fiction, notably in the novel, has undergone so liberalizing and realistic a transformation that the temptation to discuss it as a "renaissance" is nearly irresistible. To yield to this temptation here and outline the renaissance fully would be inappropriate to this discussion and impossible in terms of its prescribed scope. It is necessary, then, to repeat categorically that when creative writers dealt with Negro characters prior to 1920, departures from established and consistently perpetuated stereotypes were rare. The American novelists who created and sustained not only the "plantation tradition," but also the servile, comic, and buffoon Negro types, had imitators well into the twentieth century. Less frequent, but no less familiar, was the stereotype of "the bad nigger," the one who aspired to freedom before the war or to a better life after it. Gild the South, blacken the Negro—two sides of the same shield of the lost cause.

The first two decades after World War I, however, within the over-all context of American fiction's coming-of-age, saw not only more novels by and about Negroes, but also a consistently more realistic treatment of the Negro as a human being rather than as a symbol or type, of Negro problems as human and often universal rather than as the petty grievances of immature children in a mature society. All this, of course, connotes realism to any observer of literature, but for American literature the shift in treatment of Negro character and problems after 1920 was something more. It was, in a sense, a "new realism" if measured against the interpretation or definition of realism expounded in the 1890's by William Dean Howells. For Howells, realism was "the truthful presentation of materials" with, of course, a decided bias toward "the smiling aspects" of life. The plight of America's minorities, especially the Negro minority, in the second decade of the

1900's did not lend itself to "smiling aspects of truth," to middle-class optimism, or to regional pleasantries.

When Clement Wood published *Nigger* in 1922, he offered the American reading public a sociological novel in the truest sense, one that set a pattern that was to be emulated and approximated from then until the present decade, one that established authoritatively the beginnings of a "new realism." *Nigger* makes no case for any particular character or group; it simply traces the tragic fortunes of a Negro family from slavery to the early post-World War I years, describing its experiences as each member struggled to live in Alabama. Neither good nor bad in old stereotyped concepts, the characters are people trying to adjust not only to normal problems, but also to the added ones that their color imposes. Wood discounted both sentiment and bias in the novel, which is honest and convincing. The same year that *Nigger* was published, T. S. Stribling's *Birthright* appeared. It, too, is a sociological novel that documents the daily life of the Southern Negro with accuracy. Like Wood, Stribling analyzed his Negroes as people and showed the impact of prejudice and social injustice on them.

Stribling is best known for his trilogy, *The Store, The Forge*, and *Unfinished Cathedral*. These three novels are really social histories, though they reflect a bias of sympathy for the Negroes. They trace the fortunes of a single white family from the opening of the Civil War until the twenties. Stribling was concerned, we are told, at "the inability and unwillingness of the Southerner to think of the Negro as a human being." His history of the Vaiden family reveals very clearly the intimacy of Negro-white relationships and the dual, though overlapping, fortunes of Negroes and whites. Blood ties between Negroes and whites, while discreetly ignored, in some instances created powerful loyalties and led in turn to unexpected crises. In a moving scene Stribling described the futile effort of a white Vaiden to save his own son (by a slave girl he had raped years before) from being lynched. Like Ellen Glasgow, Stribling identified himself and his novels with explicit social forces and changes. In the third part of the trilogy, for example, he introduced a situation obviously based on the universally familiar Scottsboro case. His portrayal of seven Negro boys accused of raping an admitted prostitute is convincingly written, and it is not without an acceptable element of pathos. Their defense by an organization (obviously The National Association for the Advancement of Colored People) from the North again suggests Stribling's recognition of the Negro's progress in building organizations and developing techniques for securing legal justice and social rights. Throughout the novels there is strong evidence of the whites' tragic unawareness of Negro sensibility.

DuBose Heyward, in two novels, *Porgy* and *Mamba's Daughters*, created not only memorable and realistic accounts of Negro folk life in South Carolina, but also Negro figures of tragic proportion. Porgy, the crippled vendor, and Mamba, the intrepid matriarch whose determination and sacrifice win musical success for her granddaughter, are recognizable in universal terms of loyalty, devotion, and human compassion. Heyward, himself a South Carolinian, did not ignore the folk setting. *Porgy* is rich in descriptions of the customs, traditions, and rituals of the people of Catfish Row; in *Mamba's Daughters* there is no lack of colorful background material. The portrayals are affectionate; there is no condescension and, above all, the people are people made believable by the author's understanding and appreciation of the Negro folk. Other white writers, too, have described with warmth and intimacy the manners and customs of the Negro folk in a carefully realistic tone free from the limitations and regionalism of the condescension of the personally disinterested observer.

Julia Peterkin, perhaps best known after Heyward, created memorable folk novels dealing with Negroes who are recalled at once as individual characters rather than as rigidly defined types. *Scarlet Sister Mary*, her Pulitzer Prize novel, celebrates the amorality and nonconformist behavior of the Negro Mary, whose saga is both tragic and comic. Both *Green Thursday* and *Black April*, earlier novels, are excellent accounts of plantation life, revealing what one observer termed "an almost native comprehension" of Negro folkways. Among other writers to turn to interpretations of the Negro folk are two other South Carolinians, Edward C. L. Adams and Ambrose Gonzales, who described the customs, dialects, and folk beliefs of Gullah Negroes. At Chapel Hill, the well-known sociologist, Howard Odum, in *Rainbow Round My Shoulder* created an enduring folk hero in the person of Left Wing Jordan, who was to appear in two subsequent books. Others from Texas, Louisiana, and Mississippi recorded with varying degrees of effectiveness the speech, yarns, humor, superstitions, sermons, and customs of the Negroes of their particular regions. The over-all service of this trend to a realistic presentation of folklore was the banishing of at least some of the stereotypes of the plantation tradition. Being studiously realistic, these accounts had to reveal the humor and sorrow, the successes and failures, the bitterness and the proverbial optimism of Negroes subjected to both social and economic repressions.

The sociological fiction and the new folklore were not, however, the major achievements of Southern creative writers in the twenties and thirties. In the early twenties, young Southern writers, like writers elsewhere, embraced naturalism and repudiated the sentimental and romantic concept of the South and Southern life. Prior to 1920, one Southern writer had evaded the traditional mold of Southern writing and had defied the sentimental and sterile tradition sustained by the Southern apologists. A self-styled social historian, Ellen Glasgow from 1900 on recorded the history and social changes of her native Virginia. Her objective, incisive pictures of poor whites, white aristocracy, Negroes in their relationships to whites and to other Negroes, the Civil War, and the drastic personal (as well as over-all economic, social, and psychological) adjustments exacted by reconstruction were unprecedented. She dealt frankly with miscegenation; she satirized the overexalted standards of respectability which lingered in a Richmond years behind the times. In her last novel, when she herself was a very old woman, she focused her attention on youth and moral responsibility, predicating her point of view on a compelling situation involving an irresponsible white girl and a Negro boy of both intellect and promise. Never a naturalist in the extreme sense of the term, Ellen Glasgow was a staunch realist whose serious purpose and unquestionable achievement were to picture the South, as symbolized by Virginia, as it really was.

The major naturalists of the renaissance of Southern literature followed not only Ellen Glasgow, but also the skilled regional and realistic writers of the early twenties. Elizabeth Madox Roberts's *The Time of Man*, a beautifully written novel of Kentucky folk and a young girl's maturing, was followed by *My Heart and My Flesh*, a novel in which a white woman discovers that she is the half-sister of three Negroes living in her town. Evelyn Scott's *The Wave* recounts the grim experiences of Negroes in the Civil War with a sensitive understanding of the horrors and indignities that even the imminence of freedom did not ease. With Conrad Aiken and Sherwood Anderson, there is a substantial roster of Southern novelists who were followed in the late twenties by Thomas Wolfe, Erskine Caldwell, and William Faulkner, all of whom had something to say about the Negro and the South.

Wolfe, as a matter of fact, said very little about the Negro except as he introduced background figures. But his whole view of the South is significant: it is, in the main, the view shared by his contemporaries. In *Look Homeward, Angel*, really his own story, Wolfe's leading character, Eugene Gant, recalled the Old South as the "period where people were said to live in mansions and slavery was a benevolent institution, conducted to a constant banjo-strumming, the strewn largesses of the colonel and the shuffle-dance of his happy dependents, where all women were pure, gentle, beautiful, all men chivalrous and brave, and the Rebel horde a company of swaggering, death-mocking cavaliers."

Wolfe's hatred of the Old South, with its carry-over of pretension and sham (in spite of its poverty and confusion), intensified his violent reaction against the South, a reaction so manifest in his works, and in others by Southern naturalists. With Wolfe the hatred was bred from his own uncertainties and conflicts. Only when we recognize in his turbulent confessionals the universal and universally tragic elements of an individual's search for security or identity can we reasonably associate Wolfe's novels with other people, with a region—the South—in its fumbling and frustrating efforts to re-establish and redefined itself.

One of Faulkner's less admirable novels, *Sanctuary*, is generally credited with being an allegory of the South. The symbolism is in terms not of uncertainty, but rather of the South's ruthless destruction, its violent deflowering, analogous with the brutal ruin of the central character of the novel. Yet, if one were to carry the allegory to its full length, what could be said, in symbolic terms, of the girl's moral weakness, her self-indulgence, and her eventual total submissiveness? In his other novels, Faulkner reflects a hatred of the South which dominates Wolfe's novels. As a naturalist he sees the violence, brutality, and weakness of human nature. His characters are twisted, morally and mentally diseased, and perverted. Completely defeated by the violent changes that the Civil War incurred, unprepared or unable to adjust to a drastically changed social order, his white characters are uncertain, insecure, and without hope. *The Sound and the Fury* is typical: in an "old Southern family" we see perversion, idiocy, and alcoholism. Although the social milieu of *As I Lay Dying* is different, the same hysteria and the same futile attempt to cling to past values which obsess the Comptons obsess the family of a dead woman whose last request necessitates her being buried across country. The family, determined to honor her dying wish, is subjected to horrible and grotesque experiences as they literally carry her body through rain and mud. But it is *Absalom! Absalom!* that betrays Faulkner's hatred of miscegenation and of the potentials of incest that Southern sex mores make possible. The perplexity and confusion that white Southerners suffer as they regard the contradiction of prescribed racial attitudes and mores and the indisputable evidences of interracial alliances are crystallized in this novel. But in others, too, the mulatto theme is introduced. Joe Christmas, the half-white boy of *Light in August*, is the embittered victim of his mixed heritage and of the society that doomed him to illegitimacy and ostracism. Other Negro characters fulfill different roles. They provide the elements of stability and familiarity. They dominate and control situations. In *The Sound and the Fury*, the only stable figure is Dilsey; in *Requiem for a Nun*, a companion novel to *Sanctuary*, the Negro servant takes the dominant role and forces the still weak, indulgent Temple to hold to a bargain, marriage, rather than yield to personal weakness and self-indulgence. Minor Negro characters are shown in the entire range of human weakness, chicanery, baseness.

Intruder in the Dust, though not artistically the success of his best works, is Faulkner's most recent picture of Negro-white relations in the far South. A novel of mob violence and threatened lynching, it climaxes a series of characterizations beginning with Joe Christmas which shows Faulkner's concern for the enigmatic and inconsistent relationship between Southern whites and the Negro. One of the justifications for his receiving the Nobel Prize, in addition to his unexcelled, intensive portrayal of Southern life, was recognition of his unorthodox integrity in the treatment of the Negro.

Erskine Caldwell is invariably paired with Faulkner, but only because the two are equally brutal in their exposure of Southern decadence and degradation. Whereas Faulkner has developed a literary style and technique as important as his materials and point of view, Caldwell, though a competent writer, is frankly concerned with what he says rather than how he says it. In a succession of novels he has documented in realistic and grotesquely humorous tone the racial and economic problems of the South. Using his native Georgia as background, Caldwell has created a gallery of white rural characters and Negroes whose experiences are described in what has been called a "modern Gothic" style. His major themes are the relationship between poverty and personal degeneracy and the common denominator of poverty which should, but does not, ally poor whites and poor Negroes. In *Tobacco Road, God's Little Acre, Trouble in July*, these themes recur. Poor white is pitted against poor Negro and believes and is encouraged to believe that he is superior because of his whiteness. Equally poor, the two racial groups could strengthen their economic position through co-operative effort, but prejudice, tradition, suspicion, and intolerance prevent it. Rather, two things happen. The frustrated, hungry, insecure whites have no outlet or emotional release except as they exert pressures and physical violence against Negroes. "Baiting Negroes" and lynching, though they can never be justified, are explained, by the Caldwell thesis, as emotional outlets, entertainment really, for men who are less than human. Deprived of education, proper food, and decent housing, and with little hope of acquiring any of them, the men have, besides this thin assumption of white superiority, only sex and religion as further escapes. The exaggerated significance of each has proved offensive to some readers of the Caldwell novels, but indictment should be aimed not at this result, but at the forces that created it.

Standing apart, but no less effective as a force in both Southern thought and Southern writing, is Lillian Smith's *Strange Fruit*. Miss Smith attempts, in large measure successfully, to define the psychic forces that underlie racial prejudice and the inability of a single individual to break the force of combined prejudices. Like her subsequent volumes of nonfiction, *Strange Fruit* represents a new approach to the study of Negro-white relationships in the South. With her characteristic simplicity and directness, Lillian Smith wrote a novel of a Negro girl and a white boy genuinely in love. The story is that of average young people: neither was a particularly strong or vivid character; on the contrary, the girl's submissiveness and passivity enraged much of the genteel Negro reading public, whose main concern seemed to be that a college graduate should be capable of inflexible emotional control. But Lillian Smith's premise, it seems, is that it is a tragic irony, indeed, when a beautiful girl of education and dignity and a boy who had enough manly stamina at least to have weathered a war are not free to marry simply because of the accident (or in this case, as the girl looked white, the concept) of color. The story's power is heightened because the girl is not a "tragic octoroon" in the sense of being helpless to resolve her personal destiny in any way except a liaison with a white man. Here choice and a basic bond between the two dramatize the paradox, the inconsistency, the tragedy of a society whose social distinctions are arbitrarily determined by color. Lillian Smith does more than create a dramatic theme. With a sharp insight that only a Southerner of deep-seated conviction and real sensibility could possess, she creates the very atmosphere of a small Southern town—the insufferable heat, the stillness, the tensions, the repressed desires, the hidden fears. That people can live so intimately, so mutually interdependently, and often so affectionately, and yet live basically in a pattern of superiority and condescension as opposed to inferiority and subservience creates the strong element of both irony and tragedy.

It is an irony at once heightened by recognition of the validity of the love affair; the girl was not the victim of rape, seduction, or an enforced alliance. From childhood the two had depended on each other for companionship and reassurance because each was alone and in his own way uncertain. The need for understanding, emotional security, strength to complement weakness, and loyalty to complement ostracism are the human elements binding the tragic and doomed couple. The

The Negro in Modern American Fiction

forces that kept them apart as individuals are those which, we surmise, the author wants us to believe, create artificial and needless barriers between Negro and white people in the South.

Such other Southern novelists of the period as Hamilton Basso, William March, and Robert Rylee picked up the challenge of the South in a third-generation defiance of its sacred taboos, especially its sex mores and the subject of the Negro. Some wrote not so much in specific desire for retributive justice for the Negro as out of loyalty to realism's basic credo. Others, like Grace Lumpkin (whose *White Man* and *A Sign for Cain*, excellent pictures of smalltown Southern life, compare admirably with Lillian Smith's more mature and subtle novel), had the explicit resolve of making moral atonement. The literary revolution that started in the Midwest with Willa Cather, Carl Sandburg, and Sinclair Lewis was destined to achieve one of its greatest triumphs in the literature of the South, bringing that region its first era of outstanding cultural distinction.

In contrast to these realistic writers, progressive in the best sense of the word, was a new group of reactionary writers. In the late twenties, a group of Southern conservatives, many of whom were poets—members of the earlier Fugitives group— wrote a series of articles which were published together under the title *I'll Take My Stand*. The book was rapidly acknowledged as something of a manifesto or apologia for the Old South, the agrarian South, the aristocratic South. These men not only were opposed to industrialism, but also were resentful and critical of the new social realism that took into account the plight of the sharecroppers, the poor whites, and the Negroes. When the Agrarians were making a case for the Old South, a group of Old South novels appeared, full of familiar eulogy of the dead past and equally familiar indictments of the imposition of industrialism on the South. Outstanding examples are Stark Young's *So Red the Rose* and Margaret Mitchell's *Gone with the Wind*, two novels that reverted to the old stereotypes, the old sentimentality, and the old artificiality of plantation-tradition literature. Never were the symbols of the past more skillfully revived, as the sweeping popularity of both novels proved. Although most of the superficiality of traditional ante-bellum concepts had been stripped away by the realistic novelists and by penetrating critics of the South, the appeal of the old romantic illusion challenged that of the literature of reality.

The realistic trend was bound to influence Negro novelists. For a long time fiction by Negro authors was limited to the problem novel. DuBois's *Quest of the Silver Fleece* and Walter White's *The Fire in the Flint* are typical of the way Negro leaders incorporated racial problems into fiction. But beginning with Rudolph Fisher's semisatirical stories and his novel of Harlem, *Walls of Jericho,* Negro writers increasingly became identified with full-scale realism. Interestingly enough, the urban realism with which Fisher is identified was launched not by a Negro, but by a white author, Carl Van Vechten. In 1925, Van Vechten wrote *Nigger Heaven,* a novel based on his personal associations with and personal regard for Negroes "who had high standards, who were abreast of the best in literature, who were a credit to American culture and yet were held apart from the mainstream of American life." Widely read by both Negroes and whites, the novel not only was an education for many whites, but was also an inspiration for Negroes themselves to portray urban Negro life. Claude McKay's *Home to Harlem,* Countee Cullen's *One Way to Heaven,* and a succession of novels by Jessie Fauset, a pioneer Negro woman novelist of urban life, followed. Miss Fauset restricted herself to depicting the upper- and middle-class Negro of the North. Her main emphasis, however, was on the paradoxes and ironies of color and on the compulsion to "pass" which is a dominant force in many Negroes' lives. Walter White's *Flight* is an urban novel of "passing," though the heroine eventually returns to her Negro world; Nella Larsen's *Quicksand* shows upper-class Negroes in Harlem and Chicago, but—like its successor, *Passing*—fails, somehow, to overcome a self-conscious effort to convince the reader that the leading characters are really caught between two worlds or two cultures.

Not Without Laughter, by Langston Hughes, is a much finer realistic novel than any other so far mentioned. Set in a small town in Kansas, the novel depicts a poor Negro family that includes a boy and his overworked mother and grandmother. A simple, semiautobiographical novel, it has a sincerity and warmth as a story of childhood not to be approximated until much later, with Owen Dodson's *Boy at the Window*.

Prior to World War II, Negro writers continued in varied paths of realistic writing. Arna Bontemps delved into historical fiction with *Black Thunder,* based on a slave rebellion in 1800; his *God Sends Sunday* is a colorful story of sporting life in New Orleans and St. Louis. One of the outstanding Negro writers, Zora Neale Hurston, is not only an able folklorist, but also a trained anthropologist. In both folklore and fiction she has given an excellent inside view of Negro peasant life. *Of Mules and Men* is a collection of Florida folk tales with the hilarious and exaggerated qualities of the typical tall tales of the folk. Her novel, *Their Eyes Were Watching God,* is set in an all-colored town in Florida and is rich in its revelation of folk customs, superstitions, and accurately delineated folk speech. George Lee's *River George* is representative of still another new direction for the Negro novelist. In this novel Lee gives an excellent close-up of the sharecropper, both Negro and white. The leading figure, George, is doomed because of his education and his insistence on social rights. Waters Turpin, in a series of period novels, did what no Negro novelist previously had attempted: he traced the history of three generations of Southern Negroes. This is a bitter and discouraging history of poverty and bigotry, hatreds and a lynching. Yet somehow the Negroes survived and kept struggling in spite of the accumulation of economic and social forces against them.

World War II had its impact on literature about and by Negroes. A group of militant young liberals began writing incisively of the significance of the war for the Negro minority and the inevitability of a revolutionary shift in Southern race relations following the war's conclusion. In the main they expressed the conviction that the change would be—would have to be—preceded by or accompanied with violence. Hodding Carter's *Winds of Fear* is typical. A vigorous exposé of social tensions in a small Southern town, the novel is concerned with a white war veteran dismayed by and contemptuous of the South's continued disregard for Negro rights even after a devastating war to whose victory the Negro had contributed. Singlehandedly the veteran, as a newspaper editor, tried to stem the rising fears of the whites when Negroes challenged the economic and social traditions of white supremacy. Only with brutal murder were the Negroes temporarily silenced, and both the Negroes and the whites knew that the ultimate reckoning was yet to come.

A comparable pattern of violence and animosity, of fear and uncertainty is reflected in Robert Ardrey's *World's Beginning*, which anticipates violence and bloodshed before equitable race relations can be effected; Porteous Clark's *South Wind Blows*, an analysis of the psychological and social drives that prompt a mob to lynching; John Roeburst's *Senica, U. S. A.*, recounting a newspaper editor's abortive fight against racism; Edward Kimbrough's *Night Fight*, which shows the impact of a changing South on a traditionally conservative Mississippi planter and his son; John Hewlett's *Cross on the Moon*, dealing with the intimacies and complexities of a closely knit Negro-white community. Color paradoxes and the old octoroon theme recur in B. T. Anderson's *Southbound* and Cid Ricketts Sumner's *Quality*, but now with the new twist of the women's rejecting "passing" for useful lives as Negroes working for their own people.

There were, of course, in the forties, novels dealing with the war itself and the Negro's part in it. One of the most distinguished is James Gould Cozzens's *Guard of Honor*, which, though not a "race novel" as such, presents a penetrating and thoroughly understanding evaluation of Negro-white relationships. It is one of the best to emerge from the war literature. With superb insight Cozzens dramatizes the inequities, inconsistencies, and demoralizing factors that operated against the Negroes in the armed services. With unquestionable sincerity and forthrightness, he shows the guilt, embarrassment, and sensitive awareness of white military personnel trying to equate the insult of segregation in the armed forces with the philosophy of a nation pledged to represent, defend, and perpetuate democracy.

A significant Negro war novelist is William Gardiner Smith, whose *The Last of the Conquerors* recounts the agreeable shock and surprise of a young Negro when, on his arrival in Germany, he is unable to assume the role of "conqueror" because he finds himself susceptible to the kindliness of the German people, who, with apparent sincerity and spontaneity, accord him the simple dignity and friendly regard that any likable human being (other than the Negro) takes for granted. Never having been separated from the tensions bred of social and racial suppression, the young soldier is wary at first, but gradually in an alien land finds status as a soldier and personal dignity as a man.

The big literary achievement of the forties was Richard Wright's *Native Son*. It was in 1940 that Wright's skillful sociological realism turned a hard but brilliant searchlight on Negro urban life in Chicago and outlined the somber tragedy of Bigger Thomas in a well-studied setting of north-side wealth and south-side poverty. Artistically not the equal of the masterful short stories of Wright's *Uncle Tom's Children*, *Native Son* is nevertheless a masterful narrative; its character delineation is as skillful as that in any work of Dreiser or Farrell. The book is marred only by the author's overreliance on the Communist ideology with which he encumbered his powerful indictment of society for Bigger, the double pariah of the slum and the color line. Wright was essentially sound in his alignment of the social forces involved, but he erred in the doctrinally propagandistic tone that dominated the novel from its early sections until its angry, ineffective end. The great irony was and is that he later disavowed the ideological commitment that had cheated him of a classic in American fiction.

Not for a decade was Wright to produce another book, and then it proved so inferior to *Native Son* that it is difficult to reconcile the two. *The Outsider* is the story of a man who purportedly has "no party, no myths, no tradition, no race, no culture, and no ideas" (a man hard to envision), and who was apparently inspired by Wright's long stay in France, where he is reputed to have become closely associated with the existentialists. Bigger Thomas was convincing, symbolizing, as he did, generations of society's neglect and indifference, of suppression and fear, uneducated, really barely more than a child. Bigger is believable in spite of his inability to cope with a succession of crises. But Cross Damon, the central character of *The Outsider,* is an adult, with adult responsibilities and ties—unsatisfactory or unpleasant as they are. His "escape" into anonymity, his eventual involvement in violent crime, and his release from any moral obligation by virtue of the author's insistence that he is "nothing" render the novel pointless and purposeless.

But if Wright's second work is disappointing, that of his protégé, Ralph Ellison, is rich with promise. *Invisible Man* is a great novel. Written with force and originality, it is representative of a new level of literary achievement in both style and conception. Partially autobiographical, it is the life history of a colored boy from his early years in a Southern Negro school through his settling in New York. Conceptually it runs almost the whole gamut of class in American society and is interracial at all stages. The novel is, in fact, one of the best-integrated accounts of interaction between Negroes and whites that has yet been presented in American fiction; all the characters are portrayed in the same balance and perspective. Ellison's philosophy of characterization is incisive, realistic, and sparing of physical detail. We see a caravan of types, all registered on the sensitive but rather cynical eye of the young Negro first-person protagonist. In the South, the patronizing, well-intentioned trustee, the piously hypocritical Negro school principal, the gauche, naïve, and not very honest students, the disillusioned war veterans, and the white and black peasants, including the unforgettable Jim Trueblood, are portrayed in memorable terms. In the North, the pageant is resumed with all sorts of men and women—financiers, factory workers, pro- and anti-unionists, parlor pinks, hard-core Communists, race leaders both educated and illiterate, and the Harlem community generally. Stylistically this unrolls a flow of vivid imagery. With double symbolic meaning imposed on realism we get, in *Invisible Man,* distinctive literary quality. It is a comic novel rich in satire and sly symbolism to be interpreted at will. The hero is of the picaro tradition, and in his infinite wanderings thoroughly enjoys himself. Frank and daring, Ellison's novel is also bewildering to many readers. But the frankness and the daring coupled with the emotional intensity are an integral part of the book's success.

In 1953, a young Negro War veteran, James Baldwin, wrote

a novel entitled *Go Tell It on the Mountain*. It was promptly acclaimed as possibly the finest novel so far by a Negro author dealing with some aspects of Negro life. The leading figure, a young colored boy named John Grimes, is on the threshold of maturity, poised between submission to the narrow, confining life prescribed by his family and revolt and escape in pursuit of a wider, fuller life outside the Negro ghetto. Before he can resolve the dilemma, he is sealed into his present world because in a moment of religious inspiration and ecstasy he joins his father's church. This conversion automatically consigns him to the life of his parents, a life of work, hardship, and resignation, to be rewarded only by the promise of a better life after death. When we learn something of the family's history, we learn a great deal about their dependence on otherworldly hopes. Having been always defeated, always rejected, disillusioned by the North's failure to offer more acceptance than the South, the family had quietly placed its last hopes in religion.

Not all Negro writers of recent years have depended on Negro themes. As a clear instance on the purely popular level are the repeated successes of Frank Yerby, who writes bestselling romances exclusively. More meaningful, however, and on a far higher level is Ann Petry's *The Street*, an account of juvenile delinquency in Harlem. Her characters are Negroes, but this is incidental to her major theme. Her later novel, *Country Place*, is a nonracial story of small-town life. A major example of a Negro's using a non-Negro theme is Willard Motley's *Knock on Any Door*, an important addition to the literature of social protest. The protagonist is a young Italian-American who, like Bigger Thomas, is a victim of society's pressures. Zora Hurston's *Seraph of the Suwanee* is a local-color story of Southern whites.

Other significant novelists include Owen Dodson, whose *Boy at the Window* is a moving and sensitive study of Negro adolescence. Set in Brooklyn, the novel adds valuably to Negro portraiture in several ways—not the least of which is in presenting the Northern urban neighborhood background, which has rarely been treated in fiction. Dorothy West's *The Living Is Easy* and Chester Hime's *Third Generation* deal with the Negro middle class; each emphasizes color caste. J. Saunders Redding's *Strange and Alone*, as foreshadowed in several chapters of his earlier *No Day of Triumph*, opens up his promised exposé of Negro education in the South, with its "Jim Crow" ethics and psychological frustrations. A white novelist, Bucklin Moon, has handled the same thesis, and admirably, in *Without Magnolias*. *Beetle Creek* by William Demky reverses, with interest and profit, the usual focus of portraiture. It tells of a white recluse living precariously on the fringe of a Negro community. William Gardiner Smith's *Anger at Innocence* might have been a great proletarian story, commending itself to serious readers eager to explore the Negro "lower depths." It failed, just as *South Street*, his last book, failed—because of excessive melodrama, persistent banality, and a reportorial rather than an analytical quality.

Arthur Gordon's *Reprisal*, William Russell's *A Wind Is Rising*, and Loren Wahl's *The Invisible Glass* are three examples of novels by white authors in the early fifties. *Reprisal* is a courageous and powerful study of the psychological aftermath of lynching; *A Wind Is Rising* is the story of a repressed Delta sharecropper whose brother is involved in a murder. Both Gordon and Russell belong to the Faulkner-Caldwell school of fearless Southern fiction. Russell's real message is not to be found in the plot, but rather in his grim picture of the decaying feudal structure of the old agrarian South, the moral disintegration of the mores, the traplike vise of the old tradition, the dilemma of the dual morality, and the rising factors of challenge in the thinking and action of occasionally nonconforming whites and Negroes. In quite another vein, Wahl's *The Invisible Glass* attempts the portrayal of Negro troops in Italy, suffering at first under the injustice of a prejudiced Southern captain, only half relieved under the regime of a liberal and unprejudiced white lieutenant, and perplexed by the misunderstanding of the Italian townsfolk. A more skillful treatment of this situation might have given us the long-awaited Negro war novel.

Finally, brief reference must be made to two "big" novels —in terms of scope—by white authors. In 1952, Truman Nelson wrote *The Sin of the Prophet*, a dramatic novel or near-documentary dealing with Anthony Burns, the last runaway slave returned from Boston by virtue of the Fugitive Slave Act, and his benefactor Theodore Parker, Boston's intrepid abolitionist. Nelson's powerful thesis is suggested by his reference to Thoreau's observation that ". . . few . . . men serve the state with their consciences. . . ." Parker did, and Nelson's account of the man and his controversial times is a valuable contribution to the fiction of abolition. Three years later, in November 1955, Robert Penn Warren published *Band of Angels*. This novel, too, revolves about strong personalities—a beautiful octoroon, a slave-trader, an African hero, and so on—but its broad scope is equally important. We progress from the pre-war idyll of New Orleans through Reconstruction and into the period of the expanding West. The personal spiritual catharsis that Amantha Starr (the Negro woman) suffered may well be related to the historic periods through which she lived.

There are various schools of thought among Negro critics as to the direction Negro writers should take in employing subject matter. Should Negro writers deal with Negro themes? Or "universal" themes? Or should there be a synthesis of the two? Or should it matter?

Many Negro critics point out that for generations Negro creative expression was inevitably imitative and marked with the double provincialism of cultural immaturity and a racial sense of subordination. It ran a one-dimensional gamut from self-pity through sentimental appeal to moralizing to rhetorical threat. Most critics and artists doubtless expected too much of the Negro Renaissance, but its new vitality and independence, its pride and self-respect, and its defiance of old limitations were heartening. Yet much of the creative expression of the twenties and thirties was immature. Beginning with the broader social identifications of *Native Son* at the onset of the forties and the social discoveries of common-denominator human universals between Negro situations and others, these same critics rightly claim that Negro artistic expression has become increasingly sound and objective, less racialistic (in the limiting sense of chauvinism), but withal more racial in the better sense of being more deeply felt and projected. The third dimension of objective universality, they rightly feel, is the ultimate desideratum for a literature that seeks universal appeal and acceptance.

Suffice it to say that even in 1925 some original proponents of the Negro Renaissance forecast the result that seems to be the new consensus of the "new criticism." That is, that when the racial themes are imposed on the Negro author either from within or without, they become an intolerable and limiting artistic burden; accepted by choice, either on the ground of best-known material or preferred opportunity, they stake off a cultural bonanza. Hugh Gloster has rightly inveighed against the triple snares of "race defense, protest, and glorification," but there still remain areas of Negro life and experience which have not been fully utilized in fiction and drama. In provincial and chauvinistic renderings we have offered too much. In objective, thoroughly humanized treatment there is still need for better handling and more universal acceptance. The necessary alchemy is the universalized rendering, for the world's greatest art resides in the universalized particular experience.

Although rare, this universalized quality has appeared sporadically in Negro writing. Lewis Chandler correctly gives us the proper historical perspective, however, by reminding us how long it took American literature itself to achieve this dimension of universalized power and insight. Perhaps it would be invidious to be too specific for the current generation, though most would probably agree that the first two chapters of *Native Son* had such quality (not to mention how and why the book as a whole lost these virtues as it became more and more involved in propagandist formulas). A phenomenally early "universal particularity" is evident in Jean Toomer's *Cane*. Although the novel is Negro through and through, it is deeply and movingly human. It can be exempted from any limitation of provincialism even though it is a local-color novel. To wish for more than this is to ask that the transmuting quality of expert craftsmanship be combined with broad perspective or intuitive insight, one or the other. Russian literature achieved its great era in two ways: the cosmopolitan way of Turgenev, Tolstoi, and Chekhov, and the nativist way of Dostoevski, Gogol, and Gorki. Each way produced great writing and universal understanding for Russian experience.

The problem for the Negro writer is the final resolution of the old dilemma of the proper attitude of the Negro writer toward race materials. Agreeing as we do with Mr. Gloster's answer that the writer should "consider all life as his proper milieu, yet treat race (when he chooses) from the universal point of view, shunning the cultural isolation that results from racial preoccupation and Jim Crow esthetics," we arrive as a net result at this mandate: give us Negro life and experience in all the arts, but with a third dimension of universalized common-denominator humanity.

A final word of constructive criticism may be in order. Let us start with the paradoxical fact that out of the whole range of Negro experience, in the very areas for which the Negro author has almost monopolistic control, there has been little else than strange silence. On this matter, L. D. Reddick hints provocatively in his essay "No Kafka in the South." Let us speak plainly on this point. Three taboos seal doors that must be broken through to release original and moving revelations about Negro life and experience, but which remain unbroken. This is partly because of convention-ridden cowardice, partly because of misconceived protective strategy. If Erskine Caldwell, Lillian Smith, and William Faulkner could boldly break through the tribal taboos of the white South to release the full potentials of Southern fiction, so in turn must the Negro author break through analogous seals of Negro conventionality. The Negro intellectual is still largely in psychological bondage, not only as Reddick puts it "to the laws and customs of the local [Southern] culture," but also to the fear of breaking the taboos of Puritanism and falsely conceived conventions of race respectability. Consciously and subconsciously these repressions work great artistic harm; especially harmful is the fear of being accused of group disloyalty and "misrepresentation" in portraying the full gamut of Negro type, character, and thinking.

The releasing formula is to realize that all human beings are, basically and inevitably, human, and that even special racial complexities and overtones are only interesting variants. Why, then, this protective silence about the ambivalences of the Negro upper classes, about the dilemmas of intragroup prejudice and rivalry, about the dramatic inner paradoxes of mixed heritages, both biological and cultural, or the tragic breach between the Negro elite and the Negro masses, or the conflict between integration and vested-interest separatism in the present-day life of the Negro? These themes, among others, are great, but they decay in closed closets.

To break such taboos is the crucial challenge of the day, notwithstanding the wrath of Negro Rotarians, preachers, college presidents, and journalists. This inner tyranny must be conquered now that the outer tyranny of prejudice and intellectual ostracism is being relaxed. Perhaps, now that a few Negro authors have demonstrated the possibility of financial independence and success as writers, some of our younger talent can shake free of white-collar-job dependency on the one hand and conventional "race loyalty" on the other. If so, we can confidently anticipate an era of fuller and more objective presentation by Negro authors of their versions of contemporary living in general and of Negro life experience in particular.

CHAPTER NINE

The Negro in American Drama

DRAMA by and about Negroes has developed and matured in relationship to the developing and maturing of American drama as a whole. In 1940 Carl and Mark Van Doren observed:

> American literature has always been weakest in the department of drama. Until the present generation there has been little dramatic work worth the serious attention of the historian, and there have been few or no playwrights of deserved eminence. Not until 1890 did any arise of even respectable quality, and not until 1915 did talent of a high order enter the field.

Interestingly enough, the pioneering geniuses in the development of a native American drama recognized the Negro life and folkways as a potential source of native idioms from which a major contribution to a national drama could be developed. Eugene O'Neill, Ridgley Torrence, and Paul Green, all white writers, are representative not only of the American theater's renaissance, but also of that group of playwrights who, as Sterling Brown emphasizes, did for the Negro what Yeats, Synge, and Lady Gregory did for the Irishman. Brown recalls Yeats's plea for a movement whereby "the reality of the true Irish peasant would drive off the artificial stage Irishman."

Certainly there was a need for the true Negro to drive off the conventional stage Negro for, with rare exceptions, the Negro character in American drama had been rigidly stereotyped from his early sporadic stage appearances until 1915. These rigid stereotypes of the Negro can be understood in light of the fact that the Negro as a character has reflected successive stages of Negro social development. In the years between the Revolution and the Civil War, the predominant Negro character types were the comic buffoon and the happy, carefree slave flourishing under benevolent patronage. Because these two types were most representative of Negro character and general social maturity for the period, they were rarely abandoned. That the Negro was subtle enough or sophisticated enough to assume the guise of the jester or the complacent ward of a slave society apparently never occurred to early delineators of American society or Negro members of it. For decade after decade, the Negro character was synonymous with "comic relief," diverting antics, crude dialect, and grotesque appearance—either physically or in terms of costume. Other stereotypes were being perpetuated simultaneously. William Dunlap, as notable a playwright as America produced in the early nineteenth century, did a great deal to establish and perpetuate Yankee, French, English, Irish, as well as Negro "types."

As actor, and as motivating force for the native art known as minstrelsy, the Negro played a commanding role, even early in the nineteenth century. Edith Isaacs pointed out that in New York, in 1821, the so-called African Company of Negro Actors was performing in a makeshift theater near Bleecker and Mercer streets. The leading player of the small, highly enthusiastic group was James Hewlett, whose stellar and most triumphant roles were Othello and Richard the Third. In the neighboring area was the African Free School, which had provided education for New York's Negro children from 1787 on. One of the school's graduates was Ira Aldridge, descendant of a Senegalese chieftain. Aldridge was captivated by the theater from childhood. Educated at the University of Glasgow, he never developed an interest in any other career save that of an actor. Although he is credited with a wide repertory, he favored the Othello role, often playing it opposite Edmund Kean's Iago. His relationship to the Negro in the American theater is tenuous, for, though born in America, he later became a British subject; and though he is said to have made some short tours in America, he achieved his notable triumphs overseas. The inspiration that he provided for the American Negro was, of course, incalculable.

In the early 1820's, the Negro minstrel show evolved. Actually, the minstrel tradition did not stem from Negro performers, but from white artists who, blackfaced, imitated the dancing, singing, and humor generally ascribed to Negro ability and character. Inspired by the spontaneous and intimate entertainment accorded plantation owners by their Negro slaves, professional white entertainers developed and sustained the vogue for minstrelsy until near the end of the nineteenth century. Not until after the Civil War did Negroes begin to perform professionally. Their efforts were considerably stylized by then; a set pattern had emerged. Both Brown and Edith Isaacs describe it this way: seventeen costumed men in a half-circle traditionally dominated the first half of the program, with the master of ceremonies—the interlocutor—in the center. Singers, dancers, and two "end men" (the main comedians), invariably called Mr. Bones and Tambo, rounded out the group. The latter part of the program was more akin to a vaudeville performance—all male performers, including the one Negro-"wench" role. Interestingly enough, Negro minstrels adopted these procedures in their entirety, even to the make-up. Their native abilities and ready capacity for improvisation heightened the basic humor and appeal of the minstrel pattern, and Negroes undoubtedly prolonged its life. Of particular fame as artists were James Bland, a master ballad writer, and Billy Kersands, a dancer.

The strength of Negro minstrelsy obviously lay more in musical and picturesque extravagance than in dramatic characterization. It remained for propaganda plays to emerge, aimed at illuminating the evils of slavery, and containing distinct characters of slightly more than stereotype proportions. Thus, the humorous Topsy of *Uncle Tom's Cabin*, the forbearing and martyred Uncle Tom in the same play, and the succession of tragic octoroons represent a more serious evaluation of individual Negro character by white playwrights. It has been observed that the success of such plays would suggest that others dealing more definitively with Negro problems and character might conceivably have been written in rapid succession. It must be remembered, however, that public opinion and reaction were strong determining factors in both the writing and the producing of plays for the professional theater. The slave issue and the post-Civil War Negro problem presented constant invitations to public disapproval, a challenge that few practical playwrights were prepared to meet.

What Edith Isaacs calls "The Middle Distance" in Negro theater growth occurred in the years 1890–1917, when, as she said, "almost everything that Negro theater artists are doing today had its beginnings in the Middle Distance and much of what our theaters and concert halls and radio, and most of what our night clubs are doing, had its source or its flood tide here." These years witnessed the recognition of the spirituals as beautiful native folk music, of the Negro's contribution to modern dance—a contribution later to be identified as a distinct offshoot of ragtime,[1] and of the Negro's

---

[1] André Levinson, a contributor to Edith Isaacs's *Essays on The Arts of the Theatre* (New York: Little, Brown and Company, 1947), observed: Negro ragtime itself contributes enormously to these [dance] performances. This music, with its bewildering syncopation and rubato, its rhythmic tours de force, executed with such unimaginable dexterity, positively dazzled European audiences. This dancing, with its automaton-like quality, its marvellous flexibility and rhythmic fantasy, is as impossible for us to reproduce as it is astounding to watch.

gift to the drama of temperament rather than of tradition. Long regarded as a "natural born actor," the Negro suffered rather than gained by this estimate, for it was intended often as a confined estimate of the Negro's limitations, a simultaneous concession to his interpretative dramatic ability and disparagement of his creative abilities. In short, the Negro was evaluated as a second-rate dramatic talent: he was regarded exclusively as mimic or clown.

The art of the Negro actor (and to some extent that of the Negro playwright) has had for many years to struggle against the minstrel tradition and against the static limits of popular taste. Farce, buffoonery, and pathos overshadowed the folk comedy and folk tragedy of a dramatically endowed people until the early years of this century. Folk comedy and tragedy, until the late thirties, precluded the possibility that Negro actors or playwrights should simply portray people with universal problems unrelated to color.

Certainly the Negro experience from slavery until the present has been, and is, inherently dramatic. No minority group in America has plumbed greater emotional depths, or passed through more levels of life, or been caught in more social conflict and complication than the Negro. The essential elemental forces of great drama—epic turns of experience, tragic intensity of life, discipline and refinement of the emotions—have been accumulating for generations and are only now finding mature expression in the dramatic arts. Generations of enforced buffoonery and caricature began to give way to a more realistic interpretation of the Negro folk; today, slowly and at times almost imperceptibly, the Negro actor and playwright are functioning and creating for audiences sophisticated enough to recognize the universality of human problems and to concede the negligibility of color per se.

Even in the "Middle Distance" period, memorable personalities emerged. In 1898, Will Marion Cook, a talented composer, director, and syncopator, whose *Clorindy: The Origin of the Cake-Walk* revealed the composer's recognition of the serious potentialities of Negro ragtime, won instant recognition as a pioneer in serious Negro musical comedy. John Isham, the enterprising Negro to whom the Negro theater is indebted for the break from minstrelsy to musical comedy (insofar as Negro talent was concerned), was responsible as inspiration and impetus for operettas such as *Black Patti's Troubadours,* which repudiated the minstrel tradition. During those same years, Bert Williams, actor and humorist, was an idol of the vaudeville stage. A sensitive and brilliant performer, a true comic artist, and one of the first Negroes to be accepted in the legitimate theater, Williams merits the observation of

Booker T. Washington, quoted by Edith Isaacs at the conclusion of her succinct but moving description of Williams's career: "Bert Williams has done more for the race than I have. He has smiled his way into people's hearts. I have been obliged to *fight*."

Just a few years before 1917, a year that marked a renaissance for the Negro theater and actor, as it did for American drama as a whole, several serious "problem" plays appeared. A dramatization of Thomas Dixon's *The Clansman* proved to be as virulent as the original novel. Designed to heighten and intensify racial differences to the end of social suppression, the play intensified hostilities between Negroes and whites and "besmirched the theater." Joseph S. Cotter, Sr., a Negro playwright, wrote *Caleb, the Degenerate* in 1906, and Edward Sheldon, in *The Nigger,* introduced what has been and was to continue to be a favored theme: miscegenation and the attendant romantic, melodramatic, and often sociologically alarming implications.

In the years immediately after World War I there were increasing reflections of the playwrights' ambitions to create more honest pictures of Negroes and Negro life. The little theater and experimental theater groups gave impetus to young, untried playwrights and prompted experimentation in many areas of design, staging, and play-construction. They also encouraged serious and sensitive writers to undertake the challenging, complex task of interpreting to the theater public the Negro as an individual and a human being, liable to the same ideals, aspirations, objectives, and frustrations as any other human being. Alain Locke wrote in 1927:

> For if the first decade of intensive effort can have given us several of the most noteworthy and representative American plays that have ever been written, and can have suddenly raised the general level of plays of this subject matter from vaudeville and farce to significant folk comedy and tragedy, there is every reason to expect that another decade will fully realize Eugene O'Neill's forecast that "The possibilities are limitless and to a dramatist open up new and intriguing opportunities: the gifts the Negro can and will bring to our native drama are invaluable ones."

That O'Neill was himself deeply interested was indicated not only by his *Dreamy Kid,* a one-act play about a Harlem slum Negro torn between the urge for self-preservation and family loyalties, but also by two major contributions to the American theater. In 1920, Charles Gilpin, a Negro actor, appeared in the title role of O'Neill's *The Emperor Jones.* Gilpin was the first modern American Negro to establish himself as a serious actor of first quality, and O'Neill emerged as the first dramatist to prove that the American theater could and would accept the Negro as a subject of serious dramatic treatment.

Pressing his advantage, O'Neill three years later offered *All God's Chillun Got Wings*, a study of marriage between a Negro law student and a white girl who had been seduced by a white boy. Contrary to the expectation of violence and the prediction that the public would not tolerate the development of such a plot on the stage, the play opened without incident; another milestone was passed. In these, as in most of his other plays, O'Neill was interested in the problems of particular individuals rather than in those of groups.

A second pioneering playwright of the period, a white Southerner, Paul Green, was more frequently preoccupied with group problems. *In Abraham's Bosom*, for example, reflects the tragic struggle of a courageous and enterprising Negro to educate himself—and, in turn, others—in spite of apathy on the part both of his Negro peers and of the whites. This Pulitzer Prize play is richly colored by the playwright's sensitive awareness of the group and folk mores that produce the dilemma Abraham cannot possibly resolve. Green's talents have not been limited to this long play. Such compelling one-act plays as *The Hot Iron, White Dresses, The No 'Count Boy*, and *The Man Who Died at 12 o'clock* reflect a variety of moods ranging from the starkly tragic and bitter to the whimsy of folk superstition. *Kneel to the Rising Sun* is worthy of special comment because of its brutal pointing-up of the tragic anomaly of Southern violence, segregation, and sadism in the context of democracy's avowed declaration of individual human worth.

Other important plays of Negro life to reach Broadway during the twenties were Julia Peterkin's *Scarlet Sister Mary* and Dorothy and DuBose Heyward's *Porgy*. Each of these plays relied heavily on the novelty and charm of carefully re-created folk ways and folk speech—but both are without condescension. *Scarlet Sister Mary* was a romantic treatment of an isolated Negro community; *Porgy* combined realism and romanticism in depicting the crippled Porgy's struggle for personal happiness among the Negroes of Charleston's Catfish Row. Although these plays further demonstrated the suitability of Negro themes for the theater and developed a deeper understanding of the Negro, neither commented directly on the larger aspects of Negro-white adjustments.

During the period from 1930 to 1940 increasing evidence seemed to support the belief of Locke, O'Neill, and Torrence in the potentialities of the Negro in the theater. In ad-

The Negro in American Drama

dition to such plays of folk, exotic, or romantic appeal as Paul Green's *Roll Sweet Chariot*, Hall Johnson's *Run Little Chillun*, and Marc Connelly's *Green Pastures*, the Pulitzer Prize play whose phenomenal success and popularity did much to focus world attention on the life and talents of the Negro, there were social-problem plays like DuBose Heyward's *Brass Ankle*, Samson Raphaelson's *White Man*, and Langston Hughes's *Mulatto*, all concerned with miscegenation and its attendant problems. More important than these, however, was the social-protest play dealing with Negroes on various levels of American life. James Know Mullen's *Never No More* and Frederick Schlick's *Blood Stream* were, respectively, powerful, direct attacks on lynching and on the brutal treatment accorded Negro and white convict labor. *They Shall Not Die*, John Wexley's dramatization of the Scottsboro case, was a grim and exciting exposé of Southern "justice." Of the protest plays, *Stevedore* by Paul Peters and George Sklar was probably the most successful and important, for it not only combined authentic dialogue and skillful characterization, but also presented a forceful picture of the Negro's awakening to the consciousness of class struggle and of his final open revolt (with the help of similarly awakened whites) against racial and economic persecution.

A few years later, with Bigger Thomas, in the dramatization of Richard Wright's *Native Son*, we move out of the South and into the urban North for a dramatic trial of American society at large. Bigger Thomas was a misfit and a murderer, but the playwright's indictment was not so much of him as of the society that produced him.

Sterling Brown observed of the pre-war period:

A great deal has been done. But the note of encouragement is not the only one. These plays, for all their understanding and beauty, are beginnings, not ends. Vast areas of Negro experience and character remain unexplored. Although too many Negro critics believe that "well educated, cultured Negroes are all that is necessary for great drama, and that any play not dealing with this minority is therefore trash," it is still regrettable that the life of middle class Negroes, with its comedy and tragedy, its quieter heroism as well as its frantic striving, remains scarcely touched. Drama has room for such representation, if done honestly and thoughtfully, without the usual middle-class self-advertisement. Highlights of Southern life have been seen, but one could hardly say that the dramatic possibilities of the South have been fully realized. A deeper revelation of the folk, with the "folksiness" less stressed, is likewise waiting. Drama of the struggles of the working class are just starting to be written. The exploits of Negro history furnish a mine for the dramatist. There remains a great deal to be done.

An examination of the Broadway scene from 1945 through 1955 discloses that though the number of plays concerned with Negro themes or situations in which the Negro character played a vital part was small, some relatively untouched aspects of Negro life attracted the attention of the playwrights. A few of the plays dealt with situations involving middle-class Negroes. An early one, Philip Yordan's *Anna Lucasta*, was a study of a Negro prostitute's struggle to readjust her life. Melodramatic and at times unconvincing, the play disclosed the frustrations and the clashes of personality in an interesting family that happened to be Negro. Some observers noted that the characters in Yordan's play were not primarily Negroes; they were people, and the family could be anybody's. *Anna Lucasta* was theatrically important because it demonstrated that audiences could be attracted to a play about Negroes facing problems that did not grow out of race.

The tragedy of Nonnie, the middle-class Negro girl in the dramatization of Lillian Smith's *Strange Fruit*, develops out of a situation of racial inequality. The affair between Nonnie and her white lover is doomed from the beginning by the traditional patterns of Negro and white thinking in the South. While the love affair provides the incitement for the drama, and is treated sympathetically as a relationship beyond that of mere sex, the play is more importantly concerned with exposing the bigotries, stupidities, and violence of life in a small Southern community. The scene, for instance, in which the Negro doctor and the liberal white mill owner discuss racial inequality not only is dramatically effective, but is also a powerful, head-on attack on social injustice.

Maxine Woods's *On Whitman Avenue*, likewise concerned with a protagonist from the middle class, shifted the focus to another facet of race relations: the restrictive covenant. *On Whitman Avenue* depicts the social pressures that are brought to bear on Negroes and whites who fail to respect the sanctity of a white residential district. This attack on one of the more subtle, less spectacular aspects of racial intolerance was highlighted by the exposure of the fear-thinking that is so great an obstacle to better race relations in America. The basic theme of the play is expressed in a line of dialogue: "If men can fight and die together, they should be able to live in peace together."

To demonstrate that color is only skin deep, *Forward the Heart* by Bernard Reines used the dramatic device of the blinded white war veteran who unwittingly falls in love with a charming and cultured Negro girl. The play further urges the point that love between Negroes and whites, even when the parties concerned are intelligent and cultured people, has tragic implications in our society. While this is by no means a new idea (aspects of it were treated in *Strange Fruit*), the serious presentation of it in a new context was another step forward.

Another play to spotlight the middle-class Negro was Sarett and Herbert Rudley's *How Long Till Summer,* which examines the phychological impact of color prejudice on a little boy suddenly and brutally made aware of the fact that he is a Negro. The Rudleys make the point that neither family, nor wealth, nor power can shield a child from the hurts and anguish of being colored in America.

The Negro whose awareness of the anachronistic and incongruous character of racial intolerance in our democracy has been sharpened by his efforts to perpetuate democracy abroad was portrayed in two plays dealing with the returning veteran. The first of these, *Deep Are the Roots*, by Arnaud D'Usseau and James Gow, concerns an intelligent and confident Negro lieutenant who returns from a successful military career to be confronted with misguided, paternal, condescending liberalism on the one hand, and misunderstanding, hatred, and violence on the other—with idealistic love somewhere between. This play, a vigorous, even violent, attack on traditional Southern patterns, sharply emphasizes the bigotry of a society that requires a man to fight for the democracy he cannot share, a society that resents his success in the fight and penalizes him for having achieved manliness and independence in his experiences and position of authority in the Army.

Whereas *Deep Are the Roots* localizes its exciting action in the home of a Southern senator, *Jeb,* by Robert Ardrey, covers an extensive scene and shows its protagonist in direct conflict with good and bad Negroes and with whites. In drawing his picture of the returned veteran, a former field hand, now a decorated soldier, Mr. Ardrey writes with deep feeling and conviction and with obvious integrity. *Jeb* illustrates what can happen to a Negro who tries to break the racial barriers to employment in certain areas of the deep South. Jeb, the veteran, who has been taught to operate an adding machine in the Army, tries to make use of this skill on his return to civilian life in Louisiana. His attempt to secure a white-collar job antagonizes the whites, setting off a chain of events culminating in a near-lynching. Jeb temporarily escapes to the Northern city where he had been drugged and robbed by Negro hoodlums earlier in the play, but he finally resolves to return to the fight in the South.

In *Our Lan'*, by Theodore Ward, and in *Set My People Free*, by Dorothy Heyward, the viewpoint shifted from the contemporary to the historical scene. *Our Lan'* recounted the story of a group of freed slaves settled on an island off the coast of Georgia during the Civil War. Like any heterogeneous community of human beings, the group has its sluggards and its rascals as well as its faithful workers, and faces internal problems of individual relationships as well as the group problem of wresting a livelihood from the land. From the group emerges a leader of strength, courage, and foresight who sustains them and even, finally, inspires them to armed but hopeless resistance against threatened eviction by Federal troops. Mrs. Heyward's play is an account of the Denmark Vesey slave revolt in Charleston in 1822, a shortlived, bloody episode that should have done much to dispel the picture of the Negro as the happy, contented and submissive slave. In this, as well as in Mr. Ward's play, the Negro characters move farther and farther away from the early stereotypes.

Jean-Paul Sartre's *The Respectful Prostitute* is not really a play about a Negro at all, though a Negro fleeing from Southern justice appears in it, and the incidents presented on the stage grow out of a street brawl in which a Negro is murdered by a white man. This dramatic piece really sets a Northern girl of easy morals but decent racial attitudes against various responsible leaders of a Southern community. The leaders, employing all the pressures at their disposal, including bribery, threat, violence, and sex, finally emerge victorious, having again sustained white supremacy and the vicious pattern of Southern justice. Sartre's attack on racial inequality may be indirect and distorted, but it is powerful and it illustrates the foreigner's interest in and understanding of the American race problem.

Finally, Carson McCullers's *The Member of the Wedding*, primarily a quiet, poetic representation of a lonely little girl's quest for security, a search to belong, presents a carefully drawn picture of Berenice Brown, the Negro cook. To Frankie Adams, the little white girl, Berenice is friend, companion, and almost mother, but never the stereotype Mammy so familiar in the theater of the past. Berenice serves the dramatic purpose of helping us to see Frankie more clearly, but she is at the same time a person whose problems and attitudes receive dignified, sensitive treatment by the playwright.

This completes the immediate post-war roster of plays in the legitimate theater dealing primarily with the Negro or with Negro-white relationships. It would be unfair, however, to conclude this survey without at least passing mention of trends in areas of the theater outside the scope of this account. More and more frequently in recent plays presenting the American scene, Negro characters have been included, not for comic relief, but chiefly because an honest depiction of the scene required their presence. Examples are O'Neill's *The Iceman Cometh*, Sidney Kingsley's *Detective Story*, Samuel Spewack's *Two Blind Mice*, and Joshua Logan's *Wisteria Trees*. As usual, of course, many of the musical shows included spots for the Negro song or dance specialty, and at least three musicals were directly concerned with racial issues. *Lost in the Stars*, *South Pacific*, and *Finian's Rainbow* were notable examples of the fusing of the arts of the theater into effective dramatic pieces of sometimes subtle social propaganda and delightful entertainment.

Insofar as America's social and cultural history is concerned, the Federal Theatre was and remains a phenomenon in our annals. Designed by New Deal architects, one of innumerable projects aimed to relieve with dignity the economic and vocational stresses of talented, professionally equipped, able, nonindigent victims of the Depression years, the Federal Theatre emerged in 1935 as an explicit recognition of the fact that with the exception of New York, American cities and people in the main were unsusceptible to, unaware of, and unfamiliar with the theater. The Federal Theatre emerged in selected regions throughout the United States. No minority or special group profited more by, or developed more within, the context of the project than the Negro. The Negro's participation in the little-theater movement had been sporadic and unpredictable; with the Federal Theatre Project, the Negro actor and playwright achieved maximum recognition. According to Edith Isaacs:

> In New York, Seattle, Hartford, Philadelphia, Newark, Los Angeles, Boston and San Francisco, a survey of Negro employment on the project . . . showed 851 Negro personnel and seventy-five plays produced by their groups alone. . . . Moreover, the Federal Theatre offered Negroes excellent parts in plays by other units.[2]

[2] Writing in *The Oxford Companion to the Theatre* (Oxford University Press, 1951) Sterling Brown says: "In the early 1940s over one hundred plays included Negro actors in roles numbering nearly a thousand. But serious drama of Negro life was rare, and the Negro playwright noticeably absent. Even the plays that dealt realistically with Negro life were most often by white authors. Except for the short-lived Federal Theatre Project the Negro playwright has been without experience in the professional theatre. He has turned to the tributary theatre—community, college, and semi-professional groups—to learn and practise his craft. American Negroes by and large see little of the theatre; below the Mason Dixon line they are not allowed in the legitimate theatres, except infrequently in segregated sections." Washington, D.C., south of the Mason-Dixon Line, no longer discriminates against Negro theatergoers.

Negro colleges, although occasionally including a course in play-production or playwriting, were slow to accept theater courses as part of the regular college curriculum. For many years dramatics on the Negro college campus remained an extracurricular activity, poorly housed and too often directed by inadequately trained personnel. In recent years, however, a few Negro colleges have given academic recognition to dramatics and have acquired adequate facilities and faculties for regular instruction in basic theater courses. Fisk University, Spelman College, West Virginia Institute, Lincoln University (Missouri), Florida A. & M., and Morgan College are among the pioneeers. And at Howard University, which early took the lead among Negro colleges, a highly trained faculty of three professors offers a full program in drama, leading to a major, and looks forward to offering graduate work.

The Howard University Players, organized in 1921 by Alain Locke and Montgomery Gregory, was the official outgrowth of a less formal drama club launched at Howard before 1910 by Ernest E. Just, then professor of English. In the fall of 1949, the Players toured Scandinavia and American Army installations in Germany, presenting Ibsen's *The Wild Duck* and Heyward's *Mamba's Daughters*. The three-month tour by twenty-one students and three directors—James Butcher, Anne Cooke, and Owen Dodson—was made possible by an invitation from the Norwegian government, the co-operation of the United States Department of State and of the United States Army High Command, and the practical help of private individuals, most notably Blevins Davis. The Players were widely hailed as an artistic success, and the group, on its return, was cited as having made an outstanding contribution to international good will and understanding.

By and large, the criticism made of the tributary theater in general is applicable to the theater at Negro colleges, *i.e.*, too little has been done to encourage the writing of new plays; a too-large part of the yearly program is made up of recent popular Broadway successes; too little attention has been given to the necessity of educating audiences to good theater fare. The vast store of Negro experience available for dramatic treatment has been almost completely ignored by the Negro college theater. A noteworthy exception has been the production of Owen Dodson's *Divine Comedy* and *Bayou Legend*, the former on a religious theme, the latter an imaginative poetic adaptation of Ibsen's *Peer Gynt*. Whatever the reasons for this failure, the Negro college can no longer afford to refuse to accept its responsibility to its immediate clientele or to American culture at large. It is to be hoped that organizations like the Southern Association of Speech and Dramatic Arts, organized by Randolph Edmonds, and the Inter-Collegiate Dramatic Association, under the leadership of Fannin Belcher, with their annually increasing membership, their publications, drama exchange, and drama festivals, will do much to help the Negro college achieve its real and important contributions to the American theater.

In the 1950's, to date, three Negro authors have had plays produced on Broadway. In 1954, Louis Peterson's *Take a Giant Step* ran for several weeks on Broadway. The story of a young Negro boy burdened with the triple problem of adolescence, color, and a mother whose compulsive drive for "getting ahead" takes her family from the security of a Negro ghetto to a "mixed" or "changing" neighborhood, *Take a Giant Step* is a fairly successful problem play in which color intensifies the major conflict, but is not itself the problem.

Take a Giant Step, demanding an all-Negro cast with minor exceptions, was a boon to the Negro actor, who still must wait for plays that explicitly call for Negro parts. Although in recent years a few off-Broadway companies have cast Negroes in white roles, this is still the rare exception. Negro actors are therefore still severely limited in professional opportunities. A revival of *Porgy and Bess* in 1952 and of *Four Saints in Three Acts* the following year supplied two other outstanding vehicles for Negroes. The season of 1954–5 saw Pearl Bailey starred in *House of Flowers*, a musical whose racial tone suggested *South Pacific*. In this case, however, the liberal tone was sharply modified after initial performances.

Mrs. Patterson, written by the Negro artist and playwright Charles Seebree, in collaboration with Greer Johnson, opened on Broadway in 1954. The play deals with the ambitions, daydreams, and frustrations of a fifteen-year-old Southern Negro girl. Its run was short despite the acting and singing of Eartha Kitt in the leading role of Teddy Hicks.

Since 1940, Hollywood has been enlisted by liberal and social protest groups to promote the cause of improved social, interracial, intercultural understanding. *The Lost Weekend* certainly did a great deal to dramatize the psychological and social factors contributing to alcoholism. *Gentleman's Agreement*, a convincing and often moving film, showed the humiliating social sanctions to which Jews in America are exposed frequently and senselessly. The race theme has been handled frequently and in a variety of ways. This is as it should be because for years Hollywood had adopted the Negro stereotypes that playwrights and writers of fiction had developed. The inevitable little black boy who was part and parcel of the "Our Gang" kids, Stepin Fetchit, the perennial Mammy, and the singing stevedore (or imprisoned criminal) were all standard Hollywood props. Before 1940, *Imitation of Life* was the single exception. This full-length version of a Fannie Hurst novel was admirably done but, in spite of fine acting on the part of Louise Beavers, and indeed of most of the cast, the picture really perpetuated another Negro stereotype—the tragic (and unconvincing) octoroon.

In recent years a number of films dealing wholly or in part with Negroes have commanded respect. *Home of the Brave,* one of the best, deals with the Negro soldier; *Lost Boundaries* with the dramatic ironies and paradoxes that racial "passing" creates; *The Well* and *Intruder in the Dust* with mob psychology and mob violence. *Intruder in the Dust,* adapted from the Faulkner novel, and *The Quiet One,* a study of an urban child isolated by virtue of color and city mores, outrank even the documentaries. All of these films and some few others register new seriousness and dignity in Negro characterization; in many, a new moral dimension suggests that Hollywood will not be inept and insensitive enough to repeat the tragic blunder of *The Birth of a Nation* or, for that matter, *Gone with the Wind.*

Two questions apropos the Negro and drama are—why do we have so few Negro playwrights? What, if any, are the problems peculiar to the Negro playwright? One answer is that a playwright, like a novelist, finds it difficult to take an objective attitude about something in which he is emotionally involved. To be a part of any situation or set of circumstances, he has to know it intimately. But the playwright, beyond this intimate knowledge, must acquire a perspective on the situation or circumstance he proposes to project into a drama. Without a proper perspective he cannot possibly express himself objectively or powerfully. This psychological handicap is being overcome by the Negro playwright as he acquires wider experience, and is accorded recognition and acceptance in the one world of the theater.

A second reason might be termed the sociological handicap. Until recently the Negro has had little intimate contact with the technical side of the legitimate stage. Only occasionally on the stage as an actor, he has had no opportunity to learn the practical craftsmanship that can be acquired solely by continuous contact with the stage. This, too, is the reason why amateur Negro repertory groups remain so important for aspiring Negro actors and playwrights.

It is to be hoped that when all barriers disappear, Negro playwrights will be relieved of psychological handicaps in a society in which their familiarity with human situations will determine their success or failure. Then they will obviously be freed of the sociological problem too: as students of drama, they will have access to the professional facilities that contribute to artistic and professional growth.

CHAPTER TEN

The Negro as Artist and in American Art

WHEN, near the close of the last century, a few American Negroes began to paint and to model, it was thought strange and unusually ambitious. By most people, including the Negroes themselves, it was also thought to be the Negroes' first attempt at art. Actually, late-nineteenth-century cultural provincialism was such that art was regarded as the ultimate expression of a civilized people. That Negroes should identify themselves with the creative arts was regarded as a pretension. The Western world had yet to learn that primitive civilizations had had not only artists, but also great art. The Western world had yet to learn, too, that of the many types of primitive art that of the Negro in Africa was one of the greatest and most sophisticated. Artistic tradition and skill in all the major craft arts run back for generations, even centuries, among the principal African tribes, particularly those of the West Coast and Equatorial Africa, from which Afro-Americans are descended. These arts are wood and metal sculpture, metal-forging, wood-carving, ivory- and bone-carving, weaving, pottery-making, and skillful surface decoration in line and color. In fact, everything in the category of the European fine arts except easel painting, marble sculpture, engraving, and etching (and even the techniques of engraving and etching are represented in the surface carving of much African art) was known to Africans. Actually, therefore, the pioneer Negro artists were unknown to their American descendants; starting the Negroes' second career in art, they were unconsciously recapturing a lost artistic heritage. Actually this was a "third career," for in Brazil there had been early Negro artists.

But how was this heritage lost? The answer explains much about Negro slavery. Slavery not only transplanted the Negro physically, but also cut him off decisively from his cultural roots. By taking away his languages, abruptly changing his habits, and putting him in a strangely different civilization, slavery reduced the Negro to what might be termed "cultural zero." No matter how divided one may be as to the relative values of human civilizations, no one can really believe that the African stood, after centuries of living and a long intertribal history, at a point of "cultural zero." One of the high developments in African civilization, as in all primitive cultures, was dexterity of hand and foot and co-ordination of eye and muscle. These abilities were useful in the development of elaborate native crafts, the traditions of which had been built up on generations of trial and error. These skills were lost in the horror of the slave ship, where families, castes, and tribes were ruthlessly disrupted. When slavery later substituted the crudest body labor, providing for it only the crudest tools, it finally stultified any impulse the Negro might have had for exerting technical skill or manual dexterity. Alexander Jacovleff, a Russian artist whose drawings of African types are classic, once commented that Africa is "a continent of beautiful bodies, but above all, of beautiful hands." There is a symbolic connotation in the observation: life in Africa required skill of hand and foot, almost perfect co-ordination of nerve and muscle, so that weapons could be thrown accurately and materials woven or tied accurately. Naturally, a people endowed with these capacities and skills was able to carve, trace, or scrape; the primitive artisan was also a primitive artist.

We will never know, and cannot estimate, how much technical African skill was blotted out in America. The hardships of cotton- and rice-field labor, the crudities of the hoe, the ax, and the plow, certainly reduced the typical Negro hand to a gnarled stump incapable of fine craftsmanship even if artistic incentives, materials, and patterns had been available. But we may believe that there was some memory of beauty; by way of compensation some obviously artistic urges flowed with the peasant Negro toward the only channels of expression left open—song, graceful movement, and poetic speech. Stripped of all else, the Negro's own body became his prime and only artistic instrument; dance, pantomime, and song were the compensation for his pent-up emotions. It was environment that forced American Negroes away from the craft arts and their old ancestral skills to the emotional arts of song and dance for which they are known and noted in America. When a few Negroes did achieve contact with the skilled crafts, their work showed the latent instinct of the artisan. In the early colonial days, for example, before plantation slavery had become dominant, Negro craftsmen were well known as cabinet-makers, marquetry-setters, wood-carvers, and iron-smiths, as the workmanship of many old mansions in Charleston, New Orleans, Savannah, and other centers of colonial wealth and luxury attest.

Even in surviving, the Negro's artistry was reversed; in Africa the dominant arts were sculpture, metal-working, and weaving. In America, the Negro's chief arts have been song, dance, music, and, considerably later, poetry. African art skills were technical, rigid, controlled, and disciplined; characteristic African art expression is, therefore, sober, heavily conventionalized, and restrained. The American African arts are freely emotional, exuberant, and sentimenal. The American Negro, for example, is credited with a "barbaric love of color," which, indeed, he frequently possesses. African arts, on the other hand, are in most instances very sober and subtle in the use of color. The notion of tropical extravagance about color is a myth that facts do not sustain: in typical African art formal decoration and design are much more important than color. What we have thought "primitive" in the American Negro (his naïve exuberance, spontaneity, sentimentalism) are not characteristically African, and cannot be explained as ancestral heritage. They seem to be the result of the American Negro's peculiar experience with emotional hardships. True, they are now characteristic traits, but they represent the Negro's acquired rather than his original artistic temperament.

The Negro artist in America had to make a new beginning; he has not yet recaptured his ancestral gifts or recovered his ancient skills. He must achieve this, of course, in the medium and manner of his adopted and acquired civilization and the modern techniques of painting, sculpture, and the craft arts. But when this development finally matures, it may be expected to reflect something of the original endowment, if not as a carry-over of instinct (which many insist is unlikely), at least as a result of the proud inspiration of the reconstructed past.

In the dislocating process of being transplanted from Africa to America, Negro art and the Negro artist were somehow separated; it was generations before they came together again. In the interval, African art was forgotten; Negro themes and subject matter were neglected by artists generally, and many Negro artists regarded "Negro Art" as ghetto restriction and fled from it in protest and indignation. Now African art is both recognized and prized. Gradually American artists have come to treat Negro subjects as something more than a passing subject of secondary interest. Negro types presented with dignity and understanding are now a major theme in the program for developing a "native American art." More important, a younger generation of Negro artists has taken as one of its main objectives and opportunities the interpretation of the Negro and the development of what is now called "Negro Art." For though the Negro as a vital part of the American scene is the common property of American artists, Negro and white, he is certainly the special and particular artistic asset of his own people.

If history texts were either lost or destroyed in their entirety, we could, in large measure, rewrite history from art. A keen and perceptive eye could tell from the way in which the Negro was artistically depicted what the eighteenth, nineteenth, and twentieth centuries thought of him—or, indeed, what it thought of any other class, race, or type. Any significant change or special attitude has always been reflected in the art of the period; actually art has sometimes registered the change before it has become generally apparent in the conventional attitudes of society. For example, we may reliably judge that for the seventeenth century, the Negro was an unfamiliar figure exciting curiosity and romantic interest. This is revealed first in the blackamoor figures of the Negro king among the three magi who went to Bethlehem with gold, myrrh, and frankincense; this romantic concept of the Negro continued into the eighteenth century, when most Negroes were shown as the attendants of noblemen, in fancy and elaborate dress, symbolic of their position as petted and prized possessions. Few portraits of the Empire and Pompadour periods were complete without the traditional figure of the black page or personal attendant elegantly dressed and obviously displayed as a pet. Nor can we forget the occasional black notable or scholar whose idealized portrait reflected the admiration and sentimental interest of the eighteenth century in the Negro. *Oronooko,* a novel cited earlier in a different context, is an example; Johnson's *Rasselas* is again a case in point. Men like Juan Latino, the Spanish Negro scholar; Capitein, the Dutch Negro theologian; and others down to Samuel Brown, the learned servant of Samuel Johnson, sat for the best painters and engravers of their day. From this tradition we have the occasional, but important, Negro figure portraits by Velázquez, Rembrandt, Rubens, Goya, Reynolds, and Hogarth.

The tradition carried over into early colonial America wherever the aristocratic tradition was strong. We see it unmistakably in the portrait of George Washington's family, where the dark-brown, elegantly groomed family "retainer," Lee, is a prominent figure in the group. In fact, there is scarcely a grotesque or carelessly painted Negro figure before the beginning of the nineteenth century, the moment of the

Negro's lapse into chattel slavery and plantation bondage. Then, for a time, the Negro disappeared from painting. When he made his reappearance, it was in the background as a clownish, grotesque object setting off the glory of his master or portraying the comic subject of the master's condescending amusement. The "old faithful uncle"—later literature's "Uncle Tom," "Uncle Ned," and "Uncle Remus"—and the broad, expansive Mammy, the inevitable literary Mammy, from "Aunt Chloe," to "Aunt Jemima," were initial stereotypes. No less conventional were the jigging plantation hands (invariably in tattered jeans) and the sprawling, grinning pickaninnies. Scarcely any nineteenth-century art show was without its genre portrait study of one or more of these types, or its realistically painted or sketched portrayal of "The Plantation Quarters," "Ole Virginia Life," or some equally glorified version of the slave system. The tradition was so strong that it lasted at least forty years after the nominal fall of slavery; it has been (and to some extent still is) one of the mainstays of the literary and artistic defenses of the "lost cause" of the Confederacy. One of the cleverest arguments, if not the cleverest, was this misrepresentation of the patriarchal regime of the Southern plantation. It was against this falsification that American art had to react in the latter decades of the nineteenth century, and it was this falsification that made the Negro artist, during all that period, dread and avoid Negro subjects.

Few were able to remember that Negro subjects had been treated with dignity and even with a romantic touch in the previous century; no one dared to resume the dignified or romantic interpretation in opposition to such strong and flourishing Nordic pride and prejudice. A Negro figure, decently dressed, not obviously a peasant or servant, and without reflection of inferior status, was a rarity; a book rather than a tray in a Negro hand would have been an intolerable heresy. (To many, it might be added, it still is.) Oddly enough, no Negro painters and sculptors realized that it was their duty and opportunity to challenge this hardening tradition and stereotype. For the most part they ignored Negro subjects entirely. Yet, in spite of the Negro artist's failure to attack the stereotype, it was undermined by white artists who, for artistic rather than social reasons, were pioneers in the cause of realism. So-called "Americanists" were developing a realistic art of native types, including a new and revolutionizing portrayal of the Negro subject. Some of them, like Winslow Homer, began with sketches of the exotic Negro in the West Indies. Others started with some bias toward the plantation school, but a bias tempered by the new concept of realism which demanded *true* type portraiture. Wayman Adams can be identified with this trend. Finally, with the great realists like Robert Henri and George Luks of early-twentieth-century fame, Negro types commanded the technical thoroughness of a major artistic problem. Eventually, portrayal of Negroes was to reflect the dignity and honesty of an entirely changed artistic approach and social attitude. George Bellows, John Curry, Julius Bloch, Thomas Benton, and other artists of the twentieth century have made the Negro a subject of major interest and have interpreted him in dignified, sympathetic, even spiritual terms.

The task of the early Negro artist was to prove to a skeptical world that the Negro *could* be an artist. That world did not know that the African had been a capable artist in his native culture and that, independent of European culture, he had built up his own techniques and traditions. It had the notion that for a Negro to aspire to the fine arts was ridiculous. Before 1885, any Negro man or woman with artistic talent and ambition confronted an almost impassable barrier. Yet, in a long period of trying apprenticeship, several Negro artists surmounted both the natural and the artificial obstacles with sufficient success to disprove, but not dispel, the prevailing prejudice.

The first Negro artists in America can never be known by name, but only by their craft work. They were the woodcarvers and cabinet-makers whose skillful work went into many colonial mansions of the handcraft period. The most authentic tracing of any considerable school of master Negro craftsmen has been in connection with the famous Negro blacksmiths of New Orleans, who furnished the hand-wrought iron grilles that ornamented the balconies and step-balustrades of the more pretentious homes. Interestingly enough, they were working with an orginal African skill without knowing it, for metal-forging is one of Africa's oldest and greatest arts. However, this was retaught the Negro in his new home, and the probable reason for his almost complete monopoly of the trade was his ability to endure the extreme heat.

There are two important reasons for mentioning these nameless craft artisans: their early craftsmanship proves the artistic capacity of the group to be broader than just an occasional flowering talent of formal art at the top level, and a sound art should have a handicraft basis. Also, the development of isolated "fine art" is not a profitable way of starting the artistic education of a group. When curves were beaten out free-hand, when ornament was improvised in a quick turn of mechanical skill, when the designs were wrought from memory instead of with blueprints and calipers, there was that original creative skill out of which the best art naturally and inevitably comes.

Of the first formal Negro painter of the colonial period we have only indirect evidence—Phillis Wheatley's poem, written before 1773, to "S. M." (Scipio Moorehead), "a young African painter on seeing his works." We have the testimony of her dedicatory poem that at that time there was this young man, evidently formally trained, who painted allegorical landscapes inspired by the classics. In her poem, Phillis Wheatley describes one as symbolic of dawn, *Aurora*. Another was based on the legend of Damon and Pythias—indication of literary awareness, though we shall never know of what degree of technical ability. Like Phillis Wheatley herself, Moorehead is simply early evidence of capacity in an age that regarded such talent on the part of the Negro as too exceptional to be a serious example.

Edward Bannister, of Providence, Rhode Island, was the first Negro in America to receive real recognition as a painter. He was also a pioneer in organizing artists. He founded the Providence Art Club, still that city's leading art organization. Bannister was not a great artist. His chief interest was in marine paintings and landscapes. One of the latter, *Under the Oaks*, was awarded a medal at the Centennial Exposition in Philadelphia in 1876. Because few Bannister canvases are left, the range of his work cannot be judged except from his high standing in the art circles of his day. The fact that he was a professional painter, with professional associations, is of significance and undoubtedly had much to do with clearing the way for subsequent recognition of Negro artists. As far as is known, Bannister painted no Negroes.

Edmonia Lewis, born of mixed Negro and Indian parentage in Boston in 1854, was, as far as we know, not only the first Negro woman artist, but the first Negro sculptor. She was introduced by William Lloyd Garrison to a sculptor whose work she admired, and by the time she was twenty she was modeling portrait busts of distinction. Her bust of Robert Gould Shaw, then famous as the colonel of the first Negro Civil War regiment, attracted favorable public and artistic notice. Later, under the patronage of the Story family of Boston, Edmonia Lewis was sent to Italy, where she studied and worked for years.

By 1876 she had mastered the hard technique of sculpture, and had executed many whole figures and figure groups. Among these were a *Death of Cleopatra*, *The Marriage of Hiawatha*, a *Madonna with the Infant*, and an emancipation group, still in the possession of the Glover family in Boston, called *Forever Free*. This last is not one of her best works, technically speaking, but has great sentimental interest. It shows a muscular, scantily clad Negro freedman greeting freedom with uplifted arm and clenched fist, half in confident defiance, half in doubt, as he shelters with his right arm the half-kneeling figure of his frail wife. Artistically, Miss Lewis's best works were her portrait busts of men like Charles Sumner, John Brown, Lincoln, Longfellow, and Story. It is known that Sumner and Story posed for the artist; the Sumner bust is probably the best example of her mature style.

Another interesting Negro art pioneer was Robert Duncanson of Cincinnati. He studied in Canada, England, and Scotland. His first important painting was an allegorical interpretation of Tennyson's "Lotus Eaters." In Glasgow and London, Duncanson exhibited with much success; Moncure Conway commented that he was one of the most popular personalities in the London art circles of the time and that he enjoyed the patronage of the Duchess of Sutherland, Lord Tennyson, and other distinguished Britishers. The *London Art Journal* in 1866 credited Duncanson with being one of the outstanding landscapists of his day. He was also, however, a good figure painter, known for his historical paintings illustrative of life in the American West. His versatility, for he was also a muralist, offset his lack of true originality. Some Duncanson titles suggest the wide range of interests the painter had: *Shylock and Jessica, The Ruins of Carthage, The Battleground of the River Raisin, The Western Hunters' Encampment*.

The period covered by these pioneers is obviously that of an apprenticeship. The artists were imitative and did not reflect any organized art movement among Negroes, yet the period marks the beginnings of the Negro artist's slowly developing career. After a few outstanding colonial painters, America at large had no great artists. No master painters came until 1870, with Whistler and Winslow Homer. So, while American art generally was in its journeyman period, Negro artists, in a rather advanced apprenticeship stage, were not too far behind. Holger Cahill says in *Art in America* that "up to the period of the Civil War European critics had considered American art no more than a tasteful résumé of certain European tendencies." In following European and cosmopolitan tradition, Negro artists were following the art trends of their time.

The apprenticeship period for Negro artists coincided almost exactly with the Reconstruction era, 1865–90. From

1890 until 1914, there was a period that we might call the journeyman period. The Negro artist won world-wide recognition and won his freedom in the world of art. The leading talent of this second period was Henry Tanner, whose career vindicated the Negro artist beyond doubt. Tanner's work was never evaluated by any double standard of artistic judgment. Born in Pittsburgh in 1859, son of a bishop of the African Methodist Church, Tanner was destined for the ministry. In spite of family opposition, he was determined to be an artist. He was able to study at the Pennsylvania Academy of Fine Arts, where the sound basis of his technique was laid by a group of master instructors, including Thomas Eakins and William Case. After graduation, unable to go to Europe as he had hoped, he went to Atlanta and taught for several years. His general surroundings were uncongenial and unsympathetic, and but for the patronage of one Bishop Hartzell and his wife, Tanner might never have become more than a mediocre teacher of art.

After a summer spent sketching folk types in the North Carolina mountains, Tanner, with the help of the Hartzells, had an exhibition of his works in Cincinnati. The showing was a failure, but the Hartzells, still undaunted, decided that Tanner should be encouraged to continue his studies overseas, and they raised the necessary funds. Tanner never went to Rome; in Paris he found what he wanted in the friendship and criticism of the famous French academician, Benjamin Constant. Afterwards he enrolled at the Julien Academy and put in five years of arduous study. At home, folk types had interested him; some of his early works, like *The Banjo Lesson,* showed a capacity that, had it developed, would have made Tanner the founder of a racial school of American Negro art. But in Paris he took up one interest after another: animal sketches, then landscapes, then peasant types, and finally Biblical subjects.

By 1896 Tanner had found an interest that made his fame, an interest that though apparently remote from racial associations, was spiritually close after all. In the Paris Salon of 1896 he received honorable mention for a religious painting, *Daniel in the Lions' Den,* a curious blend of realism in the figure drawings and mystical symbolism in other features. With the assistance of Rodman Wanamaker, Tanner went to Palestine, a trip that inspired the great Biblical series that established his fame. His *Resurrection of Lazarus* was purchased by the French government for the Luxembourg Gallery Collection; this painting was followed by *Christ on the Road to Bethamy, Christ at the Home of Mary and Martha* —particularly notable for its plain, human realism—and *Re-*

turn of the Holy Women. Tanner's paintings are in the Metropolitan Museum, the Carnegie Institute, the Pennsylvania Academy, the Chicago Art Institute, and the Los Angeles Art Gallery. Besides building up a solid reputation for Tanner, this recognition and his election to the National Academy established the fact that a Negro could be an artist.

Tragically, however, in spite of having won countless honors, Tanner was embittered by the sensational publicity about his race. This was understandable, but he should have known how inevitable such a reaction was. Except for occasional family and business visits, he rarely came to America in spite of its being an excellent market for his works. He developed more and more into a studio recluse even in Paris, painting, as time went on, with increasing technical interest. His later works were dry and academic. His masters, Thomas Eakins, Jean-Paul Laurens, and Benjamin Constant, were academicians to begin with, and the one thing that would have vitalized Tanner's art more than anything else would have been a new and experimental school of racial expression. The only direct art influence directed toward his own race was occasional advice and criticism given to a few young Negro painters who sought his help. To them he was always careful to explain that he was interested in them as painters, not as Negroes.

Two young Negroes who came under Tanner's influence were William Harper and William Scott. Each found Tanner ready with artistic advice and help. Each shows the Tanner influence in his style. Harper's premature death was regarded as tragic: many felt that he was well on the way to becoming a leading landscape painter. More than just a blind follower of the romantic school, he displayed a fine balance of composition, color, and light. Scott, under the influence of Tanner's carefully studied style, was both landscape painter and muralist. The broad style of mural painting is hard to combine with the smaller-scale technique of easel painting, and few but the old masters have been successful in achieving proficiency in both. All through Scott's later career the conflict of these styles affected his work, giving his easel paintings looseness of composition and undesirable flatness. Thus, this pioneer in the important field of mural painting and the more immediately profitable type of applied painting paid something of an artistic price until, after a period in the West Indies, he recovered some of the basic artistic skill. In a newer and tighter style he created some memorable tropical sketches of Haitian peasant types.

The next Negro artistic career of significance was that of a woman artist and sculptor. Sculpture has been strangely prominent in the work of Negro artists in spite of its technical difficulties and its expensive processes; curiously, too, the majority of Negro sculptors have been women. Meta Warrick Fuller's career as a sculptor was, next to Tanner's, the greatest vindicating example of the American Negro's conquest of the fine arts. She was graduated from the Pennsylvania School of Industrial Art in 1898 and then spent three years in Paris. Her diploma pieces, *The Medusa* and *Christ in Agony*, had already attracted favorable attention, but *The Wretched*, exhibited at the Paris Salon in 1903, stamped her as a sculptor of power and originality. This and other pieces drew the commendation of Auguste Rodin, a recognition peculiarly appropriate because she had absorbed a great deal from study of this master's strong, evolutionary style. Her work of this period was of the Rodin type in both form and subject. The modeling was strong, dynamic, and definitely symbolic. The themes, as the titles show, were tragic and philosophical. *Secret Sorrow, Death on the Wing, The Man Who Laughed, John the Baptist*, and a modern grouping of *The Fates* were outstanding.

In 1907, a commission for a series of commemorative figures illustrating the history of the Negro, for the Jamestown Tercentennial Exposition, turned her interest definitely to Negro types and a more realistic style. In 1909, the artist became the wife of a New England doctor and settled in Massachusetts. A year later, a fire destroyed most of the work of her Paris period. She did not resume work actively until another commission for a series of Negro historical groups for the New York Semi-Centennial of Emancipation. From that point on, a decided change of style was evident in her work: her subjects and moods became more placid and optimistic. *Mother and Child, Life in Quest for Peace, Watching for Dawn*, and *Immigrant in America* are characteristic subjects of this later period. The later works are pleasant to contemplate, but they lack the powerful originality of the earlier pieces. One of the most significant works shows a blend of the early seriousness and somberness and the later optimism. This is *Awakening of Ethiopia*, which is represented by a semi-Egyptian female figure emerging from a casing of enveloping bands like an awakening mummy.

Another woman, May Howard Jackson, was the first Negro artist to break away from academic cosmopolitanism and turn to frank and deliberate racialism. Always attracted by Negro types, their puzzling variety and their distinctive traits, Mrs. Jackson executed a number of portrait busts: Paul

Laurence Dunbar, Kelly Miller, W. E. B. Dubois, and Francis Grimké. Others of her subjects were social and symbolic. *The Mulatto Mother and Her Child* and *Head of a Child* were attempts to portray, respectively, the dilemma of the half-caste and the significance of a new, young, emerging composite humanity. This social concern was not sentimentality reflected nor overemphasized. When a school of Negro sculpture emerges, Mrs. Jackson's work will be seen in a new perspective as noteworthy pioneering. Full maturity and freedom of her talent were denied her because of the isolations imposed by Southern prejudice.

Shortly after the turn of the twentieth century, European artists began to discover African art. The results were destined to revolutionize European art itself and to bring about an entirely new cultural evaluation of Africa and the Negro. The spiritual discovery of Africa began with artists, and was caused by their discovery of the powerful originality and beauty of African art. It was known that Africans made curious things with odd shapes and strange, primitive purposes. Missionaries have saved a few, primarily to show the state of degradation and idolatry from which Christianity was trying to save the poor, benighted heathen. In Sunday schools a favorite hymn was "The heathen in his ignorance, bowed down to wood and stone," and what we prize and cherish as African art was the damning evidence. But by the turn of the century, twenty years after the great modern imperialistic penetration of the African interior, a scientific interest in things African had developed, and elaborate museum collections had been assembled in the capitals of the European powers. In the British Museum, the Trocadéro Museum in Paris, and particularly in German museums, collections were being scientifically and methodically acquired. At best, however, this was mere collecting and scientific curiosity.

Two somewhat later events served to open European eyes to the art values of African curios. In 1897, a British military expedition had sacked and burned the ancient tribal city of Benin in West Africa as punishment for tribal raids and resistance to colonial conquest. Although much was destroyed, cartloads of cast bronze and carved ivory from the temples and the palaces were carried to England and accidentally to the auction block. Discerning critics recognized the extraordinary workmanship in carving and casting, and saw that the bronze-casting had been done by an ancient process by which the finest bronze masterpieces have been made. Acting unofficially, a young curator of the Berlin Museum bought up nearly half of this art treasure and created a reputation and a career for himself. His auction bargain turned out to be the most prized and valuable collection of African art in existence, the Benin collection of the Berlin Ethnographic Museum. Duplicates were traded to form the basis of an equally famous collection at Vienna, and the young scholar, Felix von Luschan, with a four-volume folio publication on this art and its historical background, became the outstanding authority of his generation on primitive African art.

At about the same time a group of young painters and art critics in Paris came upon some fine specimens of native African fetish carvings from the French West Coast colonies, noted their fine finish and workmanship, and began to study them. Their interest was at first purely technical, but as they became more familiar with these odd objects, the representation of forms—human, animal, and abstract—was seen to be not a crude attempt at realism but a skillful reworking of forms in simplified abstractions and deliberately emphasized symbolisms. For example, an animal or human form would be purposely distorted to fit into an element of design as a decorative pattern, or the anatomy would be distorted to emphasize an idea or create an impression of terror, strength, ferocity, fertility, virility, or any idea or mood of which the object was a symbol. It was then realized that a difference of stylistic pattern had stood between non-Africans and the correct interpretation of this African art. It was seen, too, that the breaking-down of such conventional barriers was just as necessary for the appreciation of African art as it was for the understanding of the arts of the Orient, which had been similarly misunderstood until a generation before. As a result, a new Africa was discovered, the new continent of the black man's mind. With art as a key, the secrets of African civilization were soon to be released.

This discovery of the new values of African art came at a time when younger artists were restlessly searching for a new style and a new philosophy of art. European art had become sterile by generations of inbreeding; particularly was this true of sculpture. In painting, impressionism, the older-generation style, had about exhausted the possibilities of emphasis on color, and by a natural reaction, the problem of form and design was due for a new emphasis. Cubism, expressing the new emphasis on form and abstract design, was about to emerge. The young genius destined to lead the movement, the Spanish-born, Paris-trained Pablo Picasso, was dissatisfied with the trends in post-impressionist art. He met Paul Guillaume, an art collector, and Guillaume Apollinaire, an art critic, who were pioneers in the serious appreciation of African art or *"l'art nègre,"* as it was beginning to be called. What happened can best be told in the words of a member of the group:

> What formerly appeared meaningless took on meaning in the latest experimental strivings of plastic art. We came to the realization that hardly anywhere else had certain problems of form and certain technical ways of solving them presented themselves in greater clarity or success than in the art of the Negro. It then became apparent that previous judgments about the Negro and his arts characterized the critic more than the object of criticism. The new appreciation developed instantly a new passion; we began to collect Negro art as art, became passionately interested in corrective reappraisal of it, and made out of the old material a newly evaluated thing.

The "newly evaluated thing" was that much-discussed, much-misunderstood, but powerful "modernist art." Negro art is thus one of the great original ingredients of that radical change in style which characterizes modern art. Just as Negro musical forms have been the basis of much modernism in music, Negro or African art has been a powerful force in modernism in art.

The quick conversion of the young French artists to this new interest and point of view was an art revolution in the making. A rapid succession of styles and schools arose, one after the other: cubism, expressionism, futurism, and superrealism or surrealism. All have as a common denominator the employment of form for symbolism or design rather than for realistic representation. By 1925 modernism had triumphed over tradition. The new principles of unrealistic and abstractly conventionalized design swept not only the formal arts of painting and sculpture, but also the applied arts of architectural decoration, home decoration, furniture, and eventually dress. In time every "primitive" art from Africa, Polynesia, Mexico, or Peru was ransacked for designs and stylistic suggestions.

One may say that while it was the French painters who, generally speaking, pioneered in modernism, every other modern artist has in turn felt the influence and expressed it in his own characteristic way.

While European artists were discovering Negro art, American artists were rediscovering the Negro. Worse than having completely ignored him, the American art world had treated the Negro with a biased and condescending disdain. Whether in the foreground or the background of its canvas, the Negro was only a foil for the concept of white superiority. Alone, he was invariably cast as a semicomic type without the individuality or depth that could come only from a more serious and human attitude toward him on the part of the artist and of the public. It was this stereotyped view that long handicapped the development of any artistically worth-while or meaningful portraiture of the Negro. The ultimate change in concept is doubly interesting because such a change has social and cultural as well as merely artistic significance and influence.

One might have expected the moral sympathies of Abolition and Emancipation to have worked some profound change in the public mind with regard to the Negro. However, the attention drawn to his plight only accentuated his conventional status in that mind, which forgot the types and considerable groups of Negroes whose position was far from the common lot. Reconstruction literature and art prolonged unduly the values of slavery and the slave status. More "Uncles" and "Aunties" and "plantation darkies" appeared in literature and art in the years when they were actually disappearing than had appeared before Emancipation. The newer, more modern representative Negro types were seldom, if ever, presented in fiction, drama, or pictorial art.

A changed attitude eventually came, but not because of moral or reform interest. Primarily, a new technical interest prompted the change. It began with the outline of the plantation tradition and the peasant stereotype. A few artists wanted to make their Uncle Remuses something more than sketchy, generalized types. Slowly, the romantic type-sketch and the melodramatic genre or situation picture changed to a more serious study of character or local color. The same change occurred in the portrayal of the Indian, and realism is to be credited with the obvious advance and gain. An earlier generation thrilled to badly painted pictures of Indians on horseback, in which the horses, war feathers, tomahawks, blankets, and peace pipes had more character than the Indians. Similarly, in pictures of Negroes and Negro life, the bandannas, banjos, and any other paraphernalia thought typical took precedence over legitimacy of character portrayal. To a certain extent these stereotyped concepts persist even today. On the other hand, some of the old-fashioned academicians began to be ashamed of the artistic inadequacy and general falseness of their typical paintings. As an example of growth within the general context of the plantation tradition and the Southern attitude we can cite the change in a painter like Wayman Adams. At the beginning of his career, he depended on the "big porch" and the "quarters" theme in his portrayals of "the South." In later pictures like

At Church and *Foster Johnson and His Family*, he pictured Negro types and their "local color" in realistic, individual, and highly personalized fashion.

Winslow Homer (1836–1910) was in many respects the father of this realistic movement without intending to be. He was a skillful realist, fond of the sea, ships, and fishing. In sketches made in Florida, Bermuda, and the Bahamas, and later in all the Caribbean area, he included many native Negroes. As early as 1885, Homer had painted a Negro in a straw hat and white shirt sprawled on the deck of a dismantled sailboat drifting out to sea in a tropical squall, while a white-bellied shark swam hungrily about. This was the forerunner for his best-known painting, *The Gulf Stream*, which for years hung in the Metropolitan Museum as a landmark in American realistic painting. It had a great deal to do with breaking artistic stereotypes about the Negro. It broke the cotton-patch-and-back-porch tradition—not all at once, but by starting the change. There are many later—and better—Winslow Homer portrayals of Negroes: *Rum Kay, Bermuda, The Turtle Pound, After the Tornado*, and the more mature West Indian sketches. The fact is, however, that *The Gulf Stream* marks the artistic emancipation of the Negro as subject in American art.

Since Homer's innovation, the portrayal of Negro types by both black and white American artists has become a broadening and deepening phase of realism and localism in American painting and sculpture. The work and influence of Robert Henri (1865–1929) mark a still more deliberate achievement in realism. Most of the prominent "Americanists," especially after 1910, when the Henri group organized in New York to fight academic and cosmopolitan tendencies in art, portrayed the Negro, as well as other American "types," with honesty and with realism—each in the literal sense. George Bellows, Henri's pupil, continued by including Negroes frequently in his famous boxing and sporting paintings and lithographs. With increasing enthusiasm and emphasis in terms of the new realism, George Luks, Boardman Robinson, Thomas Benton, Henry McFee, and Winold Reiss pictured the Negro in their work. Later, James Chapin, Jules Pascin, Maurice Sterne, Eugene Speicher, John Steuart Curry, Reginald Marsh, Miguel Covarrubias, and Julius Bloch were to add what might be called another dimension to the portrayal of Negro character and life. Shortly, we shall describe the works of Negro artists in this new phase

Beyond a certain point the race of a painter or sculptor is not significant. What counts in the final analysis is the adequacy of the interpretation. However, the revolution in the attitude of the white American artist toward Negro themes and subjects is in certain respects highly significant because in the first place it rests upon some subtle and slowly changing social attitude; also, it reinforces the liberalization of public opinion in a powerful way; and finally, as long as the Negro theme is subordinated among white artists or is cultivated in only a derogatory way, a pardonable reaction tends to drive the Negro artist away from an otherwise natural interest in depicting the life of his own people.

Two talented and vigorous realists came directly after Henri: George Luks (1867–1933) and George Bellows (1882–1925), the latter a pupil of Henri. Both were deeply concerned with American types and American life in realistic, unsentimentalized terms. Both had a democratic disregard for social caste and so-called artistic convention. The daring that took Luks to the immigrant street urchins led him with consistency and logic to strong and appealing paintings of Negro types. These paintings had revolutionary influence. When a talented young Negro painter had been denied a foreign scholarship, Luks gave the young artist six hundred dollars of his own. His generosity encouraged the artistic development of the most daring of the early Negro modernists—William Johnson—who, though born in Florence, South Carolina, lived both in southern France and in Denmark. The unconventionality that prompted George Bellows to re-create bar-room and prize-ring scenes in his paintings, prompted him, too, to treat the Negro. Completely dismissing the plantation tradition, Bellows disdained to paint Uncle Remuses, Aunt Chloes, Jemimas, or pickaninnies; for him Negroes were individuals. If certain Negroes lacked dignity, it was because they, like other humans, were subject to human and personal failings; their lacks were human, not racial. His consistent purpose was the portrayal of personality and a reflection of fidelity to fact. He thereby repudiated the double standard, as did all consistent and conscientious realists. More than adhering to realism in its most limited or narrow sense, Bellows carried his philosophy through to social criticism and propagandistic protest, as in two graphic indictments of lynching: *The Law Is Too Slow* and *Benediction in Georgia*.

For a later artist like Thomas Benton, Negro subjects were more than part of the search for local American color; they were spiritually representative of elements in American civilization as a whole. Benton's major concern was historical murals, though he executed many fine easel paintings. His ambition after 1924 was to paint "the epic of America." In 1925, he did a startling mural in oil entitled *The Slaves;* for all its broad, sculpturelike treatment, it says vital things about slavery never before revealed on a portrait canvas. In a single figure, one of Benton's finest works is his *Negro Boy,* chosen for the Wanamaker Prize purchase in the 1934 show of American regional art. In group figures his best work is the series depicting American life done for the murals of the Whitney Museum in New York. The significance of this work is basically national, but it has a revolutionary racial significance in that the Negro appears as an integral part of American activity with full justice accorded to his share and relative position. Benton clearly observed American life with an unprejudiced and eclectic eye; as he himself once said: "I know what camp meetings are and political rallies of the backwoods, barbecues, school house dances (with the jug in the bush)." Here obviously we have common factors of American life: the white and black peasant instead of the traditional white aristocrat and black slave.

Another pioneer of the same order was Winold Reiss. His influence exerted itself particularly upon Negro artists and Negro opinion because he was selected, in 1925, to illustrate the Harlem number of the *Survey Graphic* and subsequently *The New Negro,* which stemmed from the article. The few competent Negro artists at the time were, in the main, victims of the academy. Further, in defensive reaction to white color-prejudice they either avoided Negro types or endowed them with white characteristics in order to offset what they regarded as a prevailing overemphasis on racial traits. Actually, they frequently shared the blindness of whites who saw little or no beauty where there was real beauty of an unfamiliar kind. It was an attitude something like that of the "official Germans" of the thirties, who stressed "Aryan" blondes and ignored Aryan brunettes.

Because he was a folk painter of skill and experience and had served an apprenticeship as a portraitist of several other racial types—Norwegians, Lapps, Mexicans, Sioux—Reiss was chosen to depict the whole interesting gamut of Negro types. Artistically, the series was a great and effective revelation, not only of the range, but also of the expressiveness of Negro types. Some younger Negro artists followed the bold lead. The young Western art teacher Aaron Douglas, who went to New York to become a professional painter, and who was an exponent of "Negro Art," is a particularly important example.

In spite of the fact that the series did a great deal to create a considerable appreciation of the Negro subject and helped dissipate color prejudice in the minds of both white and Negro Americans, there were adverse reactions, particularly in "cultured" Negro circles. The Reiss drawings and their motivating creed drew the indignation of the conservatives. This reaction, all too prevalent, reconfirmed an old thesis that art, instead of mirroring what we see, teaches us what to see. True, it is hard to discover beauty in the familiar, but one phase of modern art has taught us to do just that. It was however, doubly hard with the Negro types which in America had the combined handicap of familiarity and social contempt.

Reiss began with the young poets, writers, artists, and scholars of the Negro Renaissance, but eventually did another revealing series of Southern types off the Carolina coast. The two series are among the most thorough and extensive realistic portrayals of the American Negro. In each series care was taken to treat the whole range of class and color, from the artist and the professional man to the peasant, from the quadroon and the "high yellow" to the pure black.

Other artists carried either technical or social interpretation farther. Three combined a double interest in the Negro theme. Henry McFee was one, with some powerful subject portraits; his *Negro Girl*, especially, reveals a magnificent technical ability. Eugene Speicher's admirably painted *Tennessee Negro* and Jules Pascin's *Negro Family* and *Charleston Crowd* are powerful. Extremely interesting painting in the early thirties was inspired by social themes and created by James Chapin, John Curry, Peggy Bacon, and Paul Travis, who treated the Negro in various ways, but with an interpretative power unknown to the earlier American painter. Sculptors like Jacob Epstein, Mahonri Young, Malvina Hoffman, Harold Cash, and Maurice Glickman were doing the same. After having been limited for generations to a tedious repetition of slave subjects, fugitive or suppliant, rising from chains, sculptors welcomed the realistic interpretation of the Negro.

In roughly twenty years the Negro as subject matured in art in America. Oddly enough, Negro art has come into its own by the very development most vital in contemporary American art, namely the desire to build an art free from European influences and imitation, and to root American art in the materials and themes of the native scene. We must remember that at the time the American scene was as unpopular with American artists as the Negro subject was both with him and with the academic-minded Negro artist. After a long period of disrepute Negro art has come of age as part of a vigorous over-all movement in American art.

Since the twenties, the Negro and his art have been recognized and the Negro artist has been acknowledged. No one would be foolish enough to want to restrict the Negro artist to painting racial subjects or to being merely an exponent of Negro art. Yet, as late at 1928, when the Harmon Foundation offered prizes in art to Negro artists, many artists thought color or racial chauvinism was either the motive or would be the result. But the first Harmon Award (1926) went to Palmer Hayden for *The Schooners,* a marine painting. In 1927, the award went to Laura Wheeler Waring for her portrait of a kind-faced, dignified, middle-aged Negress, entitled *Ann Washington Derrick*. The criterion was, and continued to be, good art, regardless of the subject. In the 1927 exhibition, Hale Woodruff, now a leading Negro painter, had canvases from Paris of *St.-Serven,* the *Pont Neuf,* and the *Quai de Montebello,* and Albert Smith had landscape and figure paintings from southern France and Spain. But some still thought that promoting the Negro artist involved developing Negro art as well, and that the Negro had as much to gain as the American artist in general by "coming home" spiritually. It was recalled that within a short span of time the white American artist had "come home" after generations of cosmopolitan exile, both physical and spiritual, to develop a native American art.

Prejudice made the Negro half-ashamed of himself; racial subjects were, until the early thirties, avoided or treated warily; the full race theme seldom was utilized prior to this time. As long as the Negro artist was tentative on the matter, his expression was certain to be weak and apologetic or self-conscious and falsely sophisticated. It is of great significance that a conversion in attitude seems to have occurred primarily on artistic and technical, rather than on sentimental or propagandistic, grounds. A real and vital racialism in art is a sign of objectivity and independence and gives evidence of emancipation from timidity and imitativeness. In fact, except for closer psychological contact and understanding, the relation of the Negro artist to racial subject matter is not so very different from that of his white fellow artist to the same material. To both it is important local color, racial to the one, national to the other.

After World War I, the reaction against cosmopolitan and academic tendencies in American painting which had been reflected in the works of the New York "Group of Eight" just before the War reasserted itself. The insight and daring that led Robert Henri, George Luks, and George Bellows to the new subjects of city and immigrant types and to social-document scenes also led them, with consistent logic, to do a few strong and well-observed Negro types. For the times, this was revolutionary. At this time, too, James Chapin pioneered in exploring the deeper traits of Negro subjects, while Julius Bloch portrayed unconventional and little-known aspects of Negro life and character. In the late twenties, a group of younger realists took up the Negro theme with increasing emphasis, giving their Negro subjects the added background of folk portraiture. This group brought a seasoned technique and a newly liberalized social insight to Negro type portrayal. It included Henry McFee, Maurice Sterne, Miguel Covarrubias, and Eugene Speicher.

Younger American regionalists at the time increasingly included Negro materials, revealing them dramatically as unique and typical American subject matter. Great advantages of this were the alliance of racial and local idioms and the emphasizing of common human denominators. Thomas Benton, John Steuart Curry, Anne Goldthwaite, Boardman Robinson, and Lamar Dodd added to this new understanding, despite a variety of style and outlook. Strong emphasis on the Southern folk scene still prevailed, but what a vastly different scene it is as seen through the eyes of those new regional realists! There was no perpetuation of the sentimental fictions about the Old South; there was little, if any, covering up of the social facts—even such unpleasant ones as lynching and sharecropper poverty and disillusionment. The double standard of human values was rapidly collapsing.

Negro artists from the mid-twenties on also broke with tradition in both subject and style. Artists like Aaron Douglas, Palmer Hayden, Albert Smith, Sargent Johnson, Richmond Barthé, Hale Woodruff resisted the traditionalist successfully. By the mid-thirties, a vigorous, intimate, and original documentation of Negro life was definitely under way. Fortunately, this movement did not lead the Negro artist, as had sometimes been feared, into exclusively racial art; on the contrary, it led him into the main stream of contemporary American art, as the immediately foregoing discussion has indicated. Permanently removed was the notion of the Negro as the restricted province to which the Negro might be expected to confine his artistic effort. The Negro artist was challenged to the task of self-revelation, but in a highly competitive way. The young Negro artists of the late twenties and thirties plunged into the substance of Negro life and experience and caught its characteristic idioms far more deftly than their predecessors had. The manifestly increased strength and vigor they displayed had, of course, the background of superior training and experience.. Also, we must take into account the fact that spiritual impetus must have been derived from the new conception of American culture as vitally and necessarily including the materials of Negro life.

The Negro artist was still, however, limited in terms of public support and recognition. Between 1928 and 1933, the Harmon Foundation, with five successful exhibits of the work of Negro artists, focused public and professional attention on the accomplishments and needs of Negro artists. When the Depression started, the work of the Negro artist was just beginning to receive recognition in terms of wider access to professional galleries and exhibitions. The generous inclusion of the creative Negro artist in the Federal Art Projects saved him and was largely responsible for the many young artists who did such strikingly successful work in the thirties.

Notably individual, but developed out of the academy tradition, is Aaron Douglas, also a pioneer Africanist. A student of Winold Reiss, whose work strongly influenced him, Douglas received, in an earlier period, numerous commissions to do book illustrations on Negro subjects and themes. This reinforced his desire to interpret Negro form and spirit. In turning successfully to a modernized version of African patterns, Douglas took his place beside Covarrubias as an outstanding exponent of Negro types and design-motives. He has done large-scale murals, usually on Negro or African subjects. In his easel work Douglas reflects an academic style. James A. Porter said of the easel paintings: "Douglas seldom places the Negro in a normal and plausible domestic life except in his easel paintings."

Archibald Motley is known for a severe, realistic style, as such early titles as *The Octoroon* and *Old Snuff Dipper* suggest. Later trends were to the fantastic compositions of African tribal and voodoo ceremonial, the use of lurid color schemes, and an emphasis on the grotesque.

Extreme modernists of the thirties are painters like William H. Johnson, Hale Woodruff, M. Gray Johnson, and Lesesne Wells. Diverse as their temperaments are, they show certain common features. First of all, there is the strong influence of modernism or abstract art; that is, art with emphasis on generalized forms rather than on pictorial realism or photographic detail. This mode had dominated younger American artists for at least ten years through the influence on European art of African art. Thus, an African influence twice removed acted on the Negro modernistic painters and sculptors; in being modernist, they were indirectly being African. In the second place, there was the more direct influence of the increasing popularity of the Negro theme and subject in art, with emphasis on an effort to interpret not only Negro form, but also Negro spirit.

Hale Woodruff, a modernist who acquired his techniques in France, for the most part painted landscapes and abstract formal compositions. In spite of the formalism, his color and color harmonies have a daring warmth. He has done a series of Georgia scenes in oils and black-and-white which are rich in local color and ironic observation. Extensive mural work for schools and a P.W.A. project won him praise from art critics.

Woodruff has been a ceaseless technical experimenter. Still life, landscapes, and portrait studies, in a rapid change of styles, have characterized his career. First, there was a rather luxuriant period of autumnal scenes and colors; then there were broadly drawn Negro types like *The Banjo Player* and *Washday*. After that, French landscapes in the then prevailing modernist mood; then formalistic still life; then a return to native themes: Georgia landscape like *Summer Landscapes, Autumn in Georgia,* or *Tree Forms*.

M. Gray Johnson, before his untimely death in 1934, made a substantial contribution to Negro art. James A. Porter, a fellow artist, credits him with having been "a restless experimentalist, changing styles feverishly and racing from one art creed to another, first impressionism, then cubism, then a style more directly influenced by African idioms, finally a painting of folk types and Virginia landscapes with a combination of sardonic humor and mystical pathos." Johnson's Brightwood, Virginia paintings and water colors, which he turned out rapidly just before his death, are among the most significant commentaries on the American Negro scene. There is a Southern landscape series, full of color and vivid Southern local atmosphere; there is a gallery of peasant types, and a series of swiftly executed activity scenes in water color. Johnson's death just as he was approaching maturity and had within his grasp the technical means of expressing his earlier concept of "folk soul" interpretations was a great loss.

James Wells has been not only a successful modernist painter, but also a successful pioneer of modernist methods of teaching art to children and to college students. He is primarily interested in design and composition. As a black-and-white artist in woodblock, etching, and lithograph, he has an outstanding reputation. Wells is also a painter. Several of his canvases have been purchased by and exhibited in the Phillips Gallery, Washington, D.C. This is a distinct tribute in itself, as the Gallery has one of the most authoritatively chosen collections of modernist art in the country. But while many of his paintings are ultra-modern in composition and color, they also have an unusual mystical quality: *The Wanderers,* as an example, reveals a Negro theme to some. Wells himself has said of this painting that he attempted to express "not in that sensational gusto so very often typified as Negroid, but as that which possesses the quality of serenity, has sentiment, without sentimentality and rhythmic flow of lines and tones in pure and simple forms."

Augusta Savage works in sculpture, wood-carving, modeling, painting, and applied design. She has a deep interest in Negro types, but her conceptions are often beyond her technical control. However, her *African Savage* and *Tom Tom* stimulated popular interest in primitive African types and had a constructive effect on younger artists. An effective teacher, Miss Savage developed several younger talents, including the young sculptor William Artis.

Judged by both awards and creative output, Sargent Johnson and Richmond Barthé have been the two outstanding Negro sculptors. Johnson's *Sammy,* his black porcelain bust of a Negro child, showed him committed in 1928 to a strongly simplified style. His work grew in simplicity and heavy stylizing until he was recognized as reflecting more than any other Negro sculptor the modernist mode and the African influence. His most representative work is in American Negro types, despite his excursions in other areas.

Richmond Barthé has shown particular preoccupation with the full-figure and, on occasion, group-figure compositions. He is very much disposed to do racial themes, in a less abstract, less modernistic style. Yet he is far from academic classicism or old-fashioned realism. His work includes portrait busts of distinction as well as *Mask of Black Boy, Filipino Head, The Blackberry Woman, West Indian Girl,* and African tribal types. Then comes his larger-figure work like *Torso of an Adolescent* and *African Dancer,* a full-figure study of Rose McClendon in the role of Serena in *Porgy*.

An artist, writer, and art critic who has represented a high level of achievement in various fields since the twenties is James A. Porter, head of the Department of Art at Howard University. Porter's major works include portraits and still life as well as murals. One portrait, *Sarah,* won him an honorable mention in the 1928 Harmon Exhibition; a second, *Woman Holding a Jug,* won the Arthur Schomburg Portrait Prize in 1933. Porter's numerous showings in interracial exhibitions, as well as his one-man shows, have, like his publications, done a great deal to gain more recognition for other Negro artists. He has traveled extensively, particularly in Cuba and Haiti, and is thoroughly familiar with the painting and sculpture of the two islands. In a concluding chapter of his *Modern Negro Art,* "The New Horizons of Painting," Porter refers to newer talents and includes Lois Mailou Jones, who, he says, paints "in the tradition, but not in imitation, of Cézanne," as well as Romare Bearden, Norman Lewis, Ronald Joseph, and Ernest Crichlow.

In April 1955 a Symposium was held at Howard University

in memory of Alain Locke. Numerous papers were read, including one by James Porter entitled "The Negro in Modern Art." After observing that "at least four Negro artists . . . are now well on the way to achieving . . . stature," he continues:[1]

> Three of them, Sargent Johnson, Jacob Lawrence and Eldzier Cortor, I have already mentioned. The fourth, a youngster, is one of the most versatile of the young artists. His work in many different media bears the consistency and delivers the impact of most serious and constructive realism.

Hughie Lee-Smith, to whom Porter referred, had an exhibition of his paintings at Howard University in November 1955. A young artist, Lee-Smith has won wide acclaim from art critics and from his peers. E. P. Richardson, Director of the Detroit Institute of Arts, comments, in the foreword to the Howard brochure:

> His recent development as an artist has . . . been in Detroit, a city now in full flux of transition, both inwardly and outwardly, on the strong tides of our century. . . .
>
> One of his themes is the city in transition. Old buildings, silent and tenantless, yet alive in the evening light, stand brooding among the devastations and chaos of change. The old city's day is past: but as yet one cannot discern the shape of the new. This city of ours is both troubling and beautiful in its sadness, both desolate and touched with hope.

Perhaps the art of Hughie Lee-Smith symbolizes the ultimate objective of Negro artists. For we must not expect the work of the Negro artist to be too different from that of his fellow artists. Product of the same social and cultural soil, the Negro's art has an equal right and obligation to be typically American at the same time that it strives to be typical and representative of the Negro. Ultimately the American Negro must make as distinct a contribution to the visual arts as he has made to music.

---

[1] Porter's earlier reference was this: "As the formal influence of African art declines, one still notices its effects in the work of numerous young Negro artists who annually offer their work in public exhibition. One sees it also in their blending of its idiom with effects distilled from expressionist abstraction. I have followed its course in the recent sculpture of Selma Burke, who even more recently has been chastening her art in the ever-burning fires of Renaissance classicism. Racial traditionalism and primitivism burn with even brighter flame in the abstractions of Romare Bearden, in the neo-Ethiopian symbolism of William H. Johnson, and in the occasionally retrospective forms of Richard Dempsey and Eldzier Cortor."

CHAPTER ELEVEN

Regional Nationalism in American Culture

UNTIL World War I the Negro and the "Negro problem" were regarded, for a number of reasons, as the exclusive burden of the South. The first and most obvious reason was the heavy concentration of Negroes in the South. At the close of the Civil War nearly four million Negroes lived there. Today, in spite of continuing migrations, one third of the South's population is Negro. A second reason is that in spite of the Civil War amendments and the civil-rights statutes designed to insure their being enforced, the 1880's witnessed a decline of concern by the Northerners over the enforcement of the very measures they had earlier obtained and supported. In 1875, for example, Congress adopted a statute declaring that:

> All persons within the jurisdiction of the United States shall be entitled to the full and equal enjoyment of the accommodations, advantages, facilities, and privileges of inns, public conveyances on land and water, theaters, and other places of public amusement; subject only to the conditions and limitations established by law, and applicable alike to citizens of every race and color, regardless of any previous condition or servitude.

But by 1883 the Supreme Court had ruled the statute unconstitutional, and in 1896 the famous Plessy-Ferguson Decision was handed down—the Decision that gave legal sanction to discrimination and segregation by virtue of its "separate but equal" doctrine. These two cases did three things: they opened the door for state laws to enforce segregation; they perpetuated what Justice Harlan (who dissented from both decisions) called "the badge of slavery"; and they established the first link in a long chain of legal cases which, combined with social and political changes, culminated in the Supreme Court Decision of May 17, 1954. When these cases were decided, the status of the Negro in the South had declined to something only slightly better than slavery. The Yankee, as W. J. Cash observed, "was finally giving over his long struggle actively to coerce the South." To quote Cash more fully:

> In part this was due, no doubt, to simple ennui with an endless protracting task. In part, too, it was due to the enthusiastic participation of the South in the Spanish-American War. But perhaps it was due above all to Progress. For if the adoption of the latter did not in reality mean that the South had decided to yield its ancient identity and become merely another Yankeedom, the Yankee nevertheless from the first assumed he did.

Cash makes it clear that there was "no arrival of any millennium," but that there was increasing sympathy by Northerners for Southerners, and that after 1900, when "the South . . . was making bold to nullify the Fourteenth Amendment and formally disfranchise the Negro, Henry Cabot Lodge would shrill practically alone on the floor of the Senate regarding the pressing need of sending down bayonets upon the land again—and to galleries that only grinned."

That slavery had been the foundation upon which antebellum society had rested and that it had been a moral as well as an economic and political factor in the war that had so drastically obliterated the South's entire social and economic culture—these facts served to localize the Negro, in the minds of most people, in the South. Reconstruction, with all its problems, was faced with none so severe as that of reconciliation to the fact that four million individuals (each of whom in the recent past had been politically equated as three fifths of a white man, and who, in the eyes of the law, had possessed no rights that a white man was bound to respect) had to be fitted somehow into the pattern of Southern life as citizens rather than as slaves. One sociologist, Charles Johnson, has observed rightly that actually there had been no "Negro problem" until after the Civil War; before it Negroes had been mere chattels. Thus, the infinite problems entailed by freedom—education, employment, the vote, regularized marriage, even the acquisition of a surname commanded the attention of both Northerners and Southerners.

In 1865, Congress had created a Freedmen's Bureau designed to assist the Negro to rehabilitate himself; Southerners, at the same time, in an attempt to curtail the social privileges of the recently freed Negroes, replaced the slave codes with the so-called Black Codes. The Freedmen's Bureau was dissolved in 1872; the Black Codes were never put into effect. Both, however, dramatized not only the sharply divergent attitudes entertained by Northerners eager to accord the Negro equitable treatment, and by Southerners no less eager to keep the Negro socially oppressed, but also the fact that the Negro was indeed the South's problem. Each phase of Reconstruction, most notably the decade of so-called Black Reconstruction, subjected the Constitution (and thus the Federal Government) to what Morison and Commager term an unprecedented "severe or prolonged strain." They cite the "knotty problems concerning the legal character of the War, the legal status of the seceded states after Appomattox, and the status of persons who had participated in the rebellion." Of equal challenge and perplexity was the question as to whether Congress or the President should be responsible for the practical directing or administering of Reconstruction plans. The eventual restoration of white supremacy, though it might have been predicated upon the conceded unconstitutionality of much Reconstruction legislation, was more definitely a reaction against Radical Republicans, both Northern "carpetbaggers" and Southern "scalawags" who encouraged and supported the active participation of Negroes in Southern politics. Morison and Commager say:

> Inevitably the excesses of black reconstruction aroused organized and determined opposition throughout the South. This opposition took both legal and illegal forms. In some states in which the whites were in a preponderant majority . . . the Democrats were able to recapture control of their states by regular political methods. Elsewhere, however, it was thought necessary to resort to methods that were frankly terroristic. Adopting the technique of the Radicals who had organized the Negro vote, white Southerners played upon the blacks' timidity and superstition, and made life miserable for the carpetbaggers. The latter, for instance, were apt to find themselves bystanders in a shooting affray, accidental targets for the bullets of participants. The Negroes were dealt with largely by secret societies.

The secret societies include the infamous Ku Klux Klan, whose objective was to terrorize, subdue, and control Negroes by intimidations and threats, as well as by actual physical violence. The Radical Republicans made what proved to be futile attempts to hold their ground, but time was running out, and, as we have noted, by the end of the century, the South had settled into a pattern of white supremacy and Negro oppression which was to remain more or less inexorable until World War I and its aftermath.

Because of the long tradition of the South's unrelenting preoccupation with the Negro—as a slave, as a freedman, and thereafter as an economic threat, a social menace, and a racial pariah—the South's fiction and art were dominated from their beginnings by the racial theme. Southern antebellum literature was strongly defensive of the Southern way of life, of the plantation tradition, and of the Southerner's justification of slavery—a contrived justification, to be sure, but one that white, Christian, democratic-minded Southerners forced themselves to accept and believe. But because of the defensive undertones of ante-bellum literature and the frankly, and often bitterly expressed apologistic literature of the post-bellum years, Southern literature in itself almost never rose above the regional or propagandistic level.

On the other hand, the fact that the Negro figures prominently in the literature, and that the Negro himself had made substantial contributions to regional culture in music, dance, and folklore, means that what culture the Old South might claim is in large measure indebted to the Negro's presence in a society that underwent successive social and political and, indeed, moral upheavals primarily *because* of his presence. The growing articulateness of the Negro in the South, his struggle for identification, his increasing triumph over illiteracy, and his rapidly developing determination to demand and be accorded full rights as a citizen—these forces drove Southern writers in the early twentieth century to further excesses of self-justification for continuing their pattern of racial segregation and discrimination. The results were the same: the literature failed to achieve either universality or permanance; the Negro, as the chief theme (or target), again was the only topic to inspire creative writing.

The World War I years and those which followed saw a change not only in the tone and quality of Southern literature but also in the Negro's impact on the national culture. Neither the change in Southern literature nor the expansion of Negro influence was an isolated phenomenon. There was a new temper in American literature and art, and migrants were exerting a powerful social and economic impact on the communities to which they went and on the communities they left. Over three million people left the South, for example, between 1900 and 1930; 500,000 Negroes alone moved from the South to the North between 1915 and 1918; in the early twenties another half-million moved northward. Between

1910 and 1930 the Negro population of the North jumped from 1,027,674 to 2,409,219.

These great migrations projected the Negro into the main stream of American life and culture. Because the chief migratory trend was northward to great centers of industry, the Negro's problems of adjustment were practical and local rather than exclusively racial. True, the fact that Southern whites, too, had moved to the North and to the West and had settled in big industrial centers meant that newly developed racial prejudice in these areas (a prejudice engendered by competition for employment, housing, and general public facilities) was intensified by the deep-rooted prejudices the white migrants brought with them. Yet in spite of fierce competition, ghetto housing, and usually the least desirable employment, Southern Negroes obviously preferred not to return to the South. Much of the struggle was an integral part of the larger industrial and social problem of modern living. In the twenties, also, there was the growing awareness on the part of people of sensibility that it was impossible to make generalized statements about Negroes en masse in terms of "personality," "characteristics," or "adjustment to the city."

As the Negro was being transplanted, he was also being transformed. The tide of Negro migration northward and cityward during this period cannot be explained as a blind, purposeless movement prompted by the demands of war industry, the curtailing of foreign migration, the pressure of poor crops, or the increased social terrorism in certain sections of the South and Southwest. Not labor demand, the boll weevil, or the Ku Klux Klan was a basic factor, though each was a contributing factor. A more valid explanation is that Southern Negroes, nearly two generations removed from Emancipation, had acquired enough education and social awareness to begin resenting and resisting the social sanctions exerted against them in the South. Prompted by a new vision of opportunity, by the hope of attaining social and economic freedom, by the frank gamble, in the face of heavy tolls, for an improved life and living, they moved out of the South. With each successive wave of migration, the movement of the Negro more and more paralleled the larger, the more universal, the more truly democratic pattern of aspiration for progress and change. More explicitly, the Negro was coming of age; he was repudiating the feudalism of the South, a pattern that kept him in a static role. With a courage and optimism reminiscent of frontier ideology, he was pitting himself against the city and modern, not medieval, life.

New York's Harlem is the classic example of the ultra-sophisticated urban center to which rural Negroes flocked in the twenties. The largest Negro community in the world, Harlem had the first concentration in American history of innumerable and diverse elements of Negro life. It attracted the African, the West Indian, the Negro American. It attracted the Negro of the South, who there met the Negro of the North for the first time. It brought together the man from the city and the man from the town and village, the peasant, student, businessman, professional man, artist, poet, musician, adventurer, worker, preacher, criminal, exploiter, and the social outcast. All groups came with their own motives and for their own special ends, but their greatest experience was discovering each other. Proscription and prejudice—even in the great metropolis—threw them into contact. Manhattan and Harlem were vastly superior to Southern rural areas, but not quite the "heaven" the North had been reputed to be. The mass influx of Negroes to Manhattan created the same problems and tensions that developed in Chicago and Detroit: the traditional tensions bred of too few jobs and too little housing for too many people, chiefly unfamiliar and racially "different" newcomers. Within Harlem, race sympathy and unity determined a fusing of sentiment and experience among people who, at the outset, might well have regarded their enforced association as the result of color-segregation. Actually, their association came to symbolize what might be termed a race welding. In the past, American Negroes had been a race more in name than in fact, in terms more of sentiment rather than of experience. The chief bond among them had been a condition rather than a consciousness—a problem in common rather than a life in common. In Harlem, Negro life seized upon its first chance for group expression and self-determination. Like other nascent centers of folk expression and self-determination which played a creative part in the world at the same time, Harlem, with no pretense to the political significance enjoyed by Dublin in the new Ireland or Prague in the new Czechoslovakia, played an important role for the new Negro.

Harlem was not typical, but it was significant. No one appraising the intellectual stirrings of the early twenties could possibly have said then, or say now, that the great masses of Negroes were articulate. But they were more than physically restless. The challenge of the new intellectuals among them was clear enough then and now. The race radicals and realists broke with the old philanthropic guidance, sentimental appeal, and lachrymose protest. The migrating peasant, the "man farthest down," was the most active in getting up. One of the characteristic examples of this was the professional man who migrated to recapture his followers after a vain effort to maintain in some Southern corner what for years before had seemed an established living and following. The clergyman who followed his erstwhile flock, the physician or lawyer who trailed his clients—these supplied the clues. The rank and file led; the leaders followed. A transformed and transforming psychology permeated the masses of Negroes.

When the racial leaders at the turn of the century spoke of developing race-pride, of stimulating race-consciousness, and of achieving race-solidarity, they could not have anticipated the feeling that surged up among urban Negroes of the early twenties and increasingly thereafter. Older, recognized Negro leaders and a powerful section of white opinion identified with "race work" attempted to discount the new feeling as a "passing phase," an "aftermath of the War." But it persisted; both the tone of the Negro press and the shift in popular support from the officially recognized and orthodox spokesmen to those of the independent, popular, and often radical type, unmistakable representatives of the new order, testified to it. Negroes in the Northern centers reached a stage at which tutelage, even of the best-intentioned sort, had to yield to new relationships and positive self-direction had to be reckoned in increasing measure. The American mind had to accommodate itself to a fundamentally different idea of the Negro.

The Negro, too, had to accommodate himself to a separation from the "idols of the tribe." On the one hand, the white man erred in making the Negro appear to be what would excuse or extenuate bad treatment of him; on the other hand, the Negro too often excused himself unnecessarily because of the way he had been treated. Increasingly the Negro resolved not to make discrimination an excuse for his shortcomings in either individual or collective performance. He tried to maintain a normal balance, neither bolstered by sentimental allowances nor discouraged by social discounts. To do this, he had to know himself well, exactly as he was, and to strive to be known and accepted as he was. The new scientific interest that was the intellectual basis for both realism and naturalism appealed to him as a welcome substitute for the romanticism that had bred a sentimental interest in the Negro as an exotic, as one who was martyred, or as brute "type," patronized, pitied, or excoriated.

More intelligent awareness of the Negro did not insure his being better liked or even better treated. But mutual understanding is, and always has been, undeniably basic for any ultimate co-operation or adjustment between opposing or differing forces. Increasingly, through the years, Negroes and whites have become more intelligently aware of each other as people; nothing could be more salutary for interpersonal and intercultural relationships. In the intellectual realm the Negro was studied, not merely talked about or discussed. Instead of being caricatured or typed, he was seriously portrayed as a person.

To all of this the Negro of a generation ago was keenly responsive because he realized that he was contributing a meaningful share to a new social understanding. But the desire to be understood would never by itself have opened so completely the protectively closed mind of the thinking Negro. There was still too much possibility of his being snubbed or patronized. Rather, the necessity for fuller, truer self-expression and the realization of the folly of allowing social discrimination to segregate him mentally (with the reciprocal tendency to circumscribe his own living) prompted intellectuals to abandon the "spite wall" they had built over the "color line." With the establishment of contact and a measure of rapport among the more sophisticated classes of the two races, it became increasingly evident that the conditions molding a new Negro were also molding a new American attitude.

This "new attitude" was the result or by-product of the shifts in personal, social, economic, and political philosophy which characterized the twenties. World War I is often held responsible for the greatly relaxed personal moral standards, for the despair of the "lost generation," the biting criticism of the "younger generation," and the violent rejection of internationalism. An over-all conviction arose that America was superior to any other nation, a conviction that not only antagonized Europeans and fostered an intolerable national complacency, but also provided materials with which critics like H. L. Mencken and novelists like Sinclair Lewis could attack "middle-class ideals" and the smugness, conservatism, and regimentation of American life. There was material prosperity; there was an abiding faith in materialism; certainly there was cynicism.

Woman suffrage, expanding imperialism, the direct primary—these, too, had their impact on the shift in American attitude and temper. The Prohibition Amendment represented a hitherto unprecedented assumption: that Government had the power to regulate personal conduct. The new developments in science not only led to the ultimate defeat of fundamentalism, but also reinforced the literary code of realism and naturalism.

The literary generation that crusaded against Puritanism and the genteel tradition, against stereotypes and apologies, against sentimentality and provincialism, against sex taboos and fundamentalism, also saw what Merle Curti terms "the beginnings of a new and realistic interest in American regions and American folk." The trend to full-scale social realism exemplified by the works of Sherwood Anderson, Sinclair Lewis, Theodore Dreiser, and Scott Fitzgerald was paralleled in the work of Negro writers of the same period. Claude McKay, Rudolph Fisher, George Lee, Zora Hurston, Arna Bontemps, and Jessie Fauset, for example, reached an almost full scale of self-revelation and a substantial degree of self-criticism. Negro writers of the older generation, like their white contemporaries, had had a tendency to express themselves in cautiously moral terms and guarded generalizations. Although convinced that art had the obligation of fighting social battles and compensating social wrongs, they invariably insisted on "putting the best foot forward." The young Negro writers of the twenties dealt objectively with their materials, employing a certain detachment of artistic vision, handling racial themes as neither typical nor representative. By breaking with past literary tradition, Negro writers were developing greater sophistication of style, wider and more universal appeal. And because of these advances they were becoming more and more identified with the national literary culture.

For the young Negro realists of the twenties, the motive for being racial was art. The increasing tendency was to evolve from the racial substance something technically distinctive, something that as an idiom or style would add to the general resources of art. Much of the flavor of language, flow of phrase, accent of rhythm in prose (and verse and music), and color and tone of imagery that today give distinction to Negro art was discernible in the work of Negro artists in the twenties. James Weldon Johnson's interesting experiment, in *Creation: A Negro Sermon*, of transposing dialect and carrying it through in imagery rather than in the broken phonetics of speech is a case in point. Jean Toomer added a folk lilt and a senuousness to the style of the American prose modernists. Claude McKay added Aesop and peasant irony to the social novel. Langston Hughes early displayed distinctive use of color and rhythm and a Biblical simplicity of speech at once colloquial in derivation and unquestionably artistic.

In music, racial idioms were being mixed with modern styles of expression. In painting, a racial dilemma had been reached by the twenties—a dilemma born of the fact that for years the white American artist had regarded the American scene as provincial and the Negro artist had regarded it as a ghetto. Frequently escaping to life abroad, both had retarded American art as a whole and the contribution that Negroes might have made to it. The ultimate difference was that the white artist living abroad was a voluntary expatriate, the Negro an embittered exile. When, in the early years of the present century, American realists began to turn home spiritually in an awakening appreciation of native materials, the Negro artist was not in a position to join or follow. For this racial dilemma a racial solution was necessary. It came, in the mid-twenties, from the same forces that inspired the upsurge of new, broader, more realistic and unapologetic talent in the other arts. In addition, of course, the rising tide of modernism encouraged young Negro artists away from traditionalism in both subject matter and style. Even those who did not break sharply with the academic style took up the new themes, especially by reflecting increased interest in racial subject matter. By the thirties a vigorous, intimate, and original documentation of Negro life was under way.

Fortunately, as with the parallel movement in literature, this movement in painting did not lead the Negro artist into racialist art. On the contrary, it led him into the main stream. American artists generally, as we have seen earlier, had been developing the Negro theme and subject as new native American materials. The older white artists had handled the Negro theme in a somewhat casual and superficial manner. For many young white artists of the twenties the Negro was the subject of careful and penetrating interpretation. The fact that young white American artists and their young Negro contemporaries shared this new interest in Negro life was significant. A common ground was established among young artists. The notion of the Negro as a restricted province to which the Negro artist confined his talent was removed. At the same time, the Negro artist was challenged to the task of self-revelation and forced to attempt it in competition with other artists. The poise and originality of the young artists of that period, their lack of sentimentality, and their increased realism brought them increasingly to the realization that race was a medium of expression, not an end in itself. For though their work was avowedly racial for the most part, they ranged with an increasing sense of freedom through the provinces of what might be termed a common human art. The strength and vigor of artists like Aaron Douglas, Palmer Hayden, Albert Smith, and Hale Woodruff was a reflection of superior advantages and training. Of equal, if not of greater, importance was the fact that their spiritual enlargement stemmed from the growing conception of American culture as vitally and necessarily including the materials of Negro life.

Since the twenties, then, the Negro has continued to influence our national culture. His gift of natural irony, of transfiguring imagination, of rhapsodic Biblical speech, of dynamic musical swing, of a pictorial art both racial and cosmopolitan has enriched American art.

Although the Negro was becoming a factor in national life a generation ago, and his impact on art and fiction was transcending Southern regional boundaries, he was still a potent factor in Southern life, letters, and art. Four pioneers of a new Southern regionalism symbolized not only the fact that the South, like the nation as a whole, was undergoing a metamorphosis or renaissance, but also that the Negro was still a dominant concern of Southern writers. Clement Wood's *Nigger*, T. S. Stribling's *Birthright*, DuBose Heyward's *Porgy*, and Sherwood Anderson's *Dark Laughter*—all of which have been mentioned earlier—showed that the best fiction of the new South was the realistic fiction of the Negro and of Negro life. In spite of considerable resistance from the old romantic and reactionary writers of Southern fiction, realism conquered the leading creative talents of the South. The "New South" can be described and defined variously, but at the moment no better than by pointing out how, beginning in the twenties, its literary interpreters differed from those of the "Old South."

Actually, of course, the term "New South" is ambiguous, having been applied to two periods in Southern history. Technically, the Old South ended with the close of the Civil War. It was a war peculiar to itself, for unlike other civil wars, in which defeat and victory have connoted the decline or collapse of one political faction and the ascendancy of another, the American Civil War challenged and defeated an entire civilization, a complete way of life. The classic differences between North and South in terms of climate, terrain, culture, political philosophy, and social mores are too familiar to be rehearsed. That the South's concept of a "Greek Democracy" necessitated the perpetuation of slavery is equally familiar. Plantation versus urban life, caste versus equalitarianism, oratory and apologistic literature in lieu of belles-lettres, agrarianism versus industrialism—these and other differences created a distinct cleavage between the two areas and fully justified unequivocal references to North and South. The Old South was feudal and conservative; the antebellum North, formerly torn between the romantic gospel of Emerson and the utilitarian doctrines of Webster, had capitulated to the latter by the opening of the war. It never retreated from its position of industrial leadership—a leadership that was first to defeat the South and then to reconstruct it. The New South was the initial effort of a region to resurrect itself to an entirely new life imposed from without. Thus the South had to grant freedom to its former slaves and adjust to a new political and industrial economy in which Negroes were to be accorded a legitimate place. It was not an easy task, nor one to which all Southerners were converted. Champions of the "New South Movement" were Henry Grady, Walter Hines Page, and Jabez Curry, who in the 1880's and 1890's defended industrialism, social progress, nationalism, and the Negro as an integral and important element in Southern society. Grady declared in 1886:

> The Old South rested everything on slavery and agriculture, unconscious that these could neither give nor maintain growth. The New South presents a perfect democracy, the oligarchs leading in the popular movement—a social system compact and closely knitted, less splendid on the surface, but stronger at the core—a hundred farms for every plantation, fifty homes for every palace—and a diversified industry that meets the complex need of this complex age.

Page's chief concerns were for health in educational reforms, and he constantly urged his fellow Southerners to demand free education because, as he insisted: "A public school system generously supported by public sentiment, and generously maintained by both State and local taxation, is the only effective means to develop the forgotten man." Grady, Page, and others encouraged the defeated Southerners to utilize their infinite natural resources, to initiate manufacturing and business enterprises, and to look ahead rather than back.

The term "New South" is applied also to a group of Southern liberals who, in the twenties and thirties, vehemently attacked "religious orthodoxy, puritanism, demagoguery, rural conservatism, and other undesirable aspects of the contemporary scene." Advocating industrialism, public education, good roads, schools, and health care, these twentieth-century liberals urged racial and political tolerance. But, as Francis Butler Simkins puts it, their critics knew that "the conversion of many educated Southerners to the logic of liberalism did not mean that many converts were willing to put aside inherited habits in order to live according to the new logic."

That the New Negro and the New South (of the twenties and thereafter) are interrelated can be proved by brief reference to and comment on several modern reinterpretations of the influence of the Negro on the South. W. J. Cash's *The Mind of the South*, with its unequivocal self-analysis, is a landmark among new evaluations of the South and of the Negro's role in and impact on it. Himself a Southerner, Cash had a great deal to say about the Negro, but in the broader context of a reinterpretation of the South itself. He repudiated conventional and sentimentally conceived notions of the Old South (of a character and a nature that he carefully delineates) and insisted that "New South" is a misnomer because, though there were certain post-war innovations—industrialization, commercialization—"the extent of the change and of the break between the Old South that was and the South of our time has been vastly exaggerated."

> The South [he continued], one might say, is a tree with many age rings, with its limbs and trunk bent and twisted by all the winds of the years, but with its tap root in the old South. . . .
>
> The mind of the section, that is, is continuous with the past. And its primary form is determined not nearly so much by industry as by the purely agricultural conditions of the past.

Cash stripped away the legends of white caste, insisting that in the main the South before the Civil War had been scarcely more than a frontier area with a frontier society, and that if one were to concede the existence of a Southern aristocracy, it would have to be a concession modified by the assumption that "it somehow rose up from the frontier and got to be such in forty or fifty years at best. . . ." The white Southerner, Cash tells us, was puerile in his contention of superiority to the Negro; he was thoroughly unrealistic and romantic in his outlook; he was complacent; and above all he was indelibly influenced by his proximity to the Negro.

> In this society in which the infant son of the planter was commonly suckled by a black mammy, in which gray old black men were his most loved story tellers, in which black stalwarts were among the chief heroes and mentors of his boyhood, and in which his usual, often practically his only, companions until he was past the age of puberty were the black boys (and girls) of the plantation—in this society in which by far the greater number of white boys of whatever degree were more or less shaped by such companionship, and in which nearly the whole body of whites, young and old, had constantly before their eyes the example, had constantly in their ears the accent, of the Negro, the relationship between the two groups was, by the second generation at least, nothing less than organic. Negro entered into white man as profoundly as

white man entered into Negro—subtly influencing every gesture, every word, every emotion and idea, every attitude.

What marks this point of view as "new" is the fact that emphasis had traditionally been laid on the Negro's assimilation of the white man's ways—his religion, his speech, his customs, his traditions—whereas Cash, a white Southern social historian, recognized and unhesitatingly described the reciprocal impact of white and Negro in the South.

Even more unorthodox, from the traditional Southern viewpoint, was Cash's uncompromising pronouncement on slavery:

> Wholly apart from the strict question of right and wrong, it is plain that slavery was inescapably brutal and ugly. Granted the existence, in the higher levels, of genuine humanity of feeling toward the bondsman; granted that, in the case of the house-servants at least, there was sometimes real affection between master and man; granted even that, at best, the relationship here got to be gentler than it has ever been elsewhere, the stark fact remains: It rested on force. The black man occupied the position of a mere domestic animal, without will or right of his own. The lash lurked always in the background. Its open crackle could often be heard where field hands were quartered. Into the gentlest houses drifted now and then the sounds of dragging chains and shackles, the bay of hounds, the report of pistols on the trail of the runaway. And, as the advertisements of the time incontestably prove, mutilation and the mark of the branding iron were pretty common.
>
> Just as plain was the fact that the institution was brutalizing—to white men. Virtually unlimited power acted inevitably to call up, in the coarser sort of master, that sadism which lies concealed in the depths of universal human nature—bred angry impatience and a taste for cruelty for its own sake, with a strength that neither the kindliness I have so often referred to (it continued frequently to exist unimpaired side by side, and in the same man, with this other) nor notions of honor could effectually restrain. And in the common whites it bred a savage and ignoble hate for the Negro which required only opportunity to break forth in relentless ferocity; for all their rage against the "white-trash" epithet concentrated itself on him rather than on the planters.

As Cash pointed out, the South never saw itself or slavery in these terms. Slavery was rationalized: the heathen must be Christianized; the Negro was too dependent to care for himself; he liked slavery and was happy; the Bible gave sanction to slavery; natural law divided whites and Negroes. In addition, the Negro was sentimentalized, as we have seen earlier. As Cash put it: ". . . the banjo-picking, heel flinging, hi-yi-ing happy jack of the levees and the fields" was a creation of the South, another defense mechanism.

Cash's incisive evaluation of the South and the Negro does not end with the slave period. Through the successive changes in Southern life from the ante-bellum days to 1940, he traces the impact of the Negro on Southern society—and in a vein of almost painful self-criticism. The hysteria about rape, the hatred of miscegenation, the uncertainty of Negro thought, the Southerners' determination to provide education (and that of a most inferior kind) solely to keep Negroes in prescribed "places," the deliberate exploitation of Negro tenants living in slums—all this Cash spelled out. In his concluding paragraphs he listed the South's virtues and vices. Of the latter he lists as most important "the South's too great attachment to racial values and a tendency to justify cruelty and injustice in the name of those values. . . ."

Another modern reinterpreter of the Negro and the South was Howard Odum. A folklorist and novelist as well as sociologist, Dr. Odum undertook sociological studies to prove that differences between Negroes and whites could be traced to social rather than to racial or biological sources, a difficult thesis to sustain, legitimate as it is. With some of his colleagues at the University of North Carolina Odum conducted a series of studies of Southern social and sociological problems. *Southern Regions*, published in 1936, is a comprehensive analysis of all the factors—economic, social, racial, and psychological—that contribute to the South's retarded development. This particular study was vitally important in itself, but in addition it set a pattern for other studies of comparable magnitude and importance. *These Are Our Lives*, a Federal Writers' Project, and studies by scholars from Southern universities other than the University of North Carolina, followed. One of Dr. Odum's own colleagues, Rupert Vance, wrote two outstanding books: *Human Factors in Cotton Culture* and *Human Geography of the South*. The latter contained strong arguments against the popular concept of Negro inferiority as a persisting biological axiom. Relating the concept to the South's economic plight, Vance wrote:

If biological inferiority of the whole Negro group were

a proved fact, it would, nevertheless, be to the benefit of both black and white to behave as though it did not exist. Only in this way can the section be sure of securing, in the economic sphere, the best of which both races are capable.

Henderson H. Donald's *The Negro Freedman* (1952), Herbert Aptheker's *A Documentary History of the Negro People in the United States* (1951), and Maurice Davies's *Negroes in American Society* (1949) are representative of contemporary studies that explore the full gamut of Negro cultural activity in both pre- and post-Civil War years, in church, political, and social activities. The Negro Carter Woodson had laid down the model for all studies of this sort, especially with his little-known investigation and analysis *The Mind of the Negro as Reflected in Letters Written during the Crisis, 1800–1860* (1926), clearly a forerunner of Aptheker's work. Woodson, a graduate of Berea College, the University of Chicago, and a student at both Harvard University and the Sorbonne, will always be identified by thousands as the devoted Director of the Association for the Study of Negro Life and History, which he and a few others founded in 1915. Some of his books are *Negro Makers of History* (1928), *A Century of Negro Migration* (1918), and *The Education of the Negro Prior to 1861*.

Both William Faulkner and Lillian Smith have been far from orthodox Southern writers when interpreting the Negro. Faulkner, with frank, brave introspection, has written the South's most intimate and detailed confessional. His over-all theme has been the social and economic decline, the moral corruption, and the spiritual decadence of Southern life and character, all of which he associates with the violence and ruthlessness with which the Old South was destroyed and the physical and emotional chaos of a society reconstructed in unfamiliar terms. As a stage for this, Faulkner has created an elaborate imaginary county, complete with families on all social levels. Malcolm Cowley, in his introduction to *The Portable Faulkner*, interprets the story of Faulkner's mythical Yoknapatawpha County as symbolizing the settling of the South by aristocrats (the Sartorises) and the nameless ambitious men (the Sutpens), who seized the land from the Indians with the intention of creating an enduring social order. But their plans were "accursed" by slavery, which, as an institution, ended with the Civil War. Rebuilding on the old plan was impossible because of the carpet-baggers and poor Southern whites. The descendants of the aristocrats, Cowley points out, escaped reality by way of alcohol, rhetoric, or madness.

Faulkner's violence, Cowley says, "is an example of the Freudian method turned backward, being full of sexual nightmares that are in reality social symbols."

One can accept the Faulkner saga as an allegory of the South or, as Robert Penn Warren urges, as "a legend of our general plight and problem." By that Warren is suggesting that although Faulkner's medium is the South, he is in reality documenting the history of our entire society, a society dominated by personal and acquisitive motives, a society described by Warren as suffering from "a lack of discipline, of sanctions, of community of values, of a sense of mission." Or, again, the novels may be regarded as representative of Faulkner's own ambivalent attitude toward the South. The frequently quoted question of Shreve McCannon to Quentin Compson in the novel *Absalom! Absalom!*—"Why do you hate the South?"— and Quentin's sharp response—"I don't hate it" and his repeated "I don't, I don't! I don't hate it! I don't hate it!" after he has told McCannon a grim and tragic family story based on miscegenation—might also be used as an introductory clue to the larger implication of Faulkner's novels.

Regardless of the reader's decision as to Faulkner's major intent, the fact remains that his interpretation of the Negro's role in the South is open to less speculation. Not concerned with Negroes as dominant figures, Faulkner nevertheless interprets them carefully as individuals and as plausible types, though invariably in the pessimistic terms that his consistent adherence to naturalism demands. The dependence of the whites on Negroes is emphasized in *The Sound and the Fury*, in which Dilsey, the Negro housekeeper, is not only the domestic mainstay, but also the dominant force in the household. She handles the grandmother, the girl Caddy, and Jason with varying degrees of patience and asperity, but never with subservience. Her protection of Benjy, the idiot, and her bullying of Luster again reveal the fact that, in spite of her age and frailness ("She was so old," Jason observed, "that she couldn't do any more than move hardly"), she was capable of defying Jason physically when he attempted to whip his daughter. Equally militant and outspoken is the Negro Job, who, when Jason suggests he should be working for him, observes flatly:

I works to suit de man whut pays me Sat'dy night. When I does dat, it don't leave me a whole lot of time to please other folks. Ain't nobody works much in dis country cep de boll-weevil, noways.

In "That Evening Sun Go Down," one of the collection of

stories entitled *These Thirteen*, Nancy assails her white debtor repeatedly with the taunting question: "When you going to pay me, white man? When you going to pay me, white man? It's been three times now since you paid me a cent." This in spite of the fact that the man knocked her down and kicked her until the police dragged her away. Joe Christmas, the leading character in *Light in August*, is portrayed as a victim of hypocrisy and color caste, the latter having given him a deep sense of self-repugnance when he learned of his mulatto status. These three characters are typical of the Faulkner handling of Negroes as personalities—harassed, rebuffed, embittered, but individuals.

In other instances Faulkner reflects on the whites' attitude toward Negroes, and here again, with an attitude new for a Southern white writer. When Quentin Compson went North, he reflected:

> I used to think that a Southerner had to be conscious of niggers. I thought that Northerners would expect him to. When I first came East I kept thinking You've got to remember to think of them as coloured people not niggers, and if it hadn't happened that I wasn't thrown in with many of them, I'd have wasted a lot of time and trouble before I learned that the best way to take all people, black or white, is to take them for what they think they are, then leave them alone. That was when I realized that a nigger is not a person so much as a form of behavior; a sort of obverse reflection of the white people he lives among.

Later he observes that he really missed Roskus and Dilsey. This nostalgia or emotional dependence—so paradoxical when contrasted with the blunt and often vulgar way in which the whites addressed the Negroes—is revealing. Again, Jason in *The Sound and the Fury* comments somewhat bitterly that the best places for Negroes "is in the field, where they'd have to work from sunup to sundown." And, continuing:

> They can't stand prosperity or an easy job. Let one stay around white people for a while and he's not worth killing. They get so they can outguess you about work before your very eyes. . . . Shirking and stealing and giving you a little more lip and a little more lip until some day you have to lay them out with a scantling or something.

This appraisal is strikingly contrasted with that of McCaslin, who, in "The Bear," declares that although the "Whole South is cursed, and all of us who derive from it, whom it ever suckled, white and black both, lie under the curse," it is the Negroes who will endure:

> They are better than we are. Stronger than we are. Their vices are vices aped from white men or that white men and bondage have taught them; improvidence and intemperance and evasion—not laziness; evasion: of what white men had set them to, not for their aggrandizement or even comfort but his own. . . .

This theme of the Negro's capacity to endure dominates *Go Down Moses* and *The Sound and the Fury*. In his foreword to the Modern Library edition of the latter work, Faulkner lists the characters, first the whites, with identifying biographical or descriptive data, and then the Negroes. There are four:

T. P.
> Who wore on Memphis' Beale Street the fine bright cheap intransigent clothes manufactured specifically for him by the owners of Chicago and New York sweatshops.

FRONY.
> Who married a Pullman porter and went to St. Louis to live and later moved back to Memphis to make a home for her mother since Dilsey refused to go further than that.

LUSTER.
> A man, aged 14. Who was not only capable of the complete care and security of an idiot twice his age and three times his size, but could keep him entertained.

DILSEY.
> They endured.

At the Fisk University Race Relations Institute in July 1955, Lillian Smith, speaking informally to about two hundred Negro and white race-relations experts, referred to her latest book, *Now Is the Time*. Somewhat wryly she pointed out that sophisticated New York critics had referred to her "little book" as "naïve" and "unduly simple." Miss Smith's comment to her Fisk audience was that many people in the deep South are both "naïve" and "simple," and that the profundities of professional sociology and the intellectual sophistication of its proponents would hardly have much personal meaningfulness for either Negroes or whites living in small Southern rural communities. In a community such as Miss Smith's own, for example, where a leading white preacher has had only grade schooling, the simple, eloquent explanation of the Supreme Court Decision of May 17, 1954, of its democratic and ethical meaningfulness, and of the very basic ways in which individuals can meet the challenge of integration which makes up the major content of *Now Is the Time* should prove most effective and appealing. As a matter of fact, the book is not to be underestimated; because of the direct and forthright approach of the author, it has had a widespread appeal to Northerners and Southerners alike, of more formal educational experience than the Clayton preacher. Lillian Smith's simplicity, her clarity, and her uncluttered approach to interpersonal and interracial relationships have made her an effective modern interpreter of the Southern Negro and his history, status, and problems.

For many years Lillian Smith, a white Southerner, in collaboration with Paula Schnelling, edited and distributed (often at terrifying risks) a small journal called the *North Georgia Review*. In a nonaggressive, gently persuasive fashion, the co-editors essayed to break down old misconceptions, dispel old prejudices, and introduce a fresh, positive concept of Negro-white understanding and good will.

Killers of the Dream, nonfiction, is an amplification of the point of view sometimes expressed, sometimes implied, in *Strange Fruit*. Miss Smith's thesis in this book is that sin, sex, and segregation have created the seemingly hopeless moral dilemma of the South. The title derives from the author's assertion that Southerners aspire to a good life, but that their contradiction of values as exemplified in the simultaneous practice of Christianity and segregation has nearly destroyed their dream. The added contradiction of professed allegiance to democratic doctrine and sanctioned racial exploitation heightens the guilt of white Southerners and lessens the potential survival of the dream. A later book, *Journey*, continues in much the same vein; and *Now Is the Time* candidly challenges the average layman to an awareness of his role in helping to implement the May 17, 1954 Supreme Court Decision. Fully mindful that the Decision had far-reaching social and democratic implications transcending even the cardinal issue of education, Miss Smith wrote her book "in the hope that readers will be persuaded to see that now is the time to give up segregation. . . ." The opening pages of *Now Is the Time,* dedicated "To Children Everywhere," are quoted here in part:

> Until two centuries ago, the idea of freedom was only a dream; the human being's importance was only an ideal. Tyranny and slavery were the realities of man's experience. Then, suddenly, the dream, the ideal grew into a bold and beautiful political system called democracy. Men said that never, hereafter, would human beings be satisfied with anything less. When they heard of it they would demand it as their right.
>
> Now, here were a billion people craving this new freedom, thinking of human dignity, hungering for it—and millions of them settling for new and heavier chains of bondage.
>
> Why? We knew even as we asked. We knew democracy had not met their needs. Somehow the dream had walled itself off. Somehow it had become segregated. In the eyes of Asia and Africa democracy had turned into "white democracy." They do not trust the white hands that offer them aid because, until now, those hands have given them only the bitter experiences of colonialism and white prestige. They are reluctant to accept the United States as a friend—this democracy which has never colonized any Asian or African country—because its people cling to color segregation and have laws in many states making it compulsory. . . .
>
> . . . We knew what the decision (May 17) would be. The necessities of our times had clearly determined it: not alone the world situation but the human situation here at home; in our children's lives, in our hearts and minds, made it imperative that the highest authority in our land say clearly that there is no place, today, for legal segregation in a free and democratic nation. We knew. But we wanted to hear it said aloud. And when the words came, simple and plain, a deep pride swept across America. . . .
>
> . . . White children were not mentioned in that remarkable document, but they too are deeply affected by it. For race segregation is a cruel frame that twists and misshapes the spirits of all children, no matter which side of it they are fastened to. Arrogance, complacency, blindness to human need: these hurt the heart and mind

as severely as do shame and inferiority. We hardly need
to remind ourselves of how the little Nazis' moral na-
tures were maimed by Hitler's ideas and laws to know
this is true.

White Southerners knew it so well. As we listened to the
decision, many of us were suddenly back in childhood, quietly walking through its years, remembering
its beauty, its tender moments, its sudden joy and wonder
—and its walls. Those invisible walls which we plunged
against a thousand times as we stretched out to accept
our human world. Walls that stopped our questions—
and our dreams. We were so free . . . but we did not
have the freedom to do right. For there were laws in our
states that compelled us to do wrong.

Now the Supreme Court's Decision would give this freedom back to the white child of the South. It is a very
big gift, for which many of us are deeply grateful.

These are the words of a white Southern woman writing in
1955. Although we have projected her into the discussion
of "modern reinterpretations of the Negroes," Lillian Smith
deserves to be more broadly allied with the few moderns of
Christian, or of universal moral and ethical sensibility whose
literal democratic awareness makes them both able and willing to relate our domestic moral failings to our failure to
win overwhelming and unanimous democratic support from
the millions of people of the East who must eventually ally
themselves with one or the other of today's major political
ideologies. Lillian Smith may not make a profound impression upon the nation's academicians, but she makes a sincere, fervent, intelligent, and sensible appeal to the people
not only of the South, but of the whole nation. And as, in
the final analysis, laws must be understood, supported, and
practically interpreted by the people, her contribution to
human relationships and to the promulgation of our time-
honored concept of individual social responsibility cannot
be overestimated.

Negro social scientists, too, were initiating studies in terms
of this "new approach" to an analysis of the South. An outstanding center for sociological research is at Fisk University,
in Nashville, Tennessee. There, for many years, Charles S.
Johnson (now the University's President) served as Professor of Sociology and Director of the Fisk University Institute
of Social Science. This department became one of the greatest in the country, and has been compared with social-science

centers at the University of Chicago and the University of North Carolina. With the assistance of a highly able staff that includes nationally recognized sociologists such as Preston and Bonita Valien, Dr. Johnson wrote some of modern sociology's classics. *Shadow of the Plantation* is a study of the decay of the plantation system in a Southern black-belt area. *The Collapse of Cotton Tenancy*, written in collaboration with Edwin Embree and W. W. Alexander, emphasized the need for reorganization of Southern farm practices. *The Statistical Atlas of Southern Counties* is a detailed compendium of facts about more than a thousand counties in thirteen Southern states for the five-year period 1936–41. *Growing Up in the Black Belt* recounts the handicaps suffered by colored school children in the rural South.

E. Franklin Frazier, Professor of Sociology at Howard University, is an internationally recognized sociologist. His *The Negro Family in the United States* and *The Negro Family in Chicago,* though established works, are not precisely within the scope of our consideration, but his long essay, "The Pathology of Race Prejudice," first published in the *Forum* in 1927, is a trenchant attack against the "insane nature of Southern reactions to the blacks." He says:

> Southern white people write and talk about the majesty of the law, the sacredness of human rights, and the advantages of democracy—and the next moment defend mob violence, disfranchisement, and jim crow treatment of the Negro. White men and women who are otherwise kind and law-abiding will indulge in the most revolting forms of cruelty towards black people. Thus the whole system of ideas respecting the Negro is dissociated from the normal personality, and—what is more significant for our thesis—this latter system of ideas seems exempt from the control of personality.

This (from an article characterized by a complete absence of ambivalence) is a strikingly unequivocal diagnosis to have been made nearly thirty years ago by a Negro scholar.

The men just mentioned were pioneers. Today a growing group of first-rate Negro social scientists is nationally known. Of the younger men, Ira de Reid of Haverford College is an established authority on the structure and culture of racial and ethnic populations, the Negro immigrant, and the Negro urban worker. Mozell Hill of Atlanta University is a recognized expert in social psychology, the culture of Southern poor whites, and the theoretical and methodological problems of community studies. At Howard University,

Frank Edwards, Harry Walker, and Horace Fitchett are making increasingly substantial contributions to the literature of social analysis and interpretation.

The American Negro is invariably marked as "different" and as "the exception" when he advances into the main stream of American life. The actual problem is, as few white Americans realize, that thousands of "exceptions" simply do not choose to subject themselves to the probable repudiation and insult that aspiration to personal and professional identity on the basis of merit and achievement (normal in a democratic society) invariably has brought. Thus, the Negro has been prompted, if not forced, to create his own social, civic, religious, journalistic, business, and professional outlets. The Negro press, Negro civic organizations, Negro teachers' organizations, Negro business leagues (there are some even flatly labeled "Negro Chambers of Commerce"), Negro medical and reading societies, and countless other Negro agencies and organizations testify to the fact that Negroes, denied full opportunities in American life, have had to carve out a life of their own.

Nothing has contributed so much to the sense of separateness as the long history of segregation in education, for children from their most impressionable years on were impressed with inescapable differences based on the difference of color. That Negroes—adults and children—have survived this separateness with as much emotional and psychic equanimity as they have is, or should be, a source of universal amazement, especially when one realizes that though the Negro has been driven to create his own world, his having done so has inspired his critics to insist that he prefers to live alone and apart, that he is "more comfortable with his own." This kind of circular reasoning or deduction has inspired Negrophobes to insist on delaying desegregation in education. When unintimidated Negroes insist that their children will be able to accommodate themselves to a changed educational pattern, the Negrophobes compound further irony: Well, even if they can adjust comfortably in social or psychological ways, they must not be admitted to "white schools" because they are unable to perform at an adequate intelligence level. They will undermine "white educational standards." Ignoring the fact that intelligence tests show no correlation between race and intellectual capacity, such racists blandly hold the children accountable for the results of the long-sustained system of racial segregation and discrimination. Or, as Thurgood Marshall, the brilliant chief counsel for the National Association for the Advancement of Colored People, puts it: "The whole argument reminds you of the man who killed his mother and father, but, who, when brought into court, pleaded for mercy on grounds that he was an orphan!"

With the gradual, but persistent increase in recent years of the Negro's acceptance into and absorption by the whole of American life, the Negro writer has faced an increasing dilemma. As Negroes become more and more a part of government, as they become articulate politically, as they win entree to labor unions, to civic and fraternal groups, to better employment opportunities, and to the schools and colleges of the South as well as of the East and North, the sense of racial separateness is bound to diminish. Within the past two decades the Supreme Court's concern for civil rights, with explicit reference to minority groups, has given all minorities a renewed sense of dignity and of "belonging." Thus the Negro writer is increasingly relieved of both the compulsion and the frenetic need to define and describe the "Negro problem" per se, or to attempt to defend or explain the Negro as a group entity. For the Negro writer, like any other thinking person of the present day, knows that the Negro problem is a myth, that the real problem is the bigotry of Americans who cannot or will not concede the necessity and inevitability of America's erasing what Walter White defined as "the darkest blot on its democratic record." Negro writers know, too, that problems, human experiences, and human aspirations, as well as conflicts and defeats, are universal rather than racially provincial.

Today the Negro author is moving more and more toward general subjects; the white author is more boldly and competently delineating Negro life. Each of these trends is in itself as desirable as it is inevitable, but both create confusion or questioning, best considered as the temporary stresses involved in liquidating the double literary standard and the cultural color line. Just as prejudice and segregation exacted a heavy toll in terms of literary chauvinism, integration exacts a double toll. The competition is keen, the pace swift, and the odds against success are proportionately greater in nonracial writing. Because of the exceptionally penetrating performances of contemporary white writers, the same is true of both the fiction and the social analysis of Negro life in these areas. The Negro author is faced with the problem of creating literature that might be termed "socially sane" or consonant with democratic premises. He must substantiate the thesis that in a democratic society individuals and their problems are to be seen within the whole of society rather than only within one segment of it. Negroes are rightly insisting upon a more explicit reconciliation of democratic principles and practices, and Negro writers must be equally mindful of a need for literary consistency. We cannot claim democratic rights—that connote equalitarianism, individuality, personal dignity, and the capacity for dynamic progress—and simultaneously maintain a racial subjectivity in our literature.

I have made some observations on what I regard as the ultimate synthesis of universality of point of view and the use of racial materials in fiction. Much of what was said in that context could be related to nonfiction and poetry. For just as Richard Wright, Willard Motley, Ann Petry, Ralph Ellison, and James Baldwin have achieved universals through the experiences of people who simply happen to be colored (or, as in Motley's case, are not colored at all), and as poets who happen to be Negro are increasingly widening and universalizing their themes, so the new scholarship properly identifies the Negro as an integral and inextricable part of American society. John Hope Franklin's *From Slavery to Freedom* is a classic example. Franklin's book is unprecedented as a first-rate history—ostensibly of the Negro, but really of America with proper evaluation of the Negro's share in it. It is a far cry from the conventional American histories that set aside a chapter about "the Negro" or make limited reference to his part in America's growth or perfunctory references to Crispus Attucks, Dred Scott, and the slavery issue. In subsequent works Franklin has displayed the same high quality of scholarship and a scholarly objectivity transcending the bias of racism. Another historian, Rayford Logan, in his *The Negro in American Life and Thought*, has not only performed a scholarly job, but also has made another important contribution to the new literature of "social sanity." Professor Logan's title suggests his point of view and approach: he has related the struggle of the Negro in the period 1877–1901 to the social and political struggle of the United States itself during the period. Again Benjamin Quarles's *The Negro in the Civil War* successfully and properly integrates the Negro American with American history.

Recently a number of travel books by Negroes have been published. These, too, suggest a broader, more cosmopolitan interest by Negro writers. J. Saunders Redding, an established novelist and critic, sent to India by the Department of State, has published *An American in India,* in which he recounts his experiences as lecturer and interpreter of American life to countless Indian audiences. Although any such book, based upon a comparatively brief stay in a country as alien to America as India is subject to the criticism that it lacks sufficiently penetrating insight, Redding's book is representative of an international approach and an international cultural and social identification that is altogether healthy. Carl Rowan, the talented journalist and reporter for the large midwestern daily, the *Minneapolis Tribune*, also a State Department appointee, has written of his Far Eastern experiences. Richard Wright, in *Black Power*, and Era Bell Thompson, in *Land of My Fathers*, have written of their experiences in Africa.

Somewhat earlier, in 1951, Roi Ottley, adopting the role of foreign correspondent, wrote of the Negro in present-day Europe. *No Green Pastures*, although it deals primarily with European Negroes, discusses, to some extent, the impact of American Negroes on those living in Europe and on the American Negro expatriots living abroad. Carl Rowan, in an earlier book, *South of Freedom*, described a comprehensive tour of Southern states which he made shortly after World War II in his effort to assess the racial situation.

Several Negro autobiographies in recent years merit comment, for the better ones retell the life stories of people who, in the American tradition of self-reliance and personal fortitude, have overcome traditional as well as racial handicaps to become successes in their chosen fields. W. C. Handy's autobiography tells not only of his own life, but also of the birth and history of the blues; Ethel Waters's life story, *His Eye Is On the Sparrow*, recounts her colorful experiences as a woman who, as novelist William Gardiner Smith observed, "is part of the legend of a time gone by—a time which was never quite like what we like to think it was, but whose embroidered memory persists in our national consciousness. . . ." She was able to keep abreast of the demands of several decades: the gaiety of the twenties, the lean years of the thirties; she had a concert in Carnegie Hall in the late thirties, and starred in *Member of the Wedding* in the fifties. She tells her story vividly. *Black Boy*, Richard Wright's autobiography up to the time he left the South as a young man, is a bitter denunciation of Southern mores and their impact on a colored child. It is an obvious prelude to *Native Son*. In the fall of 1955 a Negro woman published her autobiography, *The Third Door*. The author, Ellen Tarry, was, according to her publishers, "like the late Walter White, . . . in a position to choose her destiny." In short, "she, too, was fair skinned, and her calling herself a Negro was a voluntary act of allegiance that brought with it the special trials and special opportunities that confront the Negro people today." There is a certain naïveté about this observation that many Negroes will find irritating. There are countless Negroes who "look white" and have made no "voluntary act of allegiance"

—some are sophisticated and well educated, as Ellen Tarry apparently is; others are, in spite of being ethnically "colored," exactly like "poor whites" in appearance, attitude, and conduct. More important, however, is the fact that there are countless Negroes who do not "look white," but whose attitudes, aspirations, achievements—and indeed accorded recognition—are predicated upon their basic and intrinsic human and intellectual worth. These observations are not to be construed as criticism leveled at Ellen Tarry or her book. The autobiography is readable and delightful, though its essential point eludes the Negro reader who, in all probability, will think Miss Tarry's various crises less momentous than she does. Her experience, for example, of not being able to get a taxicab in a Southern city during the war years is understandable, but too familiar to command empathic response from Southern women and parents who have endured the same and worse frustrations—and humiliations—for years.

A resurgence of biographical studies of Frederick Douglass and Booker T. Washington,[1] a biography of the Chicago *Defender*'s Robert Abbott, and proposed biographies of Mary McLeod Bethune and Mary Church Terrell, both of whom were internationally known as champions of civil and particularly women's rights, indicate further the expanding literary interest in Negro life. Two outstanding biographies of distinguished Negroes are by white authors. In 1948 Ridgely Torrence wrote *The Story of John Hope*, characterized by its publishers as "one of the most important [books] ever written on the American Negro." John Hope was for many years president of Morehouse College in Atlanta, Georgia. Torrence's biography details Hope's career as an educator as well as the Negro's history during Hope's lifetime. *Doctor Dan*, by Helen Buckler, written in 1954, is the story of Daniel Hale Williams, the "first surgeon ever to operate successfully on the human heart." Helen Buckler, like the more effective modern biographers, tells a story not only of a distinguished personality, but also of his times and of his contemporaries.

In 1953, Helen Chesnutt, daughter of the Negro novelist Charles Waddell Chesnutt, published a biography of her father. Drawn from his correspondence and her own memories, the book throws definite light on the personality of a man who looms increasingly as the literary Negro of his generation. His early determination to speak objectively about

[1] The late Marquis James was preparing a biography of Washington. His untimely death is the more to be regretted because his earlier studies of Negroes were excellent. Dr. Charles Thompson, Dean of Howard University's Graduate School, has, however, just completed a definitive and well-documented life of Washington.

Negro-white relationships in the post-Civil War years takes on added significance when we realize, as is evident in his daughter's account, that the personal problem of race discrimination was satisfactorily resolved for him. In 1953, too, Philip Foner's comprehensive life of Frederick Douglass reached its third volume; the fourth volume was published in 1955.

In a class by itself is the posthumously published work of Walter White, for many years the executive secretary of the National Association for the Advancement of Colored People. Novelist, essayist, lecturer, unyielding advocate of human rights, Walter White was, as Ralph Bunche observes in his foreword to White's last book, *How Far the Promised Land?*, "always 'up front' and under fire in the cause of interracial democracy; he wrote from the trenches and the foxholes of the incessant struggle for equality for minority peoples. He lived that struggle for three decades. In a symbolic sense, he was that struggle in our times."

Walter White's concluding words in this, his last testament to the struggle for human freedom, speak eloquently for the intent of his book:

> What I have tried to do is analogous to the objective of a writer who tells the story of a long struggle against, say, tuberculosis or cancer. He knows full well that neither the complete cure nor the preventive has yet been discovered by scientists. So he relates the history of the disease and what has been done to wipe it out. He concentrates on his chosen disease and does not attempt to write a materia medica or to tell the complete story of man's battle against a host of its other ills.
>
> The job of curing and preventing man's mistreatment of another man because of his race or color in the United States or, for that matter, anywhere else in the world is not done. But we are on our way.

The previously neglected field of literary criticism comes in for welcome recognition at last. In 1953, Nathan Scott, then a professor at Howard University, now a professor at the University of Chicago, published *Rehearsals of Discomposure*, a philosophical and critical evaluation of four great contemporary literary figures: Franz Kafka, D. H. Lawrence, Ignazio Silone, and T. S. Eliot. Dr. Scott is interested in the twentieth-century problem of man—what he calls the "human predicament"—as it confronts these modern writers. After mildly rebuking academic philosophers for evading this urgent problem, he analyzes what he considers to be the common-denominator problem of the sensitive "artist-thinkers" who attempt to resolve the confusions of our culture. Actually, of course, Negro critics had appeared much earlier, but in the main their concerns had been with Negro subjects. Writing in Atlanta University's magazine of "Race and Culture," *Phylon* (Summer 1950), Ulysses Lee, himself an excellent literary critic, observed:

> Through the Thirties and into the Forties there were three critics whose ideas on literature were dominant. These were Benjamin Brawley, Alain Locke, and Sterling Brown. W. E. B. DuBois, as editor of *The Crisis*, had made his critical views known in reviews in his columns of "Opinion," and in his editorials. In his books and in separate essays he had evaluated literature by and about Negroes. But, like Stanley Braithwaite, whose twenty-five anthologies of verse and volumes of critical essays had been appearing since 1906, and James Weldon Johnson, whose introduction to the *Book of American Negro Poetry* in 1922 had provided a rationale of the Negro's creative genius leading directly into some of the ideas central to the Renaissance, DuBois after 1931 expressed himself on literary problems only in a manner incidental to his wider interests. Brawley, Locke, and Brown, however, gave the bulk of their attention to literature and to the allied arts.

Lee analyzes Brawley's work, which includes *A Short History of the American Negro, The Negro in Literature and Art in the United States,* and a text, *New Survey of English Literature.* He concludes rightly that Brawley "found little room for the expression of purely critical opinion and that which he expressed seldom changed through the years." Brown's investigations in the realm of Negro folklore have been discussed; Lee commends Sterling Brown not only for his investigations of Negro folk cultures in the South, but also for his "thorough grounding in past and contemporary literatures." Brown, as the youngest of the three critics noted —and the only one now living—does indeed exemplify the scholarly, the objective, and the sophisticated in his critical views and in his own creative writing. Blyden Jackson, Arna Bontemps, and Hugh Gloster—the first two, professors at Fisk University, Gloster a professor at Hampton Institute— are well known as critics in university circles. J. Saunders Redding frequently reviews books for *The New York Times*, and at Howard University, John Lovell, Jr., Professor of Literature and Drama, has written articles for *Theatre Arts*,

Regional Nationalism in American Culture

Phylon, and *The Crisis.* Miles Jefferson, a New Yorker, annually performs a valuable service for *Phylon,* writing a comprehensive critical report of the Negro on Broadway.

Alain Locke was a philosopher-critic, and as his friend and colleague, Dr. Eugene Holmes, observes, "equally at home in the world of letters and the arts." At the April 1955 Locke Memorial Program, Professor Holmes, himself a philosopher-critic, said of Locke:

> Locke's esthetic, literary and anthropological contributions to what he termed value relativism and cultural pluralism and to an identification with international movements also made him, for a time at least, more sympathetic to Bahaism than to the more familiar creeds. His understanding of biology and the genetics propounded by [Ernest E.] Just led him to regard anthropology as a socio-cultural discipline and to a forty-year-old belief that philosophy more properly belonged to social philosophy than to metaphysics.
>
> He used philosophical ideas to illuminate his experiences as a critic and an expert in the arts, that complex world of art and abstract world of ideas. There were no ultimates or absolutes, but the furbishing of the new—the new Negro and the new artist—subjected to criticism and analysis, and subject only to the inviolate ethos which Locke thought of as democratically based. This was his philosophical liberalism in the best sense . . .

As time goes on, the Negro author, like Negroes in general, will be increasingly *less self-conscious*—or he will not be consciously Negro as he approaches a chosen theme. The extent to which Negroes are accepted on equal footing with all other Americans in American life will determine the extent to which the Negro writer will be capable, psychologically, to view, as Hugh Gloster has put it, "all life as his milieu" without losing his "ethnic individuality."

CHAPTER TWELVE

Some Prospects of American Culture

JUST as slavery may now in perspective be viewed as having first threatened our democratic institutions and then forced them to more consistent maturity, the artistic and cultural impact of the Negro on American life must be credited with producing unforeseen constructive pressures and generating unexpected creative ferment in the literary and artistic culture of America. In cutting the Negro completely loose from his ancestral culture, slaveholders set up a unique situation between the white majority and the Negro minority. The peculiar conditions of American slavery so scrambled Africans from diverse regions and cultures of the entire continent that, the original background culture having been tribal to begin with, neither a minority language nor an ancestral tradition remains. Although a number of scholars are interested in African art and customs and in the question of African retentions in Negro art, religion, and music, the fact remains that, as Donald Young has said: "the ordinary Negro knows little or cares less about African ways of life."

Perhaps what Brown, Davis, and Lee observed in their *Negro Caravan* regarding Negro folk music may be pertinent to the over-all cultural contributions of the Negro to American culture. "Lovers of Negro folk songs," they wrote, "need not fear either its detractors or the students of origin. Neither European nor African, but partaking of elements of both, the result is a new kind of music, certainly not mere imitation, but more creative and original than any other American music." The American Negro, left no alternative but to share the language and tradition of the majority culture, brought to it inadvertently and unwittingly something of his African heritage. His folk music, folk dances, and folklore best justify this claim. The more formal developments of Negro art paralleled the Negro's successive social advances in America. During the post-Civil War years his contributions were limited by propagandistic and defense motives. With the migrations that took thousands of Negroes to urban centers during and after World War I, Negro creative artists acquired a broader, less subjective, freer tone. With the economic depression of the thirties and the revitalizing force of the New Deal, Negro artists proved themselves expressive or articulate, though propagandistic intent too frequently frustrated true artistic maturity. At the highest level, Negro artists have relegated "color" to its proper position: that of biological and aesthetic accident. The chief cultural contribution of the Negro to America, however, is in the folk arts. Of secondary importance has been the Negro's nearly exact paralleling of the literary and art history of white America.

The futility of trying to substitute an arbitrary, artificial barrier like a "color line" for a natural or accepted boundary of language, creed, or culture is obvious. Historical circumstances have made it necessary that the Negro-white minority-majority issue be settled or resolved within the context of a common culture. Any adequate understanding of the Negro's special position in American society and culture depends upon full understanding of this point, which explains why the American Negro, though forced by majority attitudes of exclusion and rejection to take on a defensive attitude of racialism, has rarely set up separate cultural values or developed divergent institutional loyalties or political objectives. On the whole, Negro racialism has remained what it has been historically: an enforced, protective counterattitude. Accordingly, although becoming more racially militant and protesting with each generation in years past, in each decade more recently, and almost daily since May 17, 1954, the American Negro is militant and protestant within the pattern of American militancy and protest.

In basic attitude and alliance with over-all American concepts and ideals, the Negro is a conformist. He believes implicitly in the promise and heritage of basic American documents, and he has applied the principles of self-reliance, personal dignity, and individual human worth to the long, rewarding fight to achieve full and unequivocal first-class citizenship. The American Negro's values, ideals, and objectives are integrally and unreservedly American. There are, of course, exceptions, but they are not unlike those which exist in all racial or religious groups or cultures, some of whose members either prefer the protection of group identity or refuse to identify themselves with the larger American issues at the expense of some narrower ones. Ignorance of the law, vested interests, and threats (particularly in deep Southern areas) of economic sanctions and physical violence militate against many Negroes' identifying themselves with the active democratic pattern. A simple case in point: In Greenbrier County, West Virginia, the County Board of Education ordered the desegregation of schools in September 1954. The order was carried out, and Negro and white children attended mixed schools for one week. Then, because of alleged threats of violence and vague rumors (later proved to be without substance), of overcrowding and dissatisfaction, the Board rescinded its order, and Negro children were sent back to the all-colored schools. Throughout the school year 1954–5 opinion was divided among both white and colored citizens. Attitudes among the latter ran the gamut from indignation at the Board's lack of courage in maintaining its position (and authority) to a frankly relieved "there's no need in going too far and too fast" position.

When, in October, 1955, the National Association for the Advancement of Colored People filed suit against the Greenbrier Board, Negro opinion was still divided, as was evidenced by the School Board's producing colored witnesses to testify in its behalf. When, on the other hand, a Negro plaintiff was asked whether or not it was true that some Negroes were anxious to preserve segregation and that Negroes in the county were not united in their opinion, the plaintiff promptly retorted that no more than any other people are Negroes united on all issues. He continued that "not all the followers of Christ are united on Sunday mornings in church," and that "when Abraham Lincoln freed the slaves there were many Negroes who did not want freedom." The witness made the point that Negroes concerned with helping themselves by following the dictates of federal law, and with getting for their children (and for themselves) the best possible citizenship opportunities, were concerned *with these values* and not with the reactionary forces, whether white or colored, who were deterrent to democracy's progress. It is interesting and gratifying to note that in this Southern West Virginia county, a Southern federal judge asked the Board of Education to initiate voluntary desegregation of schools in February 1956, and to operate *all* schools on "an indiscriminate basis" beginning in September 1956. A crowded open court in Lewisburg, West Virginia, an historic Southern town, accepted his pronouncement quietly, and with no overt evidence of displeasure—even when the judge said politely and in no more than elegantly casual conversational tones that if the Board did not comply with his ruling, he would be forced to send its members to jail.

The commitment to a common culture which is increasingly characteristic of Negroes is, naturally enough, the despair of the Negro's opponents, but it is the hope of most Negroes and of those who support his cause. Eventually the Negro will emerge completely from the social and cultural ghetto to which he has been confined too long. For the common good this will mean an inevitable democratization of the national culture.

American culture is a synthesis of diverse contributions by interpreters and appraisers of American life committed to the common idea of American democracy. There is a popular and prevailing assumption that American culture is exclusively indebted to the Anglo-Saxon tradition. Actually, of course, American ideology and culture are indebted to German influences, particularly in the realm of scholarship, philosophy, and music; and to French influences, as reflected in South Carolina and Louisiana. The Scotch-Irish, the Irish, the Scandinavians, the Jews—these and other national, racial, and religious minorities have made indisputable contributions to the common culture. The "color minorities"—that is, American Indians, Spanish-speaking Americans, and American Negroes—have made substantial contributions. With the exception of the Negro, however, these minorities have been inarticulate because of the marked condescension that has traditionally been accorded colored Americans. Spanish culture, despite its historic impact on Florida and wide areas of the Southwest, and despite our proximity to Latin America, has been shamefully ignored.

Intrinsic to the democratic idea is the concept of individual worth and dignity, the acceptance of differences as valid, valuable, and human, and the unifying force of a common belief in the transcendent value of personal freedom. Yet in spite of our American documents and our interpretative literature, we have repudiated the old values and placed an increasingly high premium not upon individuality, but upon conformity. Parallel with the rapid maturing of our industrial age after the Civil War went a decline of individualism and a substitution of class identity and values. Freedom of thought and action was curtailed, as was well exemplified, for example, by the early history of organized labor. From the years Mark Twain so colorfully labeled "The Gilded Age," until the twenties, materialism, "the cult of prosperity," and a growing nationalism dominated American thought. The latter half of the nineteenth century witnessed the abolition of slavery, but it also witnessed the birth of new social forces fundamentally as contradictory as slavery to the democratic idea.

The great social changes that began in the spiritual climate of the New Deal and were accelerated by our entry into World War II have forced America to renounce isolationism and assume a position of world leadership. The Depression contributed to a social leveling-off: the 1929 disaster drew no caste or class lines, and the impact of economic stress was borne by all. The Negro minority, as a cultural force, achieved wider and more nearly universal recognition during the thirties, when Negro writers and artists tended to relate themselves to the common social protest rather than to racial protest only. The Federal Arts Projects made it possible for young Negro artists to work with a reasonable degree of economic security and to fraternize with other artists of commensurate interests and objectives. As the decade moved on, it became increasingly apparent, in terms of the rising European totalitarianism, that America would have to redefine its democratic thesis as it was related to both politics and culture. In 1941, Franklin D. Roosevelt observed:

> There is nothing mysterious about the foundation of a healthy and strong democracy. The basic things expected by our people of their political and economic systems are simple. They are: equality of opportunity for youth and for others; jobs for those who work; security for those who need it; the ending of special privilege for the few; the preservation of civil liberties for all; the enjoyment of the fruits of scientific progress in a wider and constantly rising standard of living.

The concern for civil rights that the Roosevelt and Truman administrations evinced is reflected in the succession of civil-rights cases which came before the Supreme Court and which resulted in the Negro's being granted increasing equity in American life.

With the Negro's increasing integration into American life as a whole, he and his contributions to the social, political, and cultural fabric of the nation were more widely acknowledged and understood. In the forties, Hollywood made a conscious effort to reveal the Negro to home and overseas audiences in a sympathetic and realistic manner as opposed to the old buffoon stereotypes; and Negro musicians, dancers, and actors were widely publicized. The literature by and about Negroes tended more to universalize Negro life and experience, stressing the sameness of human experience regardless of racial difference.

When we entered World War II, we committed ourselves to a defense and perpetuation of basic democratic values. With the aftermath of the war, America was forced to convince those whom she would persuade to support democracy that the American creed is both dynamic and literally applicable to its own individual citizens. To exert moral influence and leadership abroad, Americans had to institute social changes

Some Prospects of American Culture

at home. In 1948, the President's Committee on Civil Rights reported:

> We abhor the totalitarian arrogance which makes one man say that he will respect another man as his equal only if he has "my race," "my religion," "my political views," "my social position." In our land men are equal, but they are free to be different.
>
> From these very differences among our people has come the great human and national strength of America.

This admirable restatement of America's traditional respect for diversity and individualism is part of the positive approach that Americans can and must take if we are to survive. Complacency, intolerance, resistance to change, and racial and social condescension can have no place in our thinking if we are sincere in our determination to preserve the democratic way. If we are to influence the two billion men and women who, Stringfellow Barr reminds us, are neither Russian nor American, we are going to have to convince them of our sincerity. As we extend to American minorities more and more civil and social recognition, and as they, in turn, become accepted on an equal footing in our daily life, it can be expected that, freed from the compulsion to justify their differences, they will regard differences of color or creed as distinctive, but not distinguishing, attributes. Similarly, as we take the lead in promoting world peace, we must accept wholeheartedly the fact that every society has its own cultural values and that those different from our own nevertheless carry with them some underlying likeness to our own.

The American Negro, through the years, has had to depend in large measure on humane and humanitarian values for personal and group recognition. Only in recent years has the Negro been a fairly potent force in economics and business. Even though today the Secretary of Commerce has estimated the Negroes' buying power at fifteen billion dollars per year, the fact remains that the Negro who has been pre-eminent has been so in the arts, the humanities, and popular sports. A roster of distinguished American Negroes invariably includes Paul Robeson, Roland Hayes, Marian Anderson, Dorothy Maynor, Leontyne Price, Todd Duncan, Lawrence Winters, Robert McFerrin, and William Warfield, concert and opera singers; Bill Robinson, Avon Long, Pearl Primus, Katherine Dunham, Janet Collins, dancers; Nat "King" Cole, the Mills Brothers, Lena Horne, Ella Fitzgerald, Eartha Kitt, Josh White, Harry Bellafonte, Ethel Waters, popular singers; Roy Campanella, Don Newcombe, and Jackie Robinson, baseball stars. Everybody knows of Joe Louis, Ralph Bunche, Congressman Adam Powell. They know of the veteran Illinois congressman and civil-rights leader, William Dawson, and of the new congressman from Michigan, James Diggs. The civil-rights lawyers who conceived and pleaded the education cases before the Supreme Court of the United States—the late Charles Houston, a Harvard Law School honor graduate, Thurgood Marshall, his pupil, George Hayes, and James M. Nabrit—are equally well known. Educators, such as Mordecai Johnson, President of Howard University, and Charles Johnson, President of Fisk University; civic leaders such as the late Mary Church Terrell, Mary McLeod Bethune, and Walter White; labor leaders such as Willard Townsend and A. Phillip Randolph are also well known. There have been many Negro scholars in medicine, as exemplified by the brilliant contributions of the late Dr. Charles Drew, who established the first blood bank; of the late Dr. Ernest Everett Just, whose lifelong interest in cytology culminated in his book *The Biology of the Cell Surface*, deemed by many cytologists here and abroad a forerunner to the solution of the mystery of cancer; and of Dr. Daniel Williams, a Negro surgeon who first operated on the human heart; in philosophy, as exemplified in the works of the late Alain Locke; and in practical science, as reflected in the experiments of the old-fashioned naturalist, George Washington Carver.

There are, however, among Negroes no big names internationally known in the world of business, trade, finance, or (save that of Bunche), on the large scale, diplomacy. There are no names, save that of General Benjamin O. Davis and his son, of top military officers or Negro naval officers. In short, Negroes are not identified in the eyes of Europeans, Asians, and Africans as representatives of our national aggressiveness in terms of extension of business and trade; or of our acquisitiveness in terms of our being in positions of bargaining for territorial or natural-resource gains. Our own history has made us mindful of mass suffering and appreciative of, rather than indifferent to, meditative philosophy. In the main, the traits in our modern Western world that are most baffling to the non-Western world are not generally typical of the Negro: aggressiveness, acquisitiveness, materialism, incomprehension of mass suffering, machine-mindedness, and a conditioning to overabundance.

We who have had less of the material assets, who, therefore, have not been driven by power forces, and who have attached greater significance to human values, may well have to take the lead in recasting universal social values. A rebirth of vital values is possible, Arnold Toynbee tells us, but: "It may come from some of the forgotten people who ... have not ... fallen victims to the pride and self-idolatry which may blind the great powers." The experience of the Negro in America has made him less susceptible to the pitfalls of nationalism, and this in itself may be one reason why the Negro may play a dramatic role in bringing about world democracy. The Negro has learned to detect the realities behind democratic generalizations. He has learned that, just as solemn mouthings frequently conceal differentials in domestic affairs, so they may disguise nationalistic bias in foreign relations. Sensitive to domestic discrimination, the American Negro is sensitive to the plight of oppressed and minority peoples everywhere. This sensitivity and realism, heightened by the drama of his own racial experience in America, give the Negro an unusual advantage in establishing American rapport with people traditionally skeptical of American democracy.

George N. Schuster wrote recently:

> It is obvious that the only civilization which can survive henceforth is the civilization of humanity. But it must be as broad as humanity. It must give free scope to the cultural individualism of peoples. It must be at once cooperative, a ceaselessly wrangling and a many sided civilization, wise enough to know that tension is a necessary ingredient of life.

If the only civilization that can survive is a civilization of humanity, the men and women who bring this civilization into being must be citizens of the world. Curiously enough, it has been easier for Negro Americans to be full citizens of the world than to be full citizens of their native land. This is an unfortunate (but, happily, changing) circumstance, but it is also the basis for a brilliant opportunity for the American Negro to implement both cultural democracy and the concept of cultural pluralism.

Until recent years "Americanization" of immigrants meant assimilation. "The American man would be a blended man wherein all the later and lesser colors would be lost in the initial one," Horace Kallen wrote in his essay "Cultural Pluralism and the American Idea." But nativist rejection of this sentiment "led to a reappraisal by children and grandchildren of newer Americans of their transoceanic heritages," he continued. The end results were the repudiation of the "melting pot" idea and a deliberate cultivation of differences. Says Horace Kallen, again:

> Americanization now came to denote the process by which

the diverse learn to know, to understand, and to live with one another as good neighbors in equal liberty; Americanism came to denote the union of the diverse; the American, any person convinced of the American idea, working and fighting in and through this union to bring it from faith to fact.

Thus, Americanization seeking cultural monism was challenged and is being slowly and unevenly displaced by Americanization supporting, cultivating a cultural pluralism, grounded on and consummated in the American Idea.

Because the American Negro has fought against superficial differences and intolerance for so long, he is identified with the idea of tolerance and thoroughgoing respect for all races and cultures. Cultural pluralism is indigenous to American democratic principles, though it has been placed in doubt in the course of American history. But as we face the compulsions of our time, we must restore this vital concept to our thinking and to our domestic and foreign policy.

POSTSCRIPT
1971

The American Negro's cultural achievements of the past fifteen years have been impressive. In the throes of what has been termed the Black Revolution, black creative artists are attempting to establish a legitimate black culture embracing literature, art, and music. There are, of course, still those Negro creative artists who are perplexed with the dilemma of whether or not their role is that of black artist or of artist who happens to be black. The best black artists reflect (for lack of a more explicit term) universal truths and aspirations through the medium of their black experience.

Art—all art—is an index of a people's spirit. Let us apply this maxim to contemporary Negro American painters and sculptors. The best of them reflect not only the racial experience or heritage, but an intensity of spirit and a vitality of expression. Perhaps the ten artists whose works were presented at the First World Festival of Negro Arts at Dakar, Senegal in 1966, are representative of today's black artists. The ten include: Barbara Chase, a young sculptress from Philadelphia, who has exhibited at the Spoleto Festival in Italy (1958) and the Pennsylvania Academy of Fine Arts as well as at other important art centers. A New Yorker Emilio Cruz, still under forty years old, is a painter who has exhibited in important galleries in Boston, Chicago, and New York. Sam Gilliam, a native of Mississippi but currently a Washingtonian, also a young man, has shown his acrylics on canvas at the Pan-American Union in Washington, the Mueseum of Modern Art in Buenos Aires, and the Institute of Contemporary Arts in Washington, D.C. Jacob Lawrence, somewhat older, is producing consistently well-received gouaches which have been displayed in numerous museums both in the United States and abroad. The American Society of African Culture circulated his works in Nigeria in 1962.

Norma Morgan has had showings of her engravings and drawings in Germany and Yugoslavia as well as in the United States. Robert Reid, an Atlantan who studied at Clark College, The Art Institute of Chicago, and the Parsons School of Design, has had exhibitions at the New York City Center Gallery, the James Gallery (New York), and the Osgood Gallery (New York).

Others include Charles White, who does ink drawings; Todd Williams, whose works in welded steel and iron were circulated by The American Federation of Arts in 1965–6; and Joseph Lawe, a specialist in Industrial Design, who received a medallion from the Industrial Designers Society of America in 1959, for outstanding product and graphic design. Further, the names of Hale Woodruff, Merton Dimpson, Claude Clark, Lois Pierre-Noel and Romare Bearden are significant as those of painters; William Artis and Earl Hooks are noted potters; James L. Wells is a printmaker; John Rhodes, Richard Hunt, and Selma Burke are sculptors.[1] Elizabeth Prophet, deemed by the late James A. Porter as a sculptress of "finer concentration and more fluent temperament"[2] than Augusta Savage, has concentrated on portraits in wood. The subjects, always Negro, are highly individualized.

Robert Crump, Henry Barnarn, Elizabeth Catlett, Joseph Kersey, and Zell Ingram are black sculptors who have earned varying degrees of recognition. Crump, whose early creations were in oil, later studied clay-modeling, and ultimately turned to sculpture. Barnarn's "The Head of John Brown" reflects the artist's capacity for combining, as Porter comments, "animal strength and intellectual beauty."

There are several popular artists—men and women without formal training—whose work reflects the commonplace. Everett Johnson, painter; William Edmondson, stonecutter; Horace Pippin, painter; John Hailstoack, painter; Leslie Bolling, woodcarver; Thurmond Townsend, a clay modeler, are representative popular artists who, with improved techniques, would be regarded as sophisticated artists. That this transition from "naïve" to "sophisticated" is desirable is a moot point.

Many of the most talented Negro painters have been labeled "primitives." Possibly the designation reflects the fact that some of the black artists did not receive formal training. Horace Pippin was undoubtedly the leading Negro primitive painter. Paralyzed by wounds suffered in World War I, Pippin, in spite of the handicap, painted some important works. Of these, according to Cedric Dover, writing in *American Negro Art*, "John Brown Going to His Hanging" ranks high.

In the late fifties a group of "abstract expressionists" appeared. By and large, these artists' works avoided social themes. Of the painters, Harvey Cropper, Virginia Cox, Gilbert Harris, James Weeks, Larry Compton, Charles McGee, Walter Williams, and Paul Keene were the best known. Bob Thompson has revealed the most original young talent since the period when Hale Woodruff and Jacob Lawrence were the ranking black artists. Today's expressionistic group is, in New York, represented by Jack Whitten, Larry Compton, Sonny Hodge, William White, and Joe Overstreet, all of whom use color in extreme proportions.

The recognition of Negro talent in the fine arts has long

---

[1] The following are Afro-American expatriates in Europe: Harold Cousin, sculptor; Walter Williams, Sam Middleton, Clifford Jackson, William Johnson, and Buford Delaney, painters.

[2] James A. Porter, Modern Negro Art (New York, 1967), p. 139.

prompted both individuals and organizations. As noted earlier, the Harmon Foundation in the late twenties began a series of exhibitions of the leading Negro artists of the time. Through the years the Foundation has created a permanent general collection. Under the direction of Hale Woodruff, Atlanta University developed into an art center. In 1941, Woodruff initiated annual art shows. With other painters, Woodruff established a group designed to promote creativity by black artists including Wilmer Jennings, Fred Flemister, Jewel Simon, Thomas Jefferson Flannagan, June Hector, and John Biggers. The group dubbed itself the "outhouse school," and produced prints not only of such moderate themes as Atlanta's black neighborhoods, but also of more explosive scenes, such as lynchings.

The death of James A. Porter, a long time professor at Howard University, was a loss to the art world. The University, under Porter's aegis, and that of the late Professor James Herring, whom he succeeded, had long played a leading role in fostering Negro art and artists. At Howard, James Wells, Lois Jones, David Driskell, and Albert Carter are all both practicing artists and teachers in the Art Department. The Department has trained such promising young artists as William White (who sold his prize-winning "African Metamorphosis" to the Nigerian Government).

Some black artists question the existence of "black art" even though museums and gallery owners seem to think that black art exists. Some angry young blacks "paint black." Others resist racial classification, and, even though they deal with the white artistic milieu, resist white sponsorship. They want to be classified as artists who are black—not as black artists.

These young black artists aim primarily to create an art that the black community can respect. Most are muralists who frequently paint their anger (or pride) on public walls. Boston has proffered both money and encouragement to a number of black muralists. In Washington, Detroit, and Chicago, black painters have used walls. Popular heroes, including Malcolm X, or Martin Luther King, are frequently depicted. In Detroit's "Wall of Dignity," by Bill Walker, a Chicago artist, is a painted saga of the black man's history from ancient Egypt to the present.

Today, Negro artists are working and exhibiting in the major cities both at home and abroad. Is it safe to say that their future depends on their ability to create an artists devoid of racial implications?

As we look at the Negro and contemporary music, we ask ourselves, "Are Negroes producing folk music today?" If we agree with Marion Bauer that folk music "is the unconscious expression in melody of the racial feelings, character, and interests of a people . . . without benefit of scientific training, by the common people or peasantry, which chronicles their lives in terms of design, melody, and rhythm, and has become traditional with them,"[3] we agree to the traditionally accepted definition, which has, however, been broken by various contemporary developments. First, today's folk music, unlike that of its predecessors, is not anonymous or transmitted orally from generation to generation, it is recorded; it is more formalized. Gospel music, songs of freedom, songs of protest are, and have been and are still being created in the contemporary period. Thus, a new problem has developed—that of distinguishing between "true" folk music (that of the rural folk) and the new city folk music heard in parks and in streets. *Hootenanny—The National Folk Singing Magazine*, in itself connotes the new formalism, the new functional intent of contemporary folk music.

The term "gospel music" is usually found in Pentecostal and Sanctified churches, but it is sung in Baptist and Methodist churches (black and white) not only in the small, "storefront churches" but also in the larger, more conventional ones. It is a music comprising not only traditional hymns and revival songs but also the new music of the new order. It is a spirited, antiphonal music involving group participation, not only of shouting, foot stamping and hand clapping, but also of piano, organ, and, frequently, drums, guitars and horns. Mahalia Jackson has long been regarded as the leading gospel singer. Her record "Move on Up a Little Higher" sold over a million copies. Other gospel singers include Rosetta R. Thorpe, the Ward Singers, Gospel Harmonettes, the Boyer Brothers, and the Sweet Chariots.

Freedom songs attained a new significance subsequent to the famous March on Washington, conducted in August, 1963, by the late Dr. Martin Luther King. The Freedom Singers, four young members of the Student Nonviolent Coordinating Committee (SNCC) participated, as did delegates from the Congress of Racial Equality. Of the Freedom Songs, *We Shall Overcome* is without doubt the most famous. However, all songs in the freedom movement have attained a lasting place in contemporary folk music because they describe the heroic actions of today's societal heroes and martyrs. The death of a leader, the jailing of an individual or a group, the failure of a battle for social justice prompt the creation of new songs which, in turn, frequently become chants or slogans. Typical

---

[3] Marion Bauer, "Folk Music: A General Survey," *The International Encyclopedia of Music and Musicians*, 6th ed.

of song titles are these: *The Literacy Test Song, The Ballad of Oxford, Mississippi, I Ain't Scared O' Your Jail, 'Cause I Want My Freedom Now, Talking Civil Rights, Ballad of Medgar Evers, I Can See a New Day.* The songs usually refer to words reminiscent of Birmingham, Alabama: bombing, hose, dogs, water.

In an article entitled "On the Racial Front," Leonard Feather describes how jazz musicians responded to the 1963 period of intense racial hostilities. He wrote: "In 1966 every musician, Negro or white, was more aware than ever before of the struggle for equality. . . ." He named three forms of involvement: direct musical action, through integration of one's own band or through working toward the integration of others; indirect action through support of the NAACP, the Urban League, CORE, and other similar groups; participation in freedom marches or sit-ins, and direct action with civil rights organizations.

Since the 1940's opera has become an increasingly important medium for American blacks. Mary Caldwell Dawson organized The National Negro Opera Company which presented Verdi's *Aida* at the Chicago Opera House in October 1942, and Verdi's *La Traviata* in Madison Square Garden in New York in March, two years later. In 1951, Mrs. Dawson's company performed R. Nathaniel Keith's oratorio, *The Ordering of Moses;* in May 1956 the company presented Clarence Whit's *"Ouanga."*

Zelma George, a black singer, gained national acclaim for her performance in *"The Medium,"* the work of a white composer presented at the Karamu Theatre in Cleveland. Karamu Theatre's avowed purpose has been to encourage opportunities for black performers.

The New York City Opera Company was the first major opera company to employ black singers. Pioneers were Adele Addison, Todd Duncan, Camilla Williams, Marjorie Tynes, William Brown, and Carol Bruce. Marian Anderson, the first Negro to sing with the Metropolitan Opera, was followed by William McFerris, Mattiwilda Dobbs, Grace Bumbry, Reri Grist, Leontyne Price, George Shirley, Shirley Verrett, and Felicia Weathers.

Of the men, George Shirley was the leading black tenor at the Metropolitan Opera throughout the sixties. The winner of several contests before achieving first place in the Metropolitan's Opera Auditions in 1961, Shirley is the only black male to have become permanently associated with the Metropolitan Opera.

Negro instrumentalists and conductors of the sixties include Sanford Allen, violinist with the Boston Symphony; Ann Hobson, harpist with the Cleveland Orchestra; Donald White, cellist with the Cleveland Orchestra; and Renard Edwards, violinist with the Philadelphia Orchestra. New York's Symphony of the New World included thirty-eight blacks among its roster of ninety players.

Black conductors include Dean Dixon, now with the Goteborg Symphony in Sweden; Everett Lee, now with the Frankfurt Opera in Germany; Henry Lewis, Director of the Newark, New Jersey Symphony; and Paul Freeman, Assistant Director of the Dallas, Texas Symphony Orchestra.

The outstanding black concert pianist of the contemporary period is the youthful Andrew Watts. Others are Natalie Hinderas, Sylvia Lee, Frances Walker, and Armenta Adams. Frances Cole is a leading harpsichordist; Kermit Moore, Ron Lipscomb, and Earl Madison are concert cellists.

There is currently a revival of interest in Negro music. In 1968, a group of composers organized The Society of Black Composers, Incorporated, "to provide a permanent forum for the works and thoughts of black composers, to collect and disseminate information about black composers and their activities, and to enrich the cultural life of the community at large." Assisted by a grant from Columbia University, the Society presented, during its first year, four concerts, radio and television programs, and assisted community groups that wanted to utilize the works of black composers.

In 1969, the Afro-American Music Opportunities Association, Incorporated was founded to "contribute to the enrichment of the total musical life of America." The AAMOA publishes a newsletter, sponsors concert-lectures on black music, and maintains a placement bureau for black artists and teachers. There are two neighborhood schools designed to train young black musicians: Dorothy Maynor's School of the Arts, located in New York City, and the Alma Lewis School in Boston, Massachusetts.

Black musicians have participated actively in both American and foreign music festivals and competitions. These include the Berkshire Music Center Summer Session in Massachusetts; the Bennington Composers' Conference in Vermont; the New England Festival of Two Worlds at Spoleto, Italy; the Glyndebourne Festival in England, and the Salzburg Festival in Austria.

In August 1969, the National Association of Negro Musicians, Incorporated met at St. Louis in an annual convention and also to celebrate its Golden Anniversary. Those who attended could look back with pride upon fifty years of consistent development of black American's musical history. At its inception, the Association had fewer than twelve black musicians who were nationally known. Perhaps not even the most optimistic of the founders could have imagined the changes that fifty years would bring—changes that would project the black artist and the black man's music into the vanguard of national and world culture.

What is the future of Negro music? It is parallel with the future of the Negro in America. As long as Negroes are relegated to ghetto status, Negro music will be defined by ghetto limitations. As has been noted in a different context, Negroes are a part of the American scene, living within the confines of American culture as a whole. Negro music will retain its traditional role as a link between varying Negro factions. For individual Negroes, black music will be accepted, assimilated, or rejected, in terms of the individual's attitude toward his blackness. As more individual black people move into the mainstream of American life, black music *per se* will have increasingly less meaning for them.

A final word must include a reference to contemporary jazz—now called "free jazz," the "new thing," or "the avantgarde." The new jazz, whose delineators include Cecil Taylor, Ornette Coleman, and Art Simmons, repudiates Western musical concepts, and makes the creating of music explicitly the musician's personal responsibility. Thus, the new form is reminiscent of primitive blues. LeRoi Jones has noted that "the most expressive music of any period will always be a reflection of what the Negro is at that particular time." He notes that "the most gifted blues and jazz performers (one thinks immediately of Jelly Roll Morton, Louis Armstrong, Duke Ellington, Bessie Smith, Lester Young, Billie Holiday, Charlie Parker, Thelonious Monk, Ornette V. Coleman) have always been able to speak as profoundly about the world as any other artists, and in America they have usually been able to speak more profoundly than most; certainly in terms of an American musical expression." But Jones concludes, "the enforced suppliance that has been the Negro's traditional position in America has also served to 'invalidate' Negro music as a legitimate genre of artistic expression in the eyes of most Western men, black or white."

Contemporary Negro dancers include artists well known both in America and abroad. In many instances, however, black dancers, like other black artists, have achieved renown initially in foreign countries. Arthur Mitchell is, perhaps, one of the few exceptions. At present, the only black dancer in the New York City Ballet Company, Mitchell is also director of the Dance Theater of Harlem, a new company. The company, just a year old, is totally black in membership. It performs classical ballet with notable success, and, in May 1971, appeared in a joint performance with the New York City Ballet. Mr. Mitchell's interests are eclectic: he still, for example, is identified with numerous community projects, one of which is the Jones-Haywood Studio in Washington, D. C.

Alvin Ailey, director and choreographer of the Alvin Ailey Dance Theater, is also Director in Residence of the Brok Academy of Art. This company represented the United States in tours of Africa and Europe. The recipient of numerous prizes, the company was signally honored by one offered at the International Dance Festival held in Paris in 1968. Ailey has served as choreographer for the American Ballet Theater both on and off Broadway. Although widely identified as a black company, it is, to some extent, integrated.

Sylvia Campbell, one of the few black women dancers, has performed with the Royal Netherlands Company in Amsterdam. A native of Washington, D. C., she, too, has worked with a Jones-Haywood ballet company.

Louis Johnson of Washington and New York was the choreographer for the Broadway Musical *Purlie* and was a nominee for a Tony award. Choreographer for numerous repertory companies, Johnson is at this time Choreographer in Residence for the Negro Ensemble Company of New York. For the season of 1971–2, he was appointed Choreographer in residence for the Washington Black Repertory Company, in conjunction with Mike Malone. In addition to his New York productions (which include *Black Nativity*) Johnson has done several TV shows. He has toured both the United States and Europe.

Mike Malone, a professor of dance at Federal City College and Howard University (both in Washington, D. C.) is director of Workshop for Classes in the Fine Arts. He was the choreographer for *The Great White Hope* and has worked in the television medium both in America and Europe. In 1971–2 he worked with Robert Hooks's Black Repertory Company in Washington.

Elizabeth Walton LeBlanc, a graduate of Brandeis University and the Julliard School, has performed with Martha Graham in the United States and in Europe. For six years a soloist with the Paul Taylor Dance Company, Mrs. Le Blanc is currently a teacher at Peabody Institute in Baltimore and director of and performer with her own company.

Postscript 1971

There is a new black revolutionary theater today which, in large measure, is represented by both the works and the theories of LeRoi Jones. A poet, musician, and social critic, as well as a playwright, Jones is best known for such plays as *Baptism, The 8th Ditch, Home on the Range, Dutchman, The Slave, The Toilet, Black Mass,* and *The Slave Ship.* He founded The Black Arts Repertory Theater and School in New York City where, in addition to *Dutchman,* he staged two plays, *J-E-L-L-O* and *Experimental Death Unit # 1.* The Black Arts Theater lasted seven months; thereafter, Jones moved to Newark to establish a drama group known as The Spirit House Movers and Players. He is credited with doing more than any other single black playwright to stimulate black writers for the theater. A controversial writer, Jones has been deemed by critic Howard Taubman of *The New York Times* as "one of the most gifted" dramatists of the contemporary period. Simultaneously, he has been characterized as racist and a propagandist whose abilities range from "great" to "dirty."

After the Black Arts Theater closed, black art groups developed on the West Coast, in Detroit, Washington, D. C., and on numerous college campuses including those of San Francisco State College, Fisk University, Columbia University, and Oberlin College. A "cultural ideology," greatly indebted to LeRoi Jones's philosophy, was formulated in Watts, Los Angeles, by Maulana Karenga, who established seven criteria for culture:

1. Mythology
2. History
3. Social Organization
4. Political Organization
5. Economic Organization
6. Creative Motif
7. Ethics[4]

Jones represents these criteria unreservedly. His concept of black theater is one of the Spirit as the following excerpt suggests:

> We will scream and cry, murder, run through the streets in agony, if it means some soul will be moved, moved to actual life understanding of what the world is, and what it

[4] Larry Neal, "The Black Arts Movement," The Black Aesthetic, ed. Addison Gayle, Jr. (New York, 1971), p. 278.

ought to be. We are preaching virtue and feeling, and a natural sense of the self in the world. All men live in the world, and the world ought to be a place for them to live.

Lorraine Hansberry's *A Raisin in the Sun* was designed, according to the author, to show "the clash of the old and the new, but most of all, the unbelievable courage of the Negro people." The play, however, although involving Negro characters, is essentially one that deals with common human problems confronting a family that happens to be black. Thus, Miss Hansberry's stated purpose was not explicitly realized. Nevertheless, it won the Critics' Circle Award over Tennessee Williams' *Sweet Bird of Youth* and Archibald McLeish's *J.B. A Raisin in the Sun,* which made stars of Sidney Poitier and Claudia McNeil, was the first play written by a Negro woman to appear on Broadway. A second play by Lorraine Hansberry, *"The Sign in Sidney Brustein's Window,* appeared in 1964.

Ossie Davis, who replaced Sidney Poitier in *A Raisin in the Sun* is also a playwright. Long identified with the development of black theater, Davis wrote *Purlie Victorious,* a play that falls between folk comedy and social commentary. Every stereotype of the South is held up to ridicule: the Southern Colonel, the Uncle Tom, the black mammy, integration—the entire gamut. *Purlie Victorious* is a comedy of anger—an anger directed toward those who fail to recognize that freedom for all Americans will be achieved only in proportion to the extent that black Americans enjoy true freedom.

James Baldwin's *Blues for Mister Charlie,* which opened in New York in 1964, is an impressionistic play dedicated to the memory of Medgar Evers, his widow, and children, and to that of the dead children of Birmingham. "The play," says Baldwin, "takes place in Plaguetown, U.S.A., now. The plague is race, the plague is our concept of Christianity: and this raging plague has the power to destroy every human relationship." The play deals with the murder of a young black man by a white storekeeper and in spite of its complex design, portrays brilliantly black-white relations in the contemporary South.

In 1965, Douglas Turner Ward's *Happy Ending* and *Day of Absence* ran for over a year at the St. Marks Playhouse. Mr. Ward, who undertook the leading role in each play, won the Off-Broadway Vernon Rice Drama Award for playwriting and an Obie Award for acting.

Ed Bullins is one of the most prolific contemporary black

playwrights. Bullins, currently in New York, has produced ten plays in San Francisco. On the West Coast he was also associated with LeRoi Jones. Of the many plays he has written since the sixties, *The Electronic Nigger, Come Home, The Gentleman Caller* and *In The Wine Time* are outstanding. He has been Playwright in Residence of the New LaFayette Theater. He has published essays, stories, and poetry in numerous magazines and has been Editor of *Black Theater Magazine*.

Adrienne Kennedy is a versatile young black playwright. In addition to two movies, Miss Kennedy has also written poetry and short stories. The plays include *Funnyhouse of a Negro, The Owl Answers, A Rat's Mass,* and *A Beast's Story. Funny House of a Negro* won an Obie Distinguished Play Award in 1964.

Charles Gordone won the Pulitzer Prize for drama in 1970 for *No Place To Be Somebody,* an off-Broadway production described by *Time* magazine's theater critic as a "black panther of a play," *No Place To Be Somebody* has been characterized as a "brilliant fantasia of rage, and fury, and fear; of insecurity, of love and hate, imaginatively present through the means of a symphonic blending of realism, naturalism, poetry, gangster movie melodrama, comedy, surrealism, and soul".

The play covers a fifteen year time span in the life of Johnny Williams, a black hustler who is a victim of his awareness of Black Power. The owner of a bar, Johnny is seen in the company of black and white prostitutes, gangsters, politicians, ex-convicts. Gordone says his play's meaning has to do with the question of identity. "We're all of us looking . . . to try to find out just who and what we are."

Ed Bullins apparently speaks for the new genre of black playwrights when he says:

"We don't want to have a higher form of white art in blackface. We are working towards something entirely different and new that encompasses the soul and spirit of Black people, and that represents the whole experience of our being here in this oppressive land."

In the realm of poetry Gwendolyn Brooks continues her verse of high quality. Miss Brooks' "A Bronxville Mother Loiters in Mississippi Meanwhile A Mississippi Mother Burns Bacon," recounts the inner reflections of a white woman responsible for a lynching. Dudley Randall's "Ballad of Birmingham," dealing with the bombing of a church in Birmingham, and the subsequent death of five little Negro girls begins poignantly: "Mother, dear, may I go downtown . . . and march the streets of Birmingham in the Freedom March today?"

David Harris, in his volume *De Mayor of Harlem*, writes "Keep on Pushing," LeRoi Jones writes "A Poem For Black Hearts," a tribute to Malcolm X, and Nikki Giovanni in her poem ("No Name No. 3") writes:

> They already got Malcolm,
> They already got LeRoi
> They already strapped a harness on Rap
> They already pulled Stokely's death . . ."

and again,

> "I am 25 years old
> black female poet
> Wrote a poem asking
> Nigger can you kill
> if they kill me
> it won't stop
> the revolution.

Don L. Lee in *Think Black* writes "A Poem For Black Minds" in which he notes:

> First the color/black naturally
> beautiful cannot be mixed with white-
> ness. . . . it must not
>   it's
> mine.

Another young black poet, Etheridge Knight in his *Poems From Prison*, recounts the return of Hard Rock to prison after being discharged from a hospital for the criminally insane. Another poem from the same volume, "The Violent Space," is sub-titled "Or When Your Sister Sleeps Around for Money."

James A. Emanuel, essayist and critic, has written a number of poems inspired by his son. Of these, "Emmett Till" is perhaps the most moving. It recounts the brutal murder of a black child whose only offense was a boyish whistle.

Mari Evans writes poetry in an unconventional style reminiscent of E. E. Cummings. Her poetry has been used in radio, television, and Broadway productions. Her subject matter is usually racial; her point of view frequently humorous.

Black poets today are most frequently involved in a concerted effort to effect social change through the medium of a cultural weapon—poetry.

William Melvin Kelley's *A Different Drummer* is the outstanding black novel of the sixties. Kelley, a highly sophisticated, gifted writer, employed a variety of devices and techniques in his book. A subsequent novel, *Dem*, though highly imaginative, lacks the vigor and intensity of *A Different Drummer*.

Ishmael Reed is a young writer who has taught at the University of California, Berkeley, and the University of Washington. His novel, *Yellow Back Radio Broke Down*, deals with the Loop Garoo Kid, "a black satanic cowboy," Thomas Jefferson, Lewis and Clark, Drag Gibson (a cattleman), and Big Lizzy, owner of the Rabid Black Couger Saloon. The sum total is described as "a galloping, uninhibited, astonishingly funny novel."

John A. Williams's *The Man Who Cried I Am* takes the reader through nearly thirty years of recent American history from the vantage point of an American black. The hero, Max Reddick, dying of cancer, looks back on segregated armies in World War II, bus boycotts, church burnings, and marches. What *The Man Who Cried I Am* lacks in artistic finesse is compensated for by its revelations of a modern day Negro intellectual's problems.

Other young black fiction writers include Alston Anderson, the late Frank London Brown, John Oliver Killens, Paule Marshall, Julian Mayfield, and Herbert Simmons. With rare exceptions they are *not* concerned with middle class values.

Other essayists include Lerone Bennett, Jr., author of *The White Problem in America*; Dick Gregory, author of *Nigger*; Bill Russell, author of *Go Up For Glory*; John Oliver Killens, author of *Black Man's Burden*; Malcolm X's *The Autobiography of Malcolm X*; and Gordon Parks's autobiography, *A Choice of Weapons*. The various writings of Martin Luther King, Jr., constitute some of the best prose writings by contemporary black writers. His stirring "I Have a Dream" speech is a modern classic.

Finally, a word should be said about Hollywood and its evolution in the direction of a more honest, unsentimental, non-stereotyped portrayal of Negro characters and themes. Outstanding were *Bright Road* based on a story by Elizabeth Vorman; and Harry Belafonte's *A Man is Ten Feet Tall*. Sidney Poitier was outstanding in *Lilies of the Field*. Equally outstanding was Bernie Hamilton in *One Potato, Two Potato* and *Nothing But a Man*. Marpessa Dawn, a beautiful American Negro star, appeared in *Black Orpheus*, screened in Brazil.

Melvin Van Peebles, the prolific author of five novels, is the first black man to make full-length moving pictures. His most recent, *Sweet Sweetback's Baad Asssss Song*, has been described as "a one man tour de force," since it was written, directed, and scored as well as starred in by Van Peebles. It is dedicated to "all the brothers and sisters who've had enough of the man."

Some time ago, the writer addressed an audience which included a number of young people on some of the Negro's cultural contributions to America. During the question period, a young Negro boy raised the question of why no mention had been made of the Negro in sports. It was (and is) a good question.

My answer was (and is) that the Negro's contributions to the American world of sports are too numerous and too comprehensive to be considered in a book of this length. Indeed, there have been extensive writings on the subject.

It is the most cherished hope of all black Americans today that at home, as well as abroad, we may be accorded the respect and dignity that are implicit in our American heritage.

Index

Abbott, Robert, 216
Absalom! Absalom! (Faulkner), 136, 205
Abyssinia (musical comedy), 78
Accoe, Will, 57
Adams, Edward C. L., 134
Adams, Wayman, 178
Address to the Negroes ..., An, (Hammon), 96
"Africa" (McKay), quoted, 103
Africa: A Symphonic Poem (Still), 71
African Company of Negro Actors (New York), 150
African Free School (New York), 150
Afro-American Folk Songs (Krehbiel), 52
Afro-American Symphony (Still), 71, 73
Aiken, Conrad, 135
Aldridge, Ira, 150
Alexander, W. W., 211
Alexander's Ragtime Band (Berlin), 58
All Coons Look Alike to Me (Hogan), 57
All God's Chillun Got Wings (O'Neill), 154
Allen, J. Mord, 99
Allen, Richard, 122
Allen, William, 28
America and Other Poems (Whitfield), quoted, 47
American Ballet No. 2 (Enters), 78
American Dilemma, An (Myrdal), quoted, 116
American in India, An (Redding), 214
Americana (Weidman-Humphrey), 78
Anderson, B. T., 141
Anderson, Marian, 45n, 225
Anderson, Sherwood, 135, 197, 199
Anger at Innocence (Smith), 145
Anna Lucasta (Yordan), 156
"Annie Allen" (Brooks), 113-14
Antheil, George, 66, 67
Anti-Slavery Alphabet, 122
Aptheker, Herbert, 204

Ardrey, Robert, 141, 157
Armstrong, Lous, 65, 66, 76; quoted, 63
Art in America (Cahill), quoted, 171
Artis, William, 187
As I Lay Dying (Faulkner), 136
Asbury, Bishop Francis, 19
Association for the Study of Negro Life and History, 204
Atavisms: A Dance Series (Weidman-Humphrey), 78
Atlanta University, 211, 218
Austin, Lovie, 71
Awful Sad (Ellington), 69

Bacon, Peggy, 182
Bailey, Pearl, 161
Baker, Josephine, 79
Baldwin, James, 143, 214
Ballou, Leonard, quoted, 14
Band of Angels (Warren), 145
Bandana Sketches (White), 14
Banneker, Benjamin, 19
Bannister, Edward, 170
Barber, Samuel, 75-76
Barren Ground (Glasgow), 104, 131, 163
Barthé, Richmond, 184, 187
Basso, Hamilton, 139
Bates, "Peg Leg," 79
Bayou Legend (Dodson), 160
Beale Street: Where the Blues Began (Lee), 65
"Bear, The" (Faulkner), quoted, 207
Bearden, Romare, 188, 188n
Beavers, Louise, 162
Beecher, Henry Ward, 120
Beetle Crook (Demky), 144
Behn, Aphra, 122
Beiderbecke, Leon ("Bix"), 65, 66
Belair, Felix, Jr., quoted, 76-77
Belcher, Fannin, 161
Bell, James, 97
Bellafonte, Harry, 225
Bellows, George, 169, 179-80, 183
Benét, Stephen Vincent, 105
Benét, William Rose, 105
Benezet, Anthony, 19, 115

243

Benton, Thomas, 169, 179, 180, 184
Berlin, Irving, 58, 70, 71
Berry Brothers, 79
Bethune, Mary McLeod, 216, 226
Biggs, E. Power, 75
Biographical Sketches (Mott), 122
Biology of the Cell Surface, The (Just), 226
"Birmingham Breakdown," 69
Birth of a Nation, The, 162
Birthright (Stribling), 133, 199
Black, Frank, 71
Black April (Peterkin), 134
Black Boy (Wright), 215
Black Christ, The (Cullen), 106
"Black Drop, The" (Deland), 130
Black Patti's Troubadours (Cole), 56, 152
Black Power (Wright), 215
Black Thunder (Bontemps), 140
"Black and Unknown Bards" (Johnson), quoted, 100
Bland, James, 53, 151
Bloch, Julius, 169, 179, 183
Blood Stream (Schlick), 155
Blues: An Anthology (Niles-Handy), 61, 70
Boas, Franz, 140
"Boll-weevil, where you been so long"; quoted, 55
Bontemps, Arna, 140, 198, 218
Book of American Negro Poetry, The, 35, 218
Botkin, B. A., 95 n
Bay at the Window (Dodson), 140, 144
Bradford, Roark, 95
Braithwaite, William Stanley, 101, 218; quoted, 129
Brass Ankle (Heyward), 155
Brawley, Benjamin, 218
Brewer, J. Mason, 95n
Bricks Without Straw (Tourgee), 127
"Bright sparkles in de churchyard," quoted, 82
Brooks, Gwendolyn, 112, 113-14; quoted, 112, 113
"Brothers" (Johnson), 100
Brown, John, 97, 171
Brown, Samuel, 117
Drown, Sterling, 64, 94, 103, 107, 108, 109; quoted, 44, 64, 95n, 100, 106, 108, 120, 125, 149, 150, 155, 159, 220
Brown, William Wells, 117, 120, 125
Bryant, William Cullen, 97, 98
Buckler, Helen, 218

Bunche, Ralph, 226; quoted, 217
Burke, Selma, 188
Burleigh, Harry T., 33, 69, 74, 91
Burns, Anthony, 145
Butcher, James, 160
Bynum, Charles, 65

Cable, George W., 128, 130
Cable, Thomas, 33
Cahill, Holger, quoted, 171
Caldwell, Erskine, 135, 137, 138, 145, 147
Caleb, the Degenerate (Cotter), 153
Call Me Mister, 79
Campanella, Roy, 225
Campbell, James Edwin, 99
Camptown Races (Foster), 94
Cane (Toomer), 103, 147
Careless Love, 54
Carmichael, Hoagy, 71
Carpenter, John Alden, 66, 72
Carruthers, W. A., 124
Carry Me Back to Ole Virginny Bland), 53
Carter, Benny, 69, 71
Carter, Hodding, 141
Carver, George Washington, 226
Case, William, 172
Casey Jones, 32, 53
Cash, Harold, 182
Cash, W. J., quoted, 60, 131, 191, 200-3
Castle, Irene and Vernon, 59
Castle, Willa, 139
Century of Negro Migration, A (Woodson), 204
Cesana, Otto, 72
Chadwick, George, 70
Chandler, Lewis, 146
Chapin, James, 179, 182, 183
Chapman, Maria, 122
Charlestonia (Jenkins), 71
Chesnutt, Charles Waddell, 129, 216
Chesnutt, Helen, 216
Chicago *Defender*, 216
"Chile I come from out'n slavery," quoted, 86
Clansman, The (Dixon), 129, 153
Clark, Porteous, 141
Clorindy: The Origin of the Cakewalk (Cook-Dunbar), 57, 152
Clotel (Brown), 125
Cohan, George M., 56, 58
Cole, Bob, 56, 57, 58, 59
Cole, Nat ("King"), 225
Collapse of Cotton Tenancy, The (Johnson, *et al.*), 211
Collins, Janet, 79, 225

Index

Comedy Overture on a Negro Theme (Gilbert), 70
Commager, Henry S., quoted, 13, 191
"Commemoration Ode" (Lowell), quoted, 97
Confrey, Zez, 70
"Congo, The" (Lindsay), 101, 106; quoted, 106
Connelly, Marc, 155
"Conversation on V" (Dodson), quoted, 112
Conway, Moncure, quoted, 171
Cook, Will Marion, 57, 58-59, 66, 70, 152
Cooke, Anne, 160
Cooke, John Esten, 124
Copland, Aaron, 66, 68, 72, 76
Cornish, Samuel, 118
Cortor, Eldzier, 188, 188*n*
Cotter, Joseph S., Sr., 153
Country Place (Petry), 144
Courlander, Harold, 48
Covarrubias, Miguel, 179, 184
Cowley, Malcolm, quoted, 204
Cozzens, James Gould, 141-42
Crane, Stephen, 130
Creation: A Negro Sermon (Johnson), 72, 84, 197
Creation of the World, The (Milhaud), 70
Creole Show, The, 55
Crichlow, Ernest, 188
Crisis, The, 218, 219
Cross on the Moon (Hewlett), 141
Cullen, Countee, 103, 106-7, 140; poems quoted, 103, 104, 106
Curry, Jabez, 200
Curry, John Steuart, 169, 179, 182
Curti, Merle, quoted, 197

Dabney, Ford, 59, 66
Daniel Jazz (Gruenberg), 72
"Dar ration day come once a week," quoted, 87
Dark Laughter (Anderson), 199
"Dark Symphony" (Tolson), quoted, 111
Dark Town Is Out Tonight (Cook), 57
Darrell, R. D., quoted, 69
Davies, Maurice, 204
Davis, Arthur, quoted, 120, 220
Davis, Benjamin O., 226
Davis, Benjamin O., Jr., 226
Davis, Blevins, 160
Davis, Daniel Webster, 99
Davis, Frank, 109

Dawson, William A., 41, 72, 73, 127
"Day of the War, The" (Bell), 97
De Glory Road, 40
Deep Are the Roots (D'Usseau-Gow), 157
Deep River (Harling), 72, 83
Delafosse, Maurice, 48
Deland, Margaret, 130
Delaney, Martin, 97, 117
Demky, William, 144
Dempsey, Richard, 188*n*
de Reid, Ira, 211
Detective Story (Kingsley), 159
Dett, Nathaniel, 33, 41, 74
Deutsch, Adolph, 71
Diggs, James, 226
Divine Comedy (Butcher), 160
Divine Hymns . . . (Smith), 90
Dixon, Thomas, 129
Dixon, Will, 59
Documentary History of the Negro . . ., A (Aptheker), 204
Dodd, Lamar, 184
Dodson, Owen, 140, 144, 160; poetry quoted, 112
Donald, Henderson H., 204
Douglas, Aaron, 181, 184, 185, 198
Douglass, Frederick, 19, 37, 97, 117-20, 122, 123, 216; quoted, 118-20
Dreamy Kid (O'Neill), 153
Dred (Stowe), 123
Dreiser, Theodore, 130, 142, 197
Drew, Charles, 226
DuBois, W. E. B., 16, 48, 57, 101, 139, 175, 218; quoted, 17
Dukes, West, 65
Dunbar, Paul Laurence, 57, 99-100, 129, 175, 225
Duncan, Todd, 225
Duncanson, Robert, 171
Dunham, Katherine, 77, 80, 81, 225; quoted, 42
Dunlap, William, 150
D'Usseau, Arnaud, 157
Dvořák, Antonin, 41, 57, 69, 72, 76

Eakins, Thomas, 172-173
East St. Louis Toodle-O (Ellington), 68
Ebon Chronicle (Still), 73
Edmonds, Randolph, 161
Education of the Negro . . . (Woodson), 204
Edwards, Frank, 212
Elkins, William, 56

Ellington, Duke, 66, 67, 68-69, 71, 77
Ellison, Ralph, 143, 214
Embree, Edwin, 211; quoted, 16
Emperor Jones, The (opera; Gruenberg), 72, 78
Emperor Jones, The (play; O'Neill), 153
Enters, Angna, 78
Essays on the Arts of the Theatre (Isaacs), 151n
"Ethiopa Saluting the Colors" (Whitman), quoted, 98
Europe, James Reese, 59, 64, 66, 71
Evening Thought . . . , An (Hammon), 96
Excursions (Barber), 76
Exhortation (Cook), 58

Farwell, Arthur, quoted, 74
Faulkner, William, 135, 145, 147, 162, 204-7; quoted, 206
Fauset, Arthur, quoted, 44, 45
Fauset, Jessie, 140
Federal Art Project, 185, 214
Federal Theatre Project, 78, 159, 159n, 224
Federal Writers' Project, 95n, 203, 224
Fifty Years and Other Poems (Johnson), 100
Finian's Rainbow, 79, 159
Fire in the Flint, The (White), 119n
Fisher, Rudolph, 140, 197
Fisk Jubilee Singers, 29, 33, 91
Fisk University, 75, 121, 160, 207, 210, 218, 226
Fitchett, Horace, 212
Fitzgerald, Ella, 225
Fitzgerald, F. Scott, 197
Flight (White), 140
Florida A. & M. College, 160
Foner, Philip, 217
Fool's Errand, A (Tourgee), 127
"For My People" (Walker), quoted, 110
Forge, The (Stribling), 133
Forsythe, Reginald, 71
Forward the Heart (Reines), 156
Foster, Stephen, 93-94, 99
Four Saints in Three Acts, 161
Frankie and Johnny, 32, 52, 54
Franklin, John Hope, 45
Frazier, E. Franklin, quoted, 211
Freedom's Journal, 117
From the New World (Dvořák), 74
From the Land of Dreams (Still), 71
From the New World (Dvořák), 52, 69
From Slavery to Freedom (Franklin), 214
Fuller, Meta Warrick, 174

Gaines, Francis, 125
Garies and Their Friends, The (Webb), 126
Garnet, Henry Highland, 19, 117
Garrison, William Lloyd, 118, 120, 170
Georgia Camp Meeting (Mills), 57
Gershwin, George, 62, 66, 70, 72, 161
Gift of Black Folk (DuBois), 16
Gilbert, Henry, 70
Gilpin, Charles, 153
"Gift on Board, Little Chillun," 60
Glasgow, Ellen, 104, 131, 133, 135
Glickman, Maurice, 182
Glory Road, De, 40
Gloster, Hugh, 218; quoted, 146, 147, 219
"Go Down Death" (Johnson), 100; quoted, 100
Go Down Moses (spiritual), 40
Go Down Moses (Faulkner), 207
Go Tell It on the Mountain (Baldwin), 144
Go Way Back and Sit Down (Johns), 57
God Sends Sunday (Bontemps), 140
God Struck Me Dead, 40
God's Little Acre (Caldwell), 137
God's Trombones (Johnson), 103
Goldberg, Isaac, quoted, 56-57, 60, 61
Goldmark, Rubin, 70
Goldthwaite, Anne, 184
Gone with the Wind (Mitchell), 139, 162
Gonzales, Ambrose, 134
Gonzales, Manuel, quoted, 31
Goodman, Benny, 65, 77
Gordon, Arthur, 145
Gow, James, 157
Grady, Henry, quoted, 200
Graham, Martha, 98
Grainger, Porter, 71
Grandissimes, The (Cable), 128
"Grant me that I am human . . ." (Brooks), quoted, 112
Green, Alex, 65
Green, Paul, 149, 154, 155
Green Pastures (Connelly), 155
Green Thursday (Peterkin), 134
Greenhouse, Bernard, 75

Index

Gregory, Montgomery, 160
Grimke, Angelina, 101
Grofe, Ferde, 70, 72
Growing Up in the Black Belt (Johnson) 211; quoted, 117
Gruenberg, Louis, 66, 72
Guard of Honor (Cozzens), 141-42
Guillaume, Paul, 176
Gulf Coast Blues, 54, 61
"Gwine lay my head right on de railroad track," quoted, 55

Hadley, Henry, 70
Hammon, Jupiter, 96
Hammond, John, 64
Hampton Institute, 78, 218
Handy, W. C., passim, 55, 58-62, 65, 66, 73, 215
Hansen, Howard, 71
"Harlem" (Benét), 105
Harling, Frank, 72
Harmon, Carter, quoted, 74
Harmon Foundation, 183, 184, 185, 187
Harney, Ben, 57, 65
Harper, William, 173
Harris, Joel Chandler, 33, 43, 94, 99, 127, 128
Harris, Marie, 56
Harris, Roy, 76
Hayden, Palmer, 183, 184, 202
Hayden, Robert, 111, 113; quoted, 111
Hayes, George, 226
Hayes, Roland, 33, 95n, 225
Haynes, Lemuel, 116
He Never Said a Mumblin' Word, 84
Henderson, Fletcher, 64, 66, 71
Henri, Robert, 169, 179-80, 183
Henry, Robert, 65
Henson, Josiah, 122
"Heritage" (Cullen), quoted, 106
Herskovits, Melville, J., 16, 48
Hewlett, James, 150
Hewlett, John, 141
Heyward, Dorothy, 154-55, 158
Heyward, DuBose, 104, 134, 154, 160, 199
Higginson, Thomas Wentworth, 28
Hill, E. Burlingame, 70
Hill, Mozell, 211
Hime, Chester, 144
Hindemith, Paul, 75
His Eye Is on the Sparrow (Waters), 215
Hoffman, Malvina, 182
Hoffman, Max, 57

Hogan, Enest, 57
Holman, M. Carl, 113
Holmes, Charles, 69
Holmes, Dr. Eugene, quoted, 219
Home of the Brave, 162
Home to Harlem (McKay), 140
Homer, Winslow, 168, 171, 179
Hope, John, 216
Horne, Lena, 225
Horton, Asadata Dufora, 78
Horton, George, 97
Hot and Bothered (Ellington), 68
Hot Iron, The (Green), 154
Hot Tamale Alley (Irwin), 56
House of Flowers, 161
Houston, Charles, 226
How Far the Promised Land? (White), quoted, 217
How Long till Summer (Rudley), 157
Howard University, 95n, 160, 188, 211, 212, 216n, 217, 226
Howells, William Dean, quoted, 89, 132
Huckleberry Finn (Twain), 126
Hughes, Langston, 103, 107, 140, 155, 197; poetry quoted, 102-3, 107-8
Human Factors in Cotton Culture (Vance), 203
Human Geography of the South (Vance), quoted, 203
Humoresque Nègre (Kroeger), 70
Humphrey, Doris, 78
Hurst, Fannie, 162
Hurston, Zora Neale, 45, 48, 94, 95n, 140, 144, 197
Hymns, Original and Selected ... (Smith-Jones), 90
Hymns for the Use of Christians (Smith), 90

I Don't Care If You Never Comes Back, 56
"I know moonlight, I know starlight," quoted, 82
"I wouldn't marry a black gal," quoted, 87-88
Iceman Cometh, The (O'Neill), 159
"If We Must Die" (McKay) quoted, 105
I'll Take My Stand, 139
I'm Troubled in Mind, 74
Imitation of Life (Hurst), 162
In Abraham's Bosom (Green), 154
In Dahomey, 78
In Ole Virginia (Page), 127
"In the South" (Powell), 70

Inter-Collegiate Dramatic Assn., 161
Intruder in the Dust (Faulkner), 137, 162
Invisible Glass, The (Wahl), 145
Invisible Man (Ellison), 143
Irwin, May, 56
Isaacs, Edith, 151n; quoted, 80, 150, 151, 153, 159
Isham, John, 55, 152
"I'se gwine now a-huntin' . . . ," quoted, 87
It Ain't Goin' Rain No More, 40

Jackson, Blyden, 218
Jackson, George Pullen, quoted, 90, 91
Jackson, Mahalia, 95n
Jackson, May Howard, 174
Jacovleff, Alexander, 165
James, Marquis, 216n
James, Willis, 64
Jamie, the Fugitive (Pierson), 126
Jazz (Whiteman), 70
Jazz Nocturne (Suesse), 72
Jazz Study for Two Pianos (Hill), 70
Jean (Johnson), 74
Jeb (Ardrey), 157
Jefferson, Miles, 219
Jefferson, Thomas, 115; quoted, 15, 17
Jenkins, Edmund, 71, 72
"Jesus my all to heaven is gone . . . ," quoted, 91
Joe Turner Blues, 54, 61
John Brown's Body (Benét), 105
John Henry, 32, 53; quoted, 53
Johns, Al, 57
Johnson, Billy, 56
Johnson, Charles S., 121, 210, 226 quoted, 117, 192
Johnson, Fenton, 56
Johnson, Georgia Douglas, 101
Johnson, Greer, 161
Johnson, Guy, 55; quoted, 45, 104
Johnson, Hall, 33, 155
Johnson, J. Rosamond, 33, 56, 57, 58, 59, 71, 74
Johnson, James Weldon, 33, 56, 72, 84, 100-1, 103, 197, 218; quoted, 35, 37, 44-45, 100, 101
Johnson, M. Gray, 185, 186
Johnson, Momodu, 78
Johnson, Mordecai, 226
Johnson, Sargent, 184, 187, 188
Johnson, William H., 185, 188n
Jones, Abner, 90
Jones, Lois Mailou, 187

Jones, Mme. Sissieretta, 56
Jonny spielt auf (Krenek), 70
Joplin, Scott, 57, 65
Joseph, Ronald, 188
Journey (Smith), 208
"Journey to a Parallel" (McWright), 112
Juba, 43; quoted, 43
Juba Dance (Dett), 41
Jubilee (Chadwick), 70
Jubilee Singers, 59
Jubilee Songs, 41
Jubilee Stomp (Ellington), 68
Jump Jim Crow, 43
Just, Ernest E., 160, 219, 226, see also Introduction
Just You (Johnson), 74

Kahn, Morton, 48
Kallen, Horace M., quoted, 227-28
Kay, Ulysses, 75
Kaye, Sammy, 77
Kennedy, John P., 124, 125
Kenton, Stan, 77
Kern, Jerome, 71
Kersands, Billy, 151
Killers of the Dream (Smith), 208
Kimbrough, Edward 141
"Kind Master and the Dutiful Slave, The" (Hammon), 96
King, Willis J., quoted, 13
Kingsley, Sidney, 159
Kitt, Eartha, 161, 225
Kneel to the Rising Sun (Green), 154
Knock on Any Door (Motley), 144
Koussevitsky, Serge, quoted, 67
Krehbiel, Henry, 52
Krenek, Ernst, 66, 70
Kroeger, Ernest, 70
Kykunkor (Horton), 78

La Guiablesse (Still), 78
Lambert, Constant, 70; quoted, 46, 65
Land of My Fathers (Thompson), 215
Lang, Eddie, 65
Langston, John, 118
Larsen, Nella, 140
Last of the Conquerors (Smith), 142
Latino, Juan, 167
Lawrence, Jacob, 188
Lay My Burden Down (Botkin), 95n
Leadbelly, 95n
Lee, George, 140, 197

Lee, Ulysses, quoted, 119, 218, 220
Lee-Smith, Hughie, 188
Leopard's Spots, The (Dixon), 129
"Let America Be America Again" (Hughes), 107; quoted, 107
Levee Land (Still), 71
Levee Song (White), 71
Levinson, André, quoted, 79, 151n
Lewis, D. A., 57
Lewis, Edmondia, 171
Lewis, Norman, 188
Lewis, Roscoe, quoted, 121
Lewis, Sinclair, 139, 197
Liberator, The, 118, 122
"Libretto for the Republic of Liberia" (Tolson), quoted, 111
"Lift Every Voice and Sing" (Johnson), 100
Light in August (Faulkner), 136, 206
Li'l Gal (Johnson), 58
Lincoln University, 160
Lindsay, Vachel, poetry 106; quoted, 106
"Lines to the Students of Cambridge University" (Wheatley), 97
"Litany at Atlanta" (DuBois), 101
"Little Brown Baby" (Dunbar), 101
Little Mother of Mine (Johnson), 74
Living Is Easy, The (West), 144
Locke, Alain, 95n, 154, 160, 188, 218-9, 226; quoted, 153, *see also* Introduction
Logan, Joshua, 159
Logan, Rayford, 214
Lomax, John and Alan, 64, 95, 95n
Long, Avon, 225
Longfellow, Henry W., 97, 98, 171
Look Homeward, Angel (Wolfe), 135
Lopez, Vincent, 60
"Lord he thought he'd make a man," quoted, 84
Lost Boundaries, 162
Lost in the Stars, 159
Louis, Joe, 226
Lovell, John, Jr., 218
Lowell, Amy, 101
Lowell, James Russell, 97, 98
Luks, George, 169, 180, 183
Lumpkin, Grace, 139
Lunceford, Jimmy, 66, 71
Luschan, Felix von, 176
Lyles (Miller and Lyles), 79

Lynch Town (Humphrey-Weidman), 78

McClendon, Rose, 187
McCullers, Carson, 158
McFee, Henry, 179, 182, 184
McFerrin, Robert, 225
McKay, Claude, 103, 105, 140, 197 poetry quoted, 103, 105
McWright, Bruce, 112
Madame Delphine (Cable), 128
Magic Chant (Graham), 78
Mahaly's Minstrels, 55
Mahagonny (Weill), 70
Mamba's Daughters (Heyward), 104, 134, 160
Man Who Died at 12 o'clock, The (Green), 154
Mandy Lou (Cook), 58
Maple Leaf Rag (Joplin), 57
March, William, 139
Mardi (Melville), 126
Markham, Edwin, 100, 101
Mars, Price, 48
Marsh, Reginald, 179
Marshall, Thurgood, 226; quoted, 212
Martineau, Harriet, 122
Maynor, Dorothy, 95n, 225
Meditations (Kay), 75
Melody of the Heart, The (Jones), 90
Melville, Herman, 126
Member of the Wedding, The (McCullers), 158, 215
Memphis Blues (Handy), 54, 61, 62
Milhaud, Darius, 41, 66, 70, 71
Miller and Lyles, 79
Miller, Kelly, 175
Miller, William, 90
Miller of Old Church, The (Glasgow), 131
Mills Brothers, 225
Mills, Florence, 79, 80
Mills, Kerry, 57
Mind of the Negro ... Crisis (Woodson), 204
Mind of the South, The (Cash), quoted, 200-3
"Minstrel Man" (Hughes), quoted, 200-3
Mr. Crump (Hanley), 61
Mrs. Patterson (Seebree-Johnson), 161
Mitchell, Margaret, 139, 162
Moby Dick (Melville), 126
Modern Negro Art (Porter), 187
Monster, The (Crane), 130
Mood Indigo (Ellington), 69

Moody, William Vaughn, 101
Moon, Bucklin, 144
Moorehead, Scipio, 170
Morehouse College, 216
Morgan College, 160
Morison, Samuel E., quoted, 191
"Mother to Son" (Hughes), 107
Motherwell, Hiram, quoted, 70
Motley, Archibald, 185
Motley, Willard, 144, 214
Moton, Charlotte, 78
Mott, Abigail Field, 122
M'sieu Banjo, 53
Muir, Lewis, 65
Mulatto (Hughes), 155
Mullen, James Know, 155
Music from the South (Ramsey), 95n
My Heart and My Flesh (Roberts), 135
My Lord, What a Mornin', 40, 83
My Old Kentucky Home (Foster), 94
"My ole Mistiss promise me," quoted, 86
Myrdal, Gunnar, quoted, 116, 117

Nabrit, James M., 226
Narrative of James Williams, 122
Narrative of the Sufferings of ... Clarke, 122
National Association for the Advancement of Colored People, 133, 212, 217, 222
National Negro Opera Company, 75
Native Son (Wright), 142, 146, 155, 215
Negro in America Fiction (Brown), quoted, 125
Negro in American Thought and Life, The (Logan), 214
Negro in the American Theatre, The (Isaacs), quoted, 80
Negro a Beast, The, 129
Negro Caravan, The (Brown, et al.), quoted, 120, 220
Negro in the Civil War, the (Quarles), 214
Negro Dance Unit, 78
Negro Family in Chicago, The (Frazier), 211
Negro Family in the United States, The (Frazier), 211
Negro Folk Rhymes (Talley), 46, 95n
Negro Folk Symphony (Dawson), 73
Negro Freedman, The (Donald), 204

Negro Heaven (Cesana), 72
Negro and His Songs, The (Odun-Johnson), 104
Negro in Literature and Art ... (Brawley), 218
Negro Makers of History (Woodson), 204
Negro Rhapsody (Gilbert), 70
Negro Rhapsody (Powell), 70
Negro Rhapsody, A (Goldmark), 70
Negro Slavery, by Othello: A Free Negro, quoted, 115
Negro in Virginia, The, 121
Negroes in American Society (Davies), 204
Nelson, Truman, 145
Never No More (Mullen), 155
New Negro, The, 181
New Orleans Hoe Down (Ellington), 68
Newcombe, Don, 226
Nigger (Wood), 133, 199
Nigger, The (Sheldon), 153
Nigger Jeff (Dreiser), 138
Nigger Heaven (Van Vechten), 104, 140
Night Fight (Kimbrough), 141
Nights with Uncle Remus (Harris), 128; *see also* Uncle Remus tales
Niles, Abbe, 62, 70; quoted, 62, 63
No 'Count Boy, The (Green), 154
No Day of Triumph (Redding), 144
No Green Pastures (Ottley), 215
"No Kafka in the South" (Reddick), 147
No More Auction Block, 74
Nobody Knows the Trouble I've Seen, 74, 83
North Georgia Review, 208
North Star, The, 118
Not Without Laughter (Hughes), 140
Now Is the Time (Smith), 208; quoted, 209-10

"O just let me get up ...," quoted, 91
Octoroons, The, 55
Of Mules and Men (Hurston), 140
Of New Horizons (Kay), 75
Odum, Howard, 104, 134, 203
Oh, Didn't It Rain, 40
Oh, I Don't Know, You're Not So Warm (Williams), 57
O'Higgins, Myron, 112, 113; poetry quoted, 113-14

Index

Old Black Joe (Foster), 94
Old Folks at Home, 40
"Old Lem" (Brown), quoted, 108
Old Man Blues (Ellington), 69
Oliver, Cy, 69, 71
On Slavery ("Othello"), 19
On the Town, 79
On Whitman Avenue (Woods), 156
135th Street (Gershwin), 62
One Way to Heaven (Cullen), 140
O'Neill, Eugene, 149, 153-54, 159
Ordering of Moses, The (Dett), 74
Oriental America (musical show), 56
Oroonoko (Behn), 122, 167
Osgood, Henry, 70
"Othello" (pseudonyn), 19; quoted, 115
Ottley, Roi, 215
Ouanga (White), 74, 78
Our Lan' (Ward), 158
Outsider, The (Wright), 142
Overton, Ada, 79

Page, Thomas Nelson, 99, 127, 130
Page, Walter Hines, 200
Palm Leaf Rag (Joplin), 57
Parker, Theodore, 145
Pascin, Jules, 179, 182
Passing (Larsen), 140
Perrin, Tom, 57
Pete, Peaches, and Duke, 79
Peterkin, Julia, 45, 134, 154
Peters, Paul, 155
Peterson, Louis, 161
Petry, Ann, 144, 214
Petite Ma'mselle, 53
Phillips, Wendell, 120
Phylon, 218, 219
Picasso, Pablo, 176
Pierson, Emily, 126
Pipes, William H., 95n
Planter's Victim, The (Smith), 126
Play on your Harp, Little David, 70
Polish Peasant in America, The (Thomas-Znaniecki), 50
Porgy (Heyward), 134, 154, 199
Porgy and Bess (Gershwin), 72, 161
Porter, Cole, 71
Porter, James A., 187, 188; quoted, 185, 186, 187, 188n
Portrait of Bert Williams (Ellington), 69
Powell, Adam, 228

Powell, John, 70
Price, Florence, 73
Price, Leontyne, 225
Primus, Pearl, 79, 80, 225

Quality (Sumner), 141
Quarles, Benjamin, 214
Quest of the Silver Fleece (DuBois), 139
Quicksand (Larsen), 140
Quiet One, The, 75, 162

Rademan (trombonist), 65
Ragtime Instructor (Harney), 57
Rain Song (Cook), 58
Rainbow Round My Shoulder (Odum), 134
Rainey, Ma, 64
Ramsey, Frederic, 95n
Randolph, A. Phillip, 226
Raphaleson, Samson, 155
Rasselas (Johnson), 167
Rastus on Parade (Mills), 57
Ravel, Maurice, 68, 70
Reason, Charles, 97
Red Rock (Page), 127
Reddick, L. D., 147
Redding, J. Saunders, 144, 214, 218; quoted, 13
Redman, Don, 69, 71
Rehearsals of Discomfiture (Scott), 217
Reines, Bernard, 156
Reiss, Winold, 179, 181, 185
Remond, Charles Lenox, 19
Remus. See Uncle Remus tales
"Repeal of the Missouri Compromise Considered, The" (Rogers), 97
Reprisal (Gordon), 145
Requiem for a Nun (Faulkner), 137
Respectful Prostitute, The (Sartre), 158
Rhapsody in Blue (Gershwin), 70, 71
Rhapsody Number 2 (Jenkins), 72
Richardson, E. P., quoted, 188
Rio Grande (Lambert), 70
River George (Lee), 140
Roberts, Elizabeth Madox, 135
Robinson, Bill, 79, 80, 225
Robinson, Boardman, 179, 184
Robinson, Edwin Arlington, 105
Robinson, Jackie, 226
Rocking in Rhythm (Ellington), 69
Rodgers, Richard, 71
Roeburst, John, 141

Rogers, Elymas, 97
Rogers, J. A., quoted, 61
Roll Sweet Chariot (Green), 155
Roosevelt, Franklin D., 224
  quoted, 224
Rowan, Carl, 215
Rudley, Sarett and Herbert, 157
Run Little Chillun (Johnson), 155
Rush, Benjamin, 115
Russell, Irwin, 99
Russell, Louis, 71
Russell, William, 145
Russworm, John, 117
Rylee, Robert, 139

Sahdji (Still), 73, 78
St. James Infirmary Blues, The, 46, 54
Sanctuary (Faulkner), 136, 137
Sandburg, Carl, 139
Sartre, Jean-Paul, 158
Savage, Augusta, 187
Scarlet Sister Mary (Peterkin), 134, 154
Scherzo (Hill), 70
Schlick, Frederick, 155
Schnelling, Paula, 208
Schuster, George N., quoted, 228
Scott, Evelyn, 135
Scott, Nathan, 217; quoted, 217
Scott, William, 192
Seebree, Charles, 161
Seldes, Gilbert, quoted, 63, 88
Selling of Joseph, The (Sewall), 115
Seraph of the Suwanee (Hurston), 144
Set My People Free (Heyward), 158
Sewall, Samuel, 115
Shadow of the Plantation (Johnson), 211
Sheldon, Edward, 153
Shoofly Regiment, The (Cole-Johnson), 58
Short History of the American Negro, A (Brawley), 218
"Shout! Shout! Satan's about," quoted, 85
"Shout of Color" (Cullen), quoted, 103
Silent South, The (Cable), 128
Simkins, Francis Butler, quoted, 200
Simms, William G., 124
Simpson, George, 48
Sin of the Prophet, The (Nelson), 145
Since You Went Away (Johnson), 58
Sinclair, Upton, 130
Sinfonia in E (Kay), 75
Sing Out, Sweet Land, 79
Singers, The (Work), 75
Sklar, George, 155
Slave Narrative, Its Place . . . (Starling), quoted, 120-21
Slave Narrative Sketches . . ., 122
Slave Song (White), 74
Slave Songs . . . (Allen), 28
"Slim Greer" (Brown), 108
Smith, Albert, 183, 184, 198
Smith, Bessie, 61, 64, 95n
Smith, Charles, 95n
Smith, Clara, 64
Smith, Elias, 90
Smith, Joshua, 90
Smith, Lillian, 138, 139, 147, 156, 157, 204, 207; quoted, 207, 208
Smith, Mamie, 64
Smith, W. W., 126
Smith, William Gardiner, 142, 145; quoted, 215
Smokey Mokes, 56
"Snapshots of the Cotton South" (David), quoted, 109
So Red the Rose (Young), 139
So This is Jazz (Osgood), 70
Social Harp, 91
Soliloquy (Work), 75
Solitude (Ellington), 69
Sometimes I Feel Like a Motherless child, 74
"Song of Myself" (Whitman), quoted, 98
"Song to a Negro Wash-Woman" (Hughes), 107
"Song of the Son" (Toomer), quoted, 103
Sophisticated Lady (Ellington), 69
Souls of Black Folk (DuBois), 129
Sound and the Fury, The (Faulkner), 136, 205; quoted, 205-7
South of Freedom (Rowan), 215
South Pacific, 159, 161
South Street (Smith), 145
South Wind Blows (Clark), 141
Southbound (Anderson), 141
Southern Association of Speech and Dramatic Arts, 161
Southern Plantation, The (Gaines), 125
Southern Regions, 203
"Southern Road" (Brown), 108
"Speech" (Hayden), 111;. quoted, 112
Speicher, Eugene, 179, 182, 184

Index

Spelman College, 160
Spewack, Samuel, 159
Sport of the Gods (Dunbar), 130
Stacy, Jess, 65
Starling, Marion Wilson, quoted, 120-21, 124
Starr, Amantha, 145
Statistical Atlas of Southern Counties (Johnson), 211
Sterne, Maurice, 179, 184
Stevedore (Peters-Sklar), 155
Stewart, Will, 64, 66
Still, William Grant, 41, 65, 71, 72, 78, 118
Stokowski, Leopold, 72; quoted, 67
Store, The (Stribling), 133
Story family (Boston), 171
Story of John Hope, The (Torrence), 216
Stowe, Harriet Beecher, 123-24, 151
Strange and Alone (Redding), 144
Strange Fruit (Smith), 138, 156, 157, 208
Stravinsky, Igor, 68, 71
Street, The (Petry), 144
"Street in Bronzeville, A" (Brooks), 112
Stribling, T. S., 133, 199
Stringfield, Lamar, 72
"Strong Men" (Brown), 108
Suesse, Dana, 72
Suite "In the South" (Powell), 70
Suite Virginesque (Powell), 70
Sumner, Charles, 120, 171
Sumner, Cid Ricketts, 141
"Sunset Horn" (O'Higgins), quoted, 112-13
Swallow Barn (Kennedy), 124, 125
Swanee River (Foster), 94
Swanson, Howard, 75, 76
Swing Along, Children (Cook), 58
Swing That Music (Armstrong), 63, 65

Take a Giant Step (Peterson), 161
Take It Easy (Ellington), 68
Talley, Thomas, 43, 44, 95n
Tamiris (dancer), 76
Tanner, Henry, 172-74
Ta-ra-ra Boom de Ay, 56
Tarry, Ellen, 215
Tate, Allen, quoted, 111
Taylor, Ballanta, 46, 91
Teagarden, Jack, 65

Terrell, Mary Church, 216, 226
Teschmaker, Frank, 65, 66
"That Evening Sun Go Down" (Faulkner), 205
Their Eyes Were Watching God (Hurston), 140
There'll Be a Hot Time in the Old Town Tonight, 58
"There's a camp meeting in the wilderness," quoted, 85
These Are Our Lives, 203
These Thirteen (Faulkner), 206
They Shall Not Die (Wexley), 155
Thigpen, Helen, 75
Third Door, The (Tarry), 215
Third Generation (Hime), 144
This Is The Army, 79
Thomas, William I., 50
Thompson, Charles, 216n
Thompson, Era Bell, 215
Thompson, Stith, 95
Time of Man, The (Roberts), 135
"Tired" (Johnson), quoted, 104-5
To a Mona Lisa (Work), 75
"To John Keats" (Cullen), 106
"To Nat Turner" (Brown), 108
Tobacco Road, (Caldwell), 137
Tolson, Melvin, 111, 113; poetry quoted, 111
Toomer, Jean, 103, 147; poetry quoted, 103
Torrence, Ridgley, 149, 154, 216
Tourgee, Albion, 127
"Toussaint L'Ouverture" (Robinson), 105
Townsend, Willard, 226
Toynbee, Arnold, quoted, 227
Travis, Paul, 182
Trip to Coon-Town, A (Cole-Johnson), 56
Trouble in July (Caldwell), 137
Truth, Sojourner, 118
Truth Stranger than Fiction (Henson), 122
Tubman, Harriet, 118
Turner, Jim, 65
Turner, Lorenzo, 95n
Turner, Nat, 116
Turpin, Waters, 141
Twain, Mark, 126, 223
Two Blind Mice (Spewack), 159

Uncle Ned (Foster), 94
Uncle Remus: His Songs and Sayings (Harris), 128; *see also* Uncle Remus tales
Uncle Remus tales, 32, 35, 36, 37, 43, 45, 95n, 128

Uncle Tom's Cabin (Stowe), 123-24, 151
Uncle Tom's Children (Wright), 142
Unfinished Cathedral (Stribling), 133
Up from Slavery (Washington), 129; quoted, 119

Valien, Preston and Bonita, 211
Vance, Rupert, quoted, 203
Van Doren, Carl and Mark, quoted, 149
Van Vechten, Carl, 104, 140
Venuti, Joe, 65
Vesey, Denmark, 116, 158
Villa-Lobos, Heitor, 46
Virginia Writers' Project, 121
Vodery, Will, 64, 71

Wahl, Loren, 145
Walker, David, 116
Walker, Henry, 212
Walker, Margaret, 110, 113
Walls of Jericho (Fisher), 140
Ward, Samuel Ringgold, 13, 117
Warfield, William, 225
Waring, Laura Wheeler, 183
Warren, Robert Penn, 145; quoted, 205
Washington, Booker T., 15, 119-20, 129, 216, 216n, quoted, 120, 153
Waters, Ethel, 67, 215, 225
Wave The (Scott), 135
"Way down yon'er 'un de Alerbamer way," quoted, 85
"We raise de wheat," quoted, 86
"We read in the Bible . . . ," quoted, 84
"We shall not always plant . . ." (Cullen), quoted, 104
"We wreck our love boats on the shoals," quoted, 53
Webb, Frank W., 126
Weidman, Charles, 78
Weill, Kurt, 66, 70
Weinberger, Jaromir, 66
Well, The, 162
Wells, James, 186
Wells, Lesesne, 185
"W'en I goes to die . . . ," quoted, 86
Were You There?, 84
West, Dorothy, 144
West Virginia Institute, 160
Wexley, John, 155

Wheatley, Phillis, 24, 96, 103, 170
"When de Co'n Pone's Hot" (Dunbar), 99
Whistlin' Rastus (Mills), 58
White, Clarence Cameron, 74, 78
White, Josh, 95n, 26
White, Newman Ivey, 84
White, Walter, 139, 215, 217, 226; quoted, 213
White Dresses (Green), 154
"White Houses" (McKay), quoted, 105
White Man (Ralphaelson), 155
Whiteman, Paul, 60, 70, 72
Whitfield, James, 97
Whitman, Walt, 97, 107; poetry quoted, 98, 107
Whittier, John, 122
Whittier, John Greenleaf, 97, 98
Wiley, Stella, 79
Williams, Bert, 57, 153
Williams, Charles, 78
Williams, Clarence, 71
Williams, Daniel Hale, 216, 226
Williams, James, 122
Williams, Peter, 116
Williams, Spencer, 71
Wind is Rising, A (Russell), 145
Winfield, Hewsley, 78
Winters, Lawrence, 225
Wisteria Trees (Logan), 159
Without Magnolias (Moon), 144
Wolfe, Thomas, 135, 136
Wood, Clement, 133, 199
Woodruff, Hale, 183, 184, 185, 189
Woods, Maxine, 156
Woodson, Carter, 48, 204
Woodward, Sidney, 56
Woolman, John, 19, 115
Work, John, 33, 64, 75, 83; quoted, 91
World's Beginning (Ardrey), 141
Wright, Richard, 142-43, 155, 215, 216

Yankee Doodle, 40
Yerby, Frank, 144
Yordan, Philip, 156
You May Bury Me in the East, 70
Young, Donald, quoted, 220
Young, Mahonri, 182
Young, Stark, 138

Ziegfeld, Florenz, 59
Znaniecki, Florian, 50

MENTOR and SIGNET Titles of Special Interest

☐ **THE CHRONOLOGICAL HISTORY OF THE NEGRO IN AMERICA edited by Mort Bergman.** Events, people, ideas, legislation and literature—all that constitutes the history of the Black man in America. Illustrated.
(#MW937—$1.50)

☐ **MANCHILD IN THE PROMISED LAND by Claude Brown.** The provocative bestselling autobiography revealing the spirit of a new pioneering generation of Negroes in the North who have entered the mainstream of American society as a determined, aggressive, hopeful people.
(#W5681—$1.50)

☐ **THE NEGRO REVOLUTION From Its African Genesis to the Death of Martin Luther King, Jr. by Robert Goldston.** Robert Goldston has written a provocative and well-documented analysis of Black history in this definitive work. He traces the plight of the Black people from Africa through the Civil War, post-Civil War on to the civil rights movement of today. (#Q3915—95¢)

☐ **RIGHT ON! An Anthology of Black Literature by Bradford Chambers and Rebecca Moon.** The authors describe the book as "the works of more than forty authors are presented in these pages, from the plaintive cries of the first Black poet to be stolen from Africa to the angry, fiery voices of today's Black Militants." This book will be welcomed in both schools and libraries.
(#MQ1005—95¢)

THE NEW AMERICAN LIBRARY, INC.,
P.O. Box 999, Bergenfield, New Jersey 07621

Please send me the MENTOR and SIGNET BOOKS I have checked above. I am enclosing $_____(check or money order—no currency or C.O.D.'s). Please include the list price plus 25¢ a copy to cover handling and mailing costs. (Prices and numbers are subject to change without notice.)

Name_____

Address_____

City_____State_____Zip Code_____
Allow at least 3 weeks for delivery

MENTOR and SIGNET Titles of Special Interest

☐ **BLACK VOICES: An Anthology of Afro-American Literature** edited by Abraham Chapman. Fiction, autobiography, poetry, and literary criticism by American Blacks selected from the work of well-known authors as well as younger writers whose work is being published here for the first time. Contributors include **Ralph Ellison, Richard Wright, James Weldon Johnson, James Baldwin, Gwendolyn Brooks, Langston Hughes** and **Margaret Walker.** (#ME1265—$1.75)

☐ **HARLEM** edited by John Henrik Clarke. America's foremost Black writers recreate the people, the landscape, the joy and the horror of their ghetto heartland. A unique and superb collection of tales which recapture the essence of Harlem and its people. Writers include **James Baldwin, LeRoi Jones, Maya Angelou** and **Langston Hughes.** (#Q4336—95¢)

☐ **THE SELECTED WRITINGS OF W.E.B. DUBOIS** edited by Walter Wilson with an Introduction by Stephen J. Wright. A moving testimony to a great man and his dreams. Included are selections from **The Souls of Black Folk, John Brown, Darkwater, Dusk of Dawn** and **Black Reconstruction,** his autobiographical writings, letters and personal papers all of which illuminate the man and his work. (#MW1007—$1.50)

☐ **BLACK QUARTET: Four New Black Plays by Ed Bullins, Ben Caldwell, Ronald Milner and LeRoi Jones.** Four powerful plays by the most brilliant Black playwrights of our time. Includes an introduction by Clayton Riley and a photographic insert. (#MW1332—$1.50)

THE NEW AMERICAN LIBRARY, INC.,
P.O. Box 999, Bergenfield, New Jersey 07621

Please send me the MENTOR and SIGNET BOOKS I have checked above. I am enclosing $_____(check or money order—no currency or C.O.D.'s). Please include the list price plus 25¢ a copy to cover handling and mailing costs. (Prices and numbers are subject to change without notice.)

Name_____

Address_____

City_____ State_____ Zip Code_____
Allow at least 3 weeks for delivery